THE
GREAT WESTERN
RAILWAY
150 Glorious Years

GWR
150
Official Souvenir
Authorised by British Rail Western Region

THE GREAT WESTERN RAILWAY

150 Glorious Years

General Editors

Patrick Whitehouse

&

David St John Thomas

Foreword by Bill Bradshaw
(GENERAL MANAGER, BRITISH RAIL WESTERN REGION)

Contributors include:
Patrick Whitehouse
David St John Thomas   O. S. Nock
G. F. Fiennes   Geoffrey Kichenside
P. M. Kalla-Bishop   B. K. Cooper

David & Charles

Isambard Kingdom Brunel

A DAVID & CHARLES BOOK

Hardback edition first published 1984
Reprinted 1984 (twice), 1985, 1991, 1998
Paperback edition published 1985
Reprinted 2002

Copyright © David St John Thomas and Patrick
Whitehouse, Millbrook House Ltd 1984, 1985

Distributed in North America
by F&W Publications, Inc.

A catalogue record for this book is available from
the British Library.

ISBN 0 7153 8530 5 (hardback)
ISBN 0 7153 8763 4 (paperback)

Printed in China by
Hong Kong Graphics & Printing Ltd
for David & Charles
Brunel House   Newton Abbot   Devon

Frontispiece: Waiting for the 'right away'; the fireman of Castle class 4-6-0 No 5004 Llanstephan Castle *looks back as a Paddington – Bristol train stands at Bath in 1948. It was a scene which would have changed little other than in detail for more than 60 years.*

CONTENTS

Foreword by Bill Bradshaw
(GENERAL MANAGER, BR WR)   7
Introduction   9
1   The Broad Gauge Years   23
2   Broad Gauge: Speed, Legend, and Sequel   31
3   Three Famous Stations   37
4   Locomotive Construction   54
5   Locomotive Sheds and Workshops   63
6   A Recorder Remembers   86
7   The Limited and others   94
8   Trials on other lines   106
9   Summer Saturdays   111
10 How the Passengers travelled   123
11 The Freight Scene   131
12 Signalling, Automatic Train Control and Safety   137
13 Publicity   145
14 Pioneers of Transport   156
15 Organisation and Management   160
16 The Great Western at War   166
17 Great Western into Western   168
18 Branch lines   185
19 Narrow gauge   195
20 Preservation   202
    Acknowledgements   206
    Index   207

Near the end of an era with broad
and standard gauges. 4-2-2
Great Western hauls the down Zulu
Express through Ealing in 1890.
This was the first engine to be built at
Swindon in 1846 although then as a
2-2-2. What might a broad-gauge
HST have looked like here today?
Notice the standard gauge relief lines
already in use on the left.

FOREWORD

This book is about the past. Since the age of five I have lived within earshot of the Great Western. I first worked on the Western as a student in the capacity of a temporary porter six years after Nationalisation, then in 1959 as a Traffic Apprentice. The railway I joined would tackle any job; thus I assisted with a farm removal from Swindon Town to Otterham (48 vehicles on the train); we moved Bertram Mills Circus from Bath Green Park to Cheltenham overnight (three complete trains, the first of which was loaded with the earlier acts before the show ended). I was sent to Malmesbury to learn how to secure agricultural machinery with ropes and scotches. I helped to load 144 wagons of cattle one day at Hereford. We released pigeons by the thousand. We never thought about the economics.

A General Manager's job is about the future. It is still very much about getting traffic and giving service. But it is more than ever about achieving these objectives with the least amount of resources – be these materials, rolling stock or manpower. But fierce competition from the lorry, the coach and the car mean that when we attract the business we want, we retain it by giving good service – punctuality, cleanliness, comfort, safety, frequency, speed. These were the aims of my predecessors and they were shared by all who worked for the Great Western. The loyalty which is still displayed to the former Company and its standards is in my view a desire to identify with these same qualities.

We are fortunate that much of our Region has been spared the worst of the recession. As leisure increases more and more people will want to visit the beautiful cities, countryside and coastline reached by our trains. The population we serve will grow as new industries spring up along the Western Corridor, and those seeking an early and active retirement choose our routes for their future homes. We will move increasing amounts of aggregate out of the Mendip Hills. We will have several new and rebuilt stations with easy access to the Motorway system. There will be new signalling throughout the West of England route to complement our excellent track. We will turn Paddington into a comfortable station for our passengers. New rolling stock will appear for our local trains.

We are celebrating our hundred and fiftieth anniversary, into which we will try to impart traditional GW style, confident that there have never been so many technical innovations available to us to improve the product we offer in terms of quality and price, and certain that we have a market with plenty of scope for growth.

Bill Bradshaw
GENERAL MANAGER
BRITISH RAIL, WESTERN REGION

A down express at Dunball on the Bristol & Exeter's racing ground, headed by City class No 3407 Malta.

The introduction of the Inter-City 125 High Speed Trains has revolutionised Western Region passenger services with average end to end speeds of between 85 and 90mph and about 100mph on certain intermediate sections; today's Executive trains provide seat service for refreshments to all first class passengers. A Paddington bound HST crosses Coalpit Heath viaduct in the spectacular winter of 1981/2.

INTRODUCTION

Few groups of initials have ever meant so much to so many people as GWR. In the minds of millions, they continue to spell romance, comfort, stability, good values that have been eroded, a spirit of adventure . . . and more specifically the days when the train journey was one of the best parts of a seaside or country holiday.

Many thoughts come to mind. The orderliness of Brunel's cathedral, Paddington, pannier tanks always bringing in the empty coaches a good twenty minutes before departure time. The romance of the locomotives, basically the same design across half a century that encompassed two world wars and continual revolution in most other things mechanical. The world's fastest and the world's longest non-stop trains. The Great Western's peculiarities such as Brunel's original broad gauge and the legacy of spaciousness it left; the automatic train control which made it not merely the world's safest railway, but probably the safest means of travel there has ever been in the history of man; the lower quadrant signals; the unique publicity machine turning out books for 'Boys of All Ages', jig-saw puzzles and pioneer films.

A remarkable institution, almost a way of life, or a sovereign state strung out along hundreds of miles of route? The land on either side might be governed from Whitehall; the GWR was a world apart governed and governed very firmly from Paddington. The values and the practices were often dramatically different. The two worlds, for instance, had their separate telecommunication systems, and most railwaymen would have said that the Great Western's was better than the Post Office's. A plug bought in a local shop could not be pushed into a railway socket, for the GWR had its own different design of socket and plug, along with everything else electrical and much else besides.

The railway, of course, was just the starting point. The GWR had extensive shipping, bus and lorry, and even air services. It ran docks, restaurants and hotels, designed its own linen and laundered it, published a magazine and had its own bands. In the restaurant car you read Great Western literature, drank Great Western whisky and ate Great Western biscuits with your cheese. Is it surprising that if you lived on Great Western territory you felt superior to those served by lesser railways? Part of the magic was anyway that the Great Western served much of the best-heeled and most scenic parts of Britain. But then another part of it was that the Great Western was so consciously different from other lines. It may have built the first Pacific locomotive in Britain, but it – *The Great Bear*, later converted to a Castle – was the only one it ever did build. Continuity

Fox's Wood Tunnel from the west. A sketch in J. C. Bourne's Great Western, *a magnificent tribute to the construction of the GWR published in 1846 and now a collector's piece. The print clearly shows the 7ft 0in baulk road and the care taken to fit in with the existing landscape in the form of the castellated tunnel mouth.*

A sketch reproduced from the Illustrated London News *of 17 November 1849 showing the opening of the Shrewsbury & Birmingham Railway with a double-headed train crossing the River Severn. This line was involved in the early warfare between the GWR and LNWR when each railway was seeking entrenchment north of Birmingham. Eventually it became a vital link in the Great Western's access to Chester.*

played a key role in its character, it being the only major railway to maintain its identity in the 1923 Grouping, yet no business in the 1920s and 1930s was so fond of telling its shareholders and customers about its improvements and innovations.

Such was the magic that many began admiring the GWR before ever seeing it. When they did see it they were seldom disappointed. The first glance of, say, a Castle at speed was breathtaking. The shining brass safety valve casing on top of the neatly-tapering boiler, the handsome nameplate, steam that was not smoke, and then the clear, shrill whistle, all surpassed the highest of expectations. All the human senses combined in a symphony for life when watching expresses overhaul long coal trains in Sonning Cutting, or trains round the curve coming onto the sea wall at Teignmouth, or arriving full pelt from Paddington at Birmingham Snow Hill. To travel on one of those great trains which ran for many generations and regulated the happenings over an incredibly wide area was another thrilling experience. The 1.30pm from Paddington was one such. The previous train to Plymouth would have left no less than three hours before, that to Torbay an hour-and-a-half. However generous local services might be in some areas, the GWR ran expresses sparingly, ensuring that the restaurant cars and branch line connections had the maximum of business. The 1.30 might have 15 coaches, with sections for

The buildings of Brunel's pumping station at Totnes used in connection with the atmospheric section of the South Devon Railway from September 1847 to September 1848. Similar buildings were situated at Exeter, Starcross, and Newton Abbot, and Kingskerswell on the Torquay branch.

The exterior of Bristol Temple Meads station in 1846 – an example of early Victorian mock Tudor architecture. The wording above the ground floor windows reads Great Western Railway Company Incorporated By Act of Parliament Aug 1835. *Note the Great Western horse bus.*

Taken days before the broad gauge was abolished in May 1892, this view of the north end of Torquay shows old baulk road track on the down side and more recent cross-sleepered on the up.

Facing page top:
Uphill near Weston-super-Mare around the turn of the century; 4-2-2s Nos 3020 Sultan *and 3011* Greyhound *double-head a down passenger train. Many platform extensions were built of wood (often extremely slippery in wet weather) in the first two decades of the twentieth century.*

Weymouth, the Torbay line and Cornwall. On busy days passengers would be expected to sit four abreast in third-class compartments when the northern main lines favoured only three. The attitude of the staff would imply that passengers might be important people, but so was the train important and the rules had better be obeyed.

At most stations it was the local movements that accounted for most of the activity – plus of course the mineral traffic and freight, accounting for a far higher proportion of the revenue than today. Even at main line stations like Newport, the arrival and departure of Paddington services was quite an event, demanding the stationmaster's presence. Many more trains ran to Blaenavon. Only at busy holiday times, notably summer Saturdays,

were the main lines used to capacity passenger wise. Coal trains passed through the Severn Tunnel far more frequently than expresses – and earned more money.

Between them, tourism and coal, on top of ordinary traffics, helped make the Great Western profitable. Alone of the Big Four between the wars, it had a good dividend record, and even during the 1939–45 war, its ordinary shares were daily reported by *The Times* to stand far above those of the other lines. That was the solid reality of the Great Western's difference. If occasionally one wonders if the GWR legend is nonsense, or at least wildly exaggerated, it is useful to remember what happened at the final meetings of the companies after nationalisation in 1948. The LNER directors sought compensation for loss of office, but the proposal was defeated, and so a small additional final dividend was paid to the shareholders. The GWR directors, mindful of the loss that many retired shareholders would anyway suffer from the compensation terms, did not seek anything for themselves even though the shareholders were suggesting that there be compensation at the company's final meeting, conducted almost in evangelical terms. Thus was the last homage paid to the mighty rule of Paddington, unbroken since the creation of the railway by Brunel and Gooch.

Another reason for the GWR's prosperity was the fine way in which the line had been laid out in the first place. The overseas visitor making forays out of London from the main termini quickly realised that the exit from Paddington was in a class of its own. It set a standard of excellence that influenced all Great Western men, even when building in the hillier parts of the West and Wales. Level crossings were always rare on the GW. Long trains abounded. Everything seemed better ordered and certainly was a lot cleaner. The Great Western tradition was established early and very powerfully. There was always a clear-cut Great Western way of doing things, from selecting typefaces to making sandwiches, from sending messages full of the company's own code abbreviations to the care of stations. When change took place, it happened consciously and was well-publicised, the new way immediately becoming the accepted law. This paid off handsomely, especially in the Grouping period. Many of the

Great Western in a Nutshell
The Great Western will take you to Fishguard – the nearest railway port in Britain to New York – and so to Ireland by the shortest sea passage unless you care to go as far northward as Stranraer; it will take you to Plymouth, where other ocean liners come, and to Weymouth and through to the Channel Islands. From Weymouth to Fishguard – with Bridport, Dawlish, Teignmouth, Torquay, Brixham, Kingswear, Kingsbridge, Fowey, Falmouth, the Lizard and Penzance on the Channel coast; St Ives, Newquay and Barnstaple on the Atlantic; Minehead, Watchet, Weston, Clevedon, Bristol, Newport, Cardiff, Swansea, Tenby, and the rest, on the Bristol Channel – it has more ports and seaside places on its list than on any other line . . . its longest run from London is some 305 miles, yet so many are its branches and cross country routes that its mileage, to say nothing of its motor-car work, is more than nine times as great, being 900 miles more than any other English company, and an eighth of the total mileage of all the railways in this island. . . . What with its buffet cars, breakfast cars, luncheon cars, dinner cars and sleeper cars, a journey in its trains is almost as independent as a voyage in a steamship.
From *Our Home Railways*, by W. J. Gordon (1910)

Chester station around the turn of the century with GWR 2-4-0 No 3228 standing below an array of LNWR signals. This was one of six engines built at Stafford Road works Wolverhampton in 1889 and working, in the main, from Worcester and Hereford. The class was really a modification of the 1863 Armstrong 111 class most of which were shedded at Chester.

problems of the other three main railways resulted from the fact that they were not merely trying to merge the alien traditions of their constituent parts, but indulged in much other re-organisation. Yet many politicians were impressed by the speed of change on the LMS and this – in addition to the fact that the LMS was always the largest – had much to do with Euston's influence over the whole nationalised system after 1948.

What had served the western territory well under private ownership seemed increasingly a thorn in the flesh under national. Staff were no longer promoted from within, but equally from anywhere in the country; and since the Western had much attractive country, that meant many moving in from other Regions, slowing down promotion for dedicated men who could no more have moved to ex-LNER tracks than they could have joined British Overseas Airways. For a time, Paddington fought back; chocolate-and-cream coaches re-appeared on named trains – and

14

Not everything Great Western was necessarily sparkling; some of the earlier wooden stations became dark and dreary with the passage of time as can be seen by this 1930s photograph of the old Banbury station. The photograph reflects the times well, newspaper posters headlining the British and Italian fleets while a comparatively modern bicycle leans against milk churns. The scene is dated by the GWR roundel at the top of the Passengers' Luggage notice below the Frys Chocolate advertisement. Note the leaded light window of the first class refreshment room and the wicker basket containing GWR Hotels and Restaurant Dept cups and saucers.

One of the Great Western Railway's many civil engineering achievements was the construction of the 4½-mile long Severn Tunnel. Work began in 1873 and the first train ran through on 9 January 1886, appropriately filled with South Wales coal; passenger traffic began the following December. The cost to put Cardiff one hour nearer to London and Bristol was nearly £2 million – a vast sum at the time. The reward came the following year when 7,776 trains ran through composed of over 240,000 wagons. It was Daniel Gooch's dogged tenacity which saw the work completed. It was his last big gesture to the company he had served so well. Within three years of its opening he was dead.

many more were named! – and the Region went its own diesel way with an individualistic hydraulic fleet. But this latter-day Great Westernisation is another story.

Today the Western is very much part of a national system, the second generation of diesels and the HSTs providing a faster and more frequent service than anyone could have imagined in GWR days. But you cannot make any journey without being acutely aware of the railway's origins and traditions. Physically it is still very much the Great Western Railway. It was built with such permanence that it will remain so until the last wheel turns. Paddington is still Paddington, a superbly human station, exuding history, also full of personal memories for those who have their homes in the West but come to London on important occasions, yet eminently practical for today. We follow in the path of Royalty, for here it was that Queen Victoria ended her first railway journey and from here have

Once the new cut off via Bicester and High Wycombe had been opened in 1910 (partly over the Great Western/Great Central Railway joint line) Paddington and Birmingham were brought within two hours of each other and timings with the rival LNWR route equalled. Similarly new works at Birmingham Snow Hill station made the whole route much more attractive. Five years earlier Churchward's new 4-6-0s revolutionised the motive power which had earlier been in the hands of 4-4-0s and even 4-2-2s. An early Star class locomotive heads a London express (of crimson lake coaches) near Bentley Heath, Warwickshire around 1912.

A scene from the 1920s; a 2-4-0T heads a down suburban train out of Paddington alongside a three-position upper-quadrant signal, a type installed around the first world war, but later discarded as colour-light signals took over.

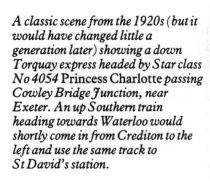

A classic scene from the 1920s (but it would have changed little a generation later) showing a down Torquay express headed by Star class No 4054 Princess Charlotte passing Cowley Bridge Junction, near Exeter. An up Southern train heading towards Waterloo would shortly come in from Crediton to the left and use the same track to St David's station.

Picturesque but less glamorous, a typical cross-country line train en route from Salisbury to Bristol near Bathampton in March 1936, headed by No 4069 Westminster Abbey.

A stopping train at Wilton on the Salisbury to Westbury cross country route: this is probably a through service from Portsmouth to Cardiff as the coaches are mostly London & South Western Railway non-corridor lavatory stock. Note the old baulk road in the siding to the right of the station and the typical GWR covered footbridge with the corrugated iron lamp hut under. The locomotive is No 3208 of the Barnum or 3206 class. They were the most successful and famous of Dean's 2-4-0s. They were the last type designed with sandwich frames and almost the last (1889) of such engines built by the Great Western, if not in the world.

departed the bodies of successive monarchs on their last journeys to final rest.

Again, Paddington provides the smoothest, least fussy exodus from London. Of course Brunel had the good fortune of being able to follow the valley of London's river, but there is rather more to it than that. No other trunk line, perhaps in the world, has required less basic alteration for increasing traffics and speeds than the original GW out of Paddington, though it should be added that the broad gauge itself never realised its potential and put a brake on progress for a generation when the GWR was not a great line. Today's trains regularly pass each other, crossing the Thames on the graceful flat-arch bridge at Maidenhead at a combined speed of 250mph, nearly half that of a jumbo jet in full flight. The railway was built for posterity; it was also built as part of the countryside through which it ran, local materials being used sympathetically, tunnel mouths and other features castellated or otherwise decorated.

Grandeur was an important ingredient in the Great Western tradition. Further away from London, the railway inherited (and indeed took part in the original planning and investment) many routes built to lower basic standards: the terrain was more difficult, money tighter, the traffic prospects less exciting. But they brought with them many grand features which played their full part among the GWR's character gallery that was exploited for publicity purposes but, more deeply, became an important part of the railway's character. Not least among them was the Royal Albert Bridge across the Tamar at Saltash, which like the Atmospheric system and the Sea Wall of the South Devon, Chepstow Bridge and the Severn Tunnel, was always good for a comment – along with the Kings, Swindon works, the 10.30 Limited, and much more.

The building of the basic system in little more than two decades was a remarkable achievement. But it was not just the building. It was the way the GWR absorbed extensions and the lines of other companies into itself, and busily went on from one improvement to another in a matter-of-fact manner. One day a valley had no railway, the next building was under way, two years later the trains started and the manner of operation firmly fixed to last until well after nationalisation. 'The system' meant just that:

Opposite:
The Great Western Railway and the Royal family always had a close affinity, Queen Victoria making her first ever railway journey from Windsor. Sometimes the occasions were sad ones, for a monarch's last journey after lying in state at Westminster Hall is to Windsor. So it was on 13 February 1952, when a Castle class 4-6-0, bearing the name and numberplates of 4082 Windsor Castle, took HM King George VI on his last journey in the LNER royal train, for the King had died at Sandringham. No 4082 was traditionally a Royal engine since at the conclusion of a royal tour of Swindon Works in April 1924 it was driven by the late King George V accompanied by Queen Mary. Consequently commemorative plates were attached to the cab sides to mark the occasion. Unfortunately the genuine No 4082 was in Swindon Works in early 1952 and not available for the funeral train so the Western Region transferred both number and name plates to No 7013 Bristol Castle, built in 1948. The deception was perpetuated to the end, for the plates never reverted to the original locomotive.

The evacuation from Dunkirk placed the railways in Southern England under considerable stress. To report on some of the activity the Great Western produced a special booklet through its Public Relations Office to commemorate the epic work done by the company in the provision of hundreds of special trains.

main lines, cross-country lines, branch lines, big and small stations, and the unstaffed halts pioneered by the GW, all had a common purpose. It was a commercial operation and the importance of boosting the receipts was never doubted. But money had to be made with dignity and efficiency, preferring the long-term to making quick profits.

Stationmasters were the local upholders of the tradition and the expectation. To talk to them was an honour. In truth, they included an odd and often lonely selection of men, but they did their job. Unthinkable that they would not answer letters, for instance. They might type them themselves on typewriters with two shift keys: press once for capitals and twice for the punctuation marks arranged above the letters. They met the important trains, helped if there was a queue at the booking office, canvassed for traffic, and ensured that important customers received their copy of the timetable. That invariably came on time, a tradition BR have sadly failed to uphold. But then the trains themselves were seldom late, or so our memory tells us. What today strikes us as a gross over-provision of equipment (one set of coaches making a single journey from West Wales to Paddington one day and returning the next) obviously helped. But so did *esprit de corps*. To delay the Bristolian was a disgrace so great that nobody risked it. And while many trains on lesser routes plodded slowly on their way to identical schedules decade by decade, making leisurely breaks for water on branch lines, it was the deities among the trains that gave everyone expectations.

The staff were not all universally good at their job, but they were loyal to the *total* system, taking pride in the record runs of the Cheltenham Flyer and the bell that the Baltimore & Ohio presented to *King George V* on its splendid American tour. Anyway, they mainly loved their work. All they wanted was to be respected and to be allowed to get on with the job, often on their own or in pairs out of direct supervision, proud to be associated with the railway that everybody knew was best and as solid as Britain itself. So even planting a rose bush or two on the platform of a wayside station contributed to the grand design. It was paternalistic, of course, but it paid off. Commendations from superior officers were treasured and became family heirlooms. Indeed, perhaps no group of working men ever kept so many records and bits and pieces relating to their jobs as the staff of the GWR. No other group was ever so fascinated over so long a period in what they were doing. The knowledge, the dedication, the self-improvement went in line with the perception that the initials GWR represented one of man's greatest achievements – even, some said, with inspiration from the Almighty as God's Wonderful Railway.

No 6016 King Edward V *just about makes it to the summit of Dainton incline at the head of the 9.30am Paddington to Plymouth express on 2 February 1959. Outwardly all is clean and Great Western but there are problems with glands leaking, and it looks as though the fireman is having a hard time to maintain steam.*

The end of the line, Penzance station in the early 1970s.

1
THE BROAD GAUGE YEARS

Broad gauge days on the Great Western can be divided into three fairly distinct periods. Brunel's original and magnificent conception and superb engineering, plus Gooch's mechanical skill, were solidly and loyally backed up by Charles Saunders, as chief executive officer of the company, and no less by Charles Russell, the great Chairman. It was an always-unanimous quartet of giant personalities, and confident in possession of 'the finest work in England' they went into the controversial time of the Battle of the Gauges with *éclat* and euphoria.

The second period was that of deep recession, in the 1850s. The first period had not been without its great anxieties for all of them. Now, when business fell off so markedly, all the golden promises vanished, and dividends were cut to almost negligible proportions, the strain told heavily upon them; by 1864 three out of the four were dead. Only Gooch survived, to return as Chairman of the company, and begin the liquidation of the broad gauge.

The third period, which lasted for exactly 20 years, covered what could be called the nostalgic era. By 1872 everything north of the original main line, and the entire route from Gloucester to Milford Haven had been converted to standard gauge, and railway students and enthusiasts like Sir William Acworth, E. L. Ahrons, and the Rev A. H. Malan, sought by every means then available to record and extol all that was left of the broad gauge, west of Bristol.

Brunel's engineering on the original main line still stands four-square today, in such classic works as Wharncliffe viaduct, Maidenhead bridge, Sonning cutting, Box tunnel, and the stately bridges and tunnel façades between Bath and Bristol; but while the gradients on the line were for the most part negligible, and the alignment supremely good, he was less successful when it came to the more detailed hardware needed for running the trains. The distinctive bridge rails, laid on longitudinal timbers, were stiff and rigid as he intended them to be; but they gave a very hard and unyielding ride, and when towards the end of the broad gauge era certain sections began to be renewed with cross-sleepered chaired track, with bullhead rails, the enginemen always said that their locomotives were at least 'one coach better' than on the old longitudinals. Ironically, one of the greatest advantages of the old 'baulk road', as it was usually known, was the far greater ease with which the gauge could be altered from broad to standard! All that was needed was to cut the cross-transoms, and slew one rail across, whereas on the sections that had been relaid with cross-sleepers the fact that the GWR had adopted fang bolts for fixing the chairs, instead

From *Herepath's Railway Journal* The Baulk Road 1838
At present it is known that on many parts of those lines in which stone blocks are used, a large force must be maintained to preserve the road in sufficient order for the passage of the engines. Directly as a train passes, a gang of workmen appears, whose task it is to raise and adjust the blocks over which the engine has just passed, lest the succeeding train should be thrown off the track, or otherwise damaged. Nothing of this kind, I apprehend, can happen on the Great Western Railway. If a partial subsidence of the embankment or packing takes place, it may cause an increased resistance and some uneasiness in the passage of the trains, but as all the timbers are firmly connected together into one frame-work, and are supported at various points, there is no danger of the rails losing gage, or being loosened at their points of junction. To say nothing, therefore, of the greater safety thus secured, both to passengers and workmen, there can be little doubt that, after a short time, there will be a great saving to the company in that most expensive item of charge "maintenance of way."

Reproduction of the title page of J. C. Bourne's epic volume of engravings commemorating the construction of the Great Western Railway in 1835.

An excellent example of a Brunel overall station roof. The opening day at Cheddar, 3 August 1869 with a Bristol & Exeter Railway 4-4-0 saddle tank entering with a mixed train from Yatton.

of coach screws, increased the complications of gauge conversion.

Down in the West Country the ingeniously designed and highly picturesque timber trestle viaducts were symbolical of the broad gauge era. Some of them, notably on the Falmouth branch, survived into the 1930s; their design, and the details of their construction, were of such professional interest as to inspire a learned article in *The Railway Engineer* by one of the most distinguished 20th Century civil engineers of the GWR, H. S. N. Whiteley, who then, in 1931, was Divisional Engineer, Plymouth. The South Devon Railway and the Cornwall Railway, single-tracked at first, were built on what was virtually a 'shoe-string', compared to the depth of purse available for the original Great Western main line. It is interesting, though, to recall that long before Brunel journeyed west of Exeter the West Country timber trestle viaducts had a prototype in Sonning Cutting, built to carry an occupation road over the excavation east of the deepest part, where the Bath Road bridge was built.

One of the most remarkable, lengthiest, and yet shortest lived of the timber trestle viaducts was not in South-West England at all, but in South Wales, where the main line into Swansea crossed the valley at Landore. The approach spans on both sides were carried over the marshy ground on trestles similar to those used at the tidal creeks to the west of Saltash, except that there were very many more of them at Landore; but the central span, of no less than 110ft, was also entirely in timber. Unlike the viaducts for the South Devon and Cornwall Railways, Landore was designed to carry a double line.

Another characteristic of the broad gauge era was the all-over roof design of the smaller passenger stations. A criticism that was frequently made of the British railways when many country stations were still in use, and town to town and village to village travel by train was still the rule rather than the exception, was that the stations themselves were unconscionably draughty. On the Great Western and its associated broad gauge lines Brunel in many cases would seem to have forestalled such criticism, not only providing all-over roofs, beneath a shallow gabled section, but building end walls behind which waiting passengers could shelter from cold winds. The interior could be very dark and gloomy at times, and an enclave for smoke and condensed steam to linger. One of the largest of such stations was Swansea; but the all-over roof type survived in very many localities, even at important main line stations like Taunton, until the 1920s and still exists at Frome.

There is little doubt that in propagating his great conception of a rail gauge much wider than anything used hitherto on railways, Brunel was the victim of a major misjudgment, not of engineering nor of railway operating practice, but of human nature. Despite the fact that the railway mileage in Great Britain, built or already authorised by the time the Great Western obtained its Act of Incorporation, greatly exceeded that which he initially planned to build on the broad gauge, Brunel seems to have been confident that when his railway was in operation its all-round superiority would be so obvious that everyone else would want to change. That, of course, was a complete underestimate of the tenacity of the English character, which when faced with severe opposition promptly digs in to withstand a siege! And of course the spread of the 4ft 8½in gauge, the standard of the future, was so rapid that in a very short time it was Brunel himself who was completely encompassed by this narrow gauge, as it was

Standard Time

It is not generally realised that when railways first started they were greatly inconvenienced by the fact that local or actual sun time was used in the country. As the Great Western Railway, with its associates the Bristol & Exeter and South Devon Railways and later the Cornwall and West Cornwall Railways, ran from East to West they were more affected than railways running northwards from London which more or less kept on the same meridian (and hence time). The difference in local time between Paddington and Truro is as much as twenty minutes, and in order to work a standard timetable Paddington or Greenwich time was adopted throughout the system. It was not until 1852 that there was direct telegraph communication from London to Plymouth and commencing from 1 November 1852, a standard time signal was sent to all stations at 10am. When the Cornwall Railway opened in 1859 this was extended through to Truro. At two minutes to 10am all telegraph operators were warned to keep the lines clear so that the station clocks could be checked when the signal came through at 10am. In the provinces at this period time was generally derived from the church clocks or the railways, there being no regular public 'Time' service in operation. It will be seen that as the railways spread throughout the country so the adoption of standard time developed. An unusual way in which the time signal was passed on was at Penzance Station. Here the telegraph clerk stood at the door of his office and when the time signal came through blew a horn, which was a signal for the guard of the 10am up Cornish Riviera Express to give the engine driver the 'Right Away'.

From *The Centenary of the Cornwall Railway*, by R. J. Woodfin

A contemporary engraving of Ealing Haven station in 1840. Note the flat arch bridge, the commodious station and the second class coach placed at the front of the train to protect first class passengers from soot and dirt. Like contemporary road coaches, passengers' luggage is strapped to the coach roofs.

then called. But Brunel carried Russell, Saunders and Gooch with him, and with the extension of the broad gauge to the Bristol & Exeter Railway the situation, nationwide, looked like getting into such a muddle that Parliament set up a Royal Commission on Railway Gauges in July 1845.

In the flood of evidence presented to the Commissioners there was a highly significant distinction between that presented by the protagonists of the narrow and broad gauge parties. Robert Stephenson, Locke, Vignoles, and others who were building narrow gauge lines, having answered the questioning in such a way as to present an almost complete symposium of their life's work, did not argue against the broad gauge on technical grounds, but purely on the increasing lack of uniformity, and of the inconvenience of changing from one to the other at junction points. Gooch on the other hand took exactly the opposite line, and gave a monumental survey of the superiority of the broad gauge, not only in theory and promise for the future but in solid achievement; and even though the Great Western then extended no further than its original termini at Paddington and Bristol, the statistics of its performance were startling in their superiority over the others.

Railway	Total annual loco-miles	Average weight of trains, tons		Average speed of passenger trains, mph
		Passenger	Goods	
London & Birmingham	1,414,941	42.4	162	20
Grand Junction	870,000	43.5	152	20.8
South Western	743,000	36	121	24
Great Western	1,622,700	67	265	27½

The Great Western was thus carrying by far the heaviest loads, and was also making the highest average speeds.

Nevertheless, by the report of the Gauge Commissioners the broad

gauge stood condemned, purely because on the basis of total route-mileage in 1845 it was so heavily outnumbered. Recommendations were made for eliminating it forthwith, but first the Board of Trade, and then Parliament so watered down the report, that not only was the original extent of the broad gauge left intact, but broad gauge trains from Paddington were able to penetrate as far west as Penzance by the very substantial extensions made to it afterwards – to Plymouth by 1849, to Swansea by 1850, to Haverfordwest by 1854, to Weymouth by 1857, to Truro by 1859, and by the laying of mixed gauge over the hitherto standard-gauge West Cornwall Railway. The line from Truro, on standard gauge, had been opened as early as 1852. Mixed gauge was also laid as far north as Wolverhampton, and over the London & South Western line from Exeter to Barnstaple.

The first part of the extension into South Wales was not quite in accordance with Brunel's plan. Having taken the line to Gloucester through the Cotswolds, and come down on the western side through Stroud and Stonehouse, he intended to go straight on, and cross the

Severn where the estuary narrows at Awre. But a variety of local interests combined to block this scheme, though it was eventually the Admiralty which put an end to it by forbidding any kind of bridge downstream from Gloucester. And so Brunel went on to build another 160 miles of broad gauge main line from Gloucester through Newport, Cardiff, and the outskirts of Swansea to Carmarthen, and later to Haverfordwest before eventually extending to tidewater at New Milford. The line from Chepstow to Swansea was opened as early as 1850, but the completion of the route awaited the finishing of the unique tubular bridge over the River Wye at Chepstow, and this did not take place until 1853.

Another great broad gauge line would have been that proposed by Brunel for conveyance of the Irish Mail, for which his project was put forward in opposition to that of Robert Stephenson, who proposed going along the North Wales coast, crossing the Menai Strait and making Holyhead the packet station. Brunel proposed to take the broad gauge north-westwards from Oxford, via Worcester, Ludlow, and Montgomery; thence, tunnelling under the flanks of Cader Idris, to pass Dolgelly and so round the shores of Cardigan Bay to a new packet station at Port Dinlleyn, on the Lleyn peninsula near the present village of Nevin. But the Holyhead route was preferred, and the broad gauge never penetrated to the north-west of Oxford.

The lengthy broad gauge main line through South Wales was short lived, and by 1872 its entire length had been converted to standard gauge. It is a pity that the observers who wrote so entertainingly of the later years of the broad gauge west of Bristol did not have earlier counterparts who

The end of another line in the 1870s, New Milford's extensive layout, better used than it was to be in later decades when the emphasis switched to Fishguard.

could have regaled us with tales of the trains running to Swansea, Carmarthen, Haverfordwest and New Milford. The celebrated Gooch 8ft 4-2-2s did not work on the Gloucester line, or beyond, where some intriguing and little known coupled engines were at work. When the line was first opened throughout, in 1853, the famous Gooch 2-2-2s of the Fire Fly class were used, having 7ft dia driving wheels and 16in by 20in cylinders. But in 1855 Gooch obtained from Robert Stephenson & Company the ten large 4-4-0s of the Lalla Rookh class, having 7ft dia coupled wheels and 17in by 24in cylinders. These engines had inside frames throughout, and as in the 4-2-2s the leading wheels were not carried on a bogie. Both the axles had bearings in the main frames, and to shorten the length of rigid wheelbase the wheels were spaced so close together as to give a very 'squashed-up' appearance.

From all accounts the Lalla Rookh class do not appear to have been very successful engines, and had a way of leaving the road. They were followed by a class of 2-4-0s with 6ft 6in coupled wheels, and 16in by 24in cylinders that seem to have met requirements on the South Wales main line rather better. But the conversion of the gauge in 1872 made the majority of these four-coupled engines redundant, and by the summer of 1881 all had been scrapped, 2-4-0s and 4-4-0s alike.

Extent of the Broad Gauge, including mixed gauge, in the late 1860s. Only one or two more lines were built to the broad gauge in the South West after this.

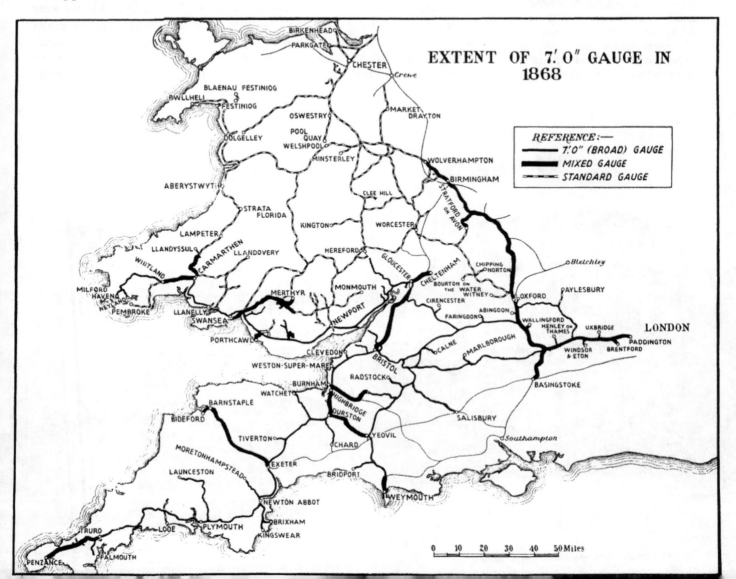

By that time, except on the line west of Exeter, broad gauge activities were being very much curtailed. The thin end of the wedge had been driven into the broad gauge edifice in 1860, when in compliance with the Act that authorised amalgamation with the Shrewsbury railways, mixed gauge was laid in between Oxford and Basingstoke, using the station avoiding line at Didcot, and the west curve connecting directly to the Berks & Hants line at Reading. This allowed through standard gauge traffic to pass from the north to the London & South Western line. In the following year the mixed gauge was laid from Reading to Paddington, and even at that early date the writing was indeed on the wall.

Despite these encroachments the great majority of the older Great Western men remained unshakeably loyal to the spirit of the broad gauge, and sincerely felt that they had in it that 'extra' which the other companies had not got. All who had anything to do with the broad gauge, its locomotives and trains, had a tremendous sense of pride in the job, a superiority complex, particularly at a station like Bristol Temple Meads, where Gooch's beautiful 8ft singles came abreast of the Midland engines. Actually those famous engines, which had been so much in advance of their time when introduced in 1847, had dropped very much behind in the course of their 40-odd years' existence. Although they had a large amount of heating surface the boiler pressure was only 140lb/sq in and there were standard gauge 4-2-2s on other railways with a nominal tractive effort nearly 50 per cent greater. Nevertheless, to the very end the Gooch eight-footers had a magnificent presence unsurpassed by any of their contemporaries, and they nobly personified the broad gauge to the end.

There were twenty-nine of Daniel Gooch's famous 8ft singles though there were individual variations in detail. From 1871 onwards the majority were replaced by new engines officially regarded as rebuilds. Lord of the Isles (originally named Charles Russell *though never running as such) was shown at the Great Exhibition of 1851 and hauled a Directors' special train to Birmingham on 1 October 1852, coming to grief at Aynho when it ran into the back of the previous train. It was withdrawn in 1884, exhibited at Chicago in 1893 and broken up by Churchward in 1906. The photograph shows this famous engine prepared to haul a special train for the Sultan of Turkey.*

2

BROAD GAUGE: SPEED, LEGEND, AND SEQUEL

The opening of the Bristol & Exeter Railway throughout, on 1 May 1844, was signalled by a locomotive performance of which there had been no parallel, anywhere in the world. The special train carrying the invited guests from London was scheduled not only to cover the 194 miles in an overall time of only five hours, an average speed of 39mph inclusive of stops, but to be worked by the same engine. At that time there were no larger engines than Daniel Gooch's Fire Fly class 2-2-2s, of 1840, and of these the *Orion* was chosen. These engines burned coke, and with this there would be less chance of conditions deteriorating in the firebox on so long a run. There were no such things as water troughs at that time, so intermediate stops would have been necessary to fill up the tender tank. Gooch himself, then no more than 27 years of age, drove the engine, and leaving Paddington at 7.30am they arrived in Exeter in exactly the five hours scheduled. What was perhaps more remarkable was that not only was the same engine used for the return trip, but that once again, with Gooch driving all the way, they cut 20min off the five-hour schedule, and averaged 41½mph.

The five-hour Exeter expresses went into regular operation from 10 March 1845, with intermediate stops at Didcot, Swindon, Bath, Bristol and Taunton. These totalled 21min, giving a running average speed of 41¾mph; but from 12 May in that same year, in anticipation of the coming fight before the Gauge Commission, a full half-hour was cut from the time. This was before the days of the compulsory refreshment stop at Swindon, and the time there was cut from ten to a single minute! Even so the running average was accelerated to 45¼mph, a speed that the narrow gauge partisans could not touch. But the restaurant people at Swindon were furious and brought an action against the GWR. Litigation dragged on through the autumn of 1845, but eventually the Railway had to concede defeat. Not so Daniel Gooch however, and by cutting the running times he made up the extra nine minutes spent at Swindon, and still made the Paddington–Exeter run in 4½ hours, a running average speed of 46¾mph. At that time the fastest start-to-stop runs, both at 49mph, were from Paddington to Didcot, and from Bristol to Taunton.

From December 1847 an additional stop was put in at Bridgwater, and far from requiring any extra time on this account, the overall time was *cut* by a further five minutes, and all the quickening came from a truly audacious acceleration of the Paddington–Didcot time from 65 to 55min. As the distance is 53 miles, the Gooch 4-2-2s, which by that time had taken up the running, were required to make a start-to-stop average of 58mph

Daniel Gooch
Gooch was brought up in an engineering environment. He owed his introduction to railways to his acquaintance with George Stephenson, and learned the civil engineering side from his brother Tom, a senior assistant to Robert Stephenson. Daniel was working with his brother on the Manchester & Leeds Railway when he applied for the post of Locomotive Superintendent on the Great Western. Brunel gave him the job, and on 18 August 1837 Gooch took up his appointment at Paddington. He was still six days short of his twenty-first birthday.

Gooch had, indeed, jumped in at the deep end, and no doubt coping with the unpromising early Great Western engines, and fending off an impatient Board of Directors, helped to produce the man of later years. However irascible some Directors may have been when stung by public criticism of delays and breakdowns, the Board evidently recognised Gooch's dedication and competence for he was instructed to prepare designs for new engines. His eight-foot singles are among the classic locomotives, and he was an able and adroit defender of the 7ft gauge before the Gauge Commission of 1845–46. He had planned the locomotive works at Swindon which opened in 1843.

Gooch's reputation in the Board Room was now established, and although he resigned as Locomotive Superintendent in 1864 to spend more time on outside business activities he returned to Paddington in 1865 as Chairman.

over this first stage of the journey. In regular service however the engines were always changed at Bristol. The trains were very light, even by later broad gauge standards, and rarely exceeded about 60 tons behind the tender. The scheduled time from London to Bristol was increased by 5min to 2hr 35min in October 1848, to include a stop at Chippenham, and gave a running average of 51¼mph. Nevertheless a series of fuel consumption tests made in the early spring of 1849 by the distinguished consulting engineer Daniel Kinnear Clark showed that strict time was not often kept, even with trailing loads of no more than 60 tons, and that the coke consumption varied from 30 up to 38lb per mile – very heavy in relation to the light loads hauled. The Gooch 4-2-2s were indeed hauling little more than their own weight.

A legend persisted that on 11 May 1848 the run from Paddington to Didcot was made in 47½min at a start-to-stop average speed of 67mph. The word 'legend' is used advisedly, because attempts have been made at various times to disprove this claim, if not to assert its impossibility of achievement. Some years ago however two professional engineers of high academic distinction jointly made a careful analysis of all the available evidence, including that contained in a paper that Gooch himself read before the Institution of Civil Engineers in 1848, and came to the conclusion that the claim of such a record had some justification.

In the discussion on his paper Gooch said that they were in the *habit* of running from Paddington to Didcot in between 48 and 50min, and that the specially fast run was made in the presence of Capt Simmons, one of the Inspecting Officers of the Board of Trade. Furthermore he quoted the water consumption as 1,550gal, or roughly 30gal to the mile, and stated that the steam cut-off in the cylinders was at 15in, in a stroke of 24in, or 62 per cent. This would in any case be considered very hard working, and would account for the high fuel consumption, even though the total

A down express – on what is today's down relief lines – passes through Twyford over separate standard- and broad-gauge connections to a siding, beside which work has started on the right on building what were to become the main line tracks between Paddington and Reading. Shunting would have been a hazardous business.

weight of the train – engine, tender and coaches – was only 115 tons. To average 67mph from start to stop would have entailed continuous running at over 70mph for much of the distance. The engine concerned in the making of this run was the *Great Britain*.

Such a run would have been quite exceptional at that time in railway history, and so far as maximum speed was concerned, the highest that was reported with one of these engines was attained when Brunel and Gooch were testing them, when brand new. Then, driven all-out down Dauntsey bank, with its gradient of 1 in 100, the maximum they could get was 78mph. At this distance in time it is rather pointless to try and theorise as to the working of these broad gauge engines, and how in the euphoric early days they had to be thrashed to make the speeds they did. In his evidence before the Gauge Commissioners in 1845 Gooch submitted some indicator diagrams taken off the 2-2-2 engine *Ixion*, of the Fire Fly class, which showed that at 60mph the regulator was full open, and cut-off no less than 66 per cent; but the diagram also shows that there was surprisingly little drop in pressure from the rated 50lb/sq in during the period of admission. It would have been interesting to see indicator cards taken from the big 4-2-2 engines when running the Paddington–Didcot 55min train. When D. K. Clark was making his extensive tests of fuel consumption, Gooch, as recorded later in his diaries, rode on the buffer beam of the engines to take the indicator diagrams. This was before the days when a temporary shelter would be created round the front of an engine to protect men engaged in such work.

From 1847 to 1852 the 9.50am Exeter express from Paddington was without doubt the fastest train in the world – on its normal timing that is,

A splendid bird's eye view of convertible 2-4-0 No 14, on an up passenger train near Bathampton.

33

This year was memorable in Railway annals as bringing to an end the celebrated "Broad Gauge;" and it happened that on the 20th May, on going down to Windsor in readiness for the Queen's journey to Scotland, on my arrival at Paddington, I was eye-witness to a memorable scene on the departure of the 5.0 p.m. train from Paddington to the West of England. It was the last broad gauge train that ran out of London, and as it reached its destination it closed the long record of the Great Western Brunel Gauge service in the West. The way in which the retreat of the broad gauge stock was managed on the morrow, when the lines were being narrowed and no possibility would exist for the transit of such vehicles, is a study in railway working, and required a splendid organisation and scheming, on the part of the Superintendent's Department to keep the traffic going, to make sure of the safe retirement of all the broad gauge stock to its old home at Swindon; and a most rapid development on the part of the Engineering Department in bringing the rails into position for the narrow gauge service.

The small volume of printed regulations issued by Mr. Burlinson for this final termination of one system and starting of another is a curiosity in its way.

The mixed gauge existed from Truro to Penzance. On this, of course, the broad gauge was simply disused, so the task consisted in converting the broad to the narrow gauge between Exeter and Truro and the branches connected. The men to conduct the operation had to be taken to destinations by special broad gauge trains; space being reserved in one compartment of each carriage for their tools. The men amounted to a perfect army, and their empty vehicles formed the last broad gauge running on the system.
From *Railway Reminiscences*, by G. P. Neale

quite apart from any special spurts. It received the nickname of 'The Flying Dutchman', after the famous racehorse that won both the Derby and the St Leger in 1849. That it was a tough job for the enginemen was generally recognised, so much so that the phrase 'stoking the Dutchman' became a synonym for hard physical work. The fireman would have to shovel roughly a ton of coke in the 55min run to Didcot. But alas this brilliant performance could not be sustained, and in the Spring of 1852 deceleration began, eventually with the withdrawal of the fast Exeter service altogether. With the financial fortunes of the Great Western seriously declining the cancellation of the 'Flying Dutchman' had an echo in the austere post-war aftermath in 1947, when the 'Cornish Riviera Express' was temporarily withdrawn.

In broad gauge days, in face of competition from the London & South Western, a new Flying Dutchman was put on in March 1862, leaving Paddington at 11.45am and once again running to Exeter in 4½hr. At first, as previously, a stop at Didcot was included, in 57min from Paddington; but in general much difficulty was experienced in keeping time and from June 1864 the Didcot stop was abandoned, and the train was still allowed 90min for the 77.3 miles to Swindon, thenceforward non-stop. The average speed of 51½mph was immeasurably easier than 56mph from Paddington to Didcot. But even this timing was subsequently eased out drastically and by the summer of 1867 the Flying Dutchman was allowed 105min from Paddington to Swindon, only 44mph. This was the prelude to being taken off for the second time.

The Great Western's legendary reputation for speed was now fading almost into oblivion. The train was reinstated two years later, only at the instigation of the Bristol & Exeter Railway, to reach Exeter in 4¾hr from Paddington, but it was wretchedly slow on the Great Western, and achieved its overall time only by some much brisker running over the B&E. But if the Dutchman was slow how can the rest of the GWR passenger service be described? Of nine down trains between Paddington and Bristol in the early 1870s only one covered the 118½ miles in three hours; the rest varied between 3hr 5min and a heroic 6hr 25min. When the London & South Western put on a new train in 4½ hours from Waterloo to Exeter, the Great Western was stirred to accelerate the Dutchman to a 4¼hr run, with a timing of 87min over the 77.3 miles from Paddington to Swindon, and 51min for the 44¾ miles from Bristol to Taunton; this schedule remained in operation for the rest of the life of the broad gauge.

While the Paddington–Swindon run at an average of 53¼mph was commendable, there were by that time keen observers to report on how it was done, or not done, as was more frequently the case! The point-to-point scheduling of the train was not a good example of railway operating psychology, for the hard run down to Swindon was followed by a very easy run of 38min, over the generally favourable 29½ miles on to Bath. The result was that drivers were in the habit of losing two or three minutes on the first stage, and regaining it on the next.

Sir William Acworth got a footplate pass to see how it was done, intending to make a very quick turn-round at Swindon. The down

Racing between Taunton and Bristol, a 2-2-2 convertible takes up the mail through Flax Bourton.

Dutchman was due to arrive at 1.12pm and the up to leave at 1.18, also with 87min allowed for the run up to Paddington. There was a strongish cross-wind and a load heavier by one coach; but the driver and fireman obliged with a harder run than usual and reached Swindon on time; but as they were running in Acworth reported the driver as saying: 'If you hadn't been here, I should have been five minutes late into Swindon this morning, and have saved five or six hundredweight of coal'. The privileged observer was able to hurry across and board the engine of the up Dutchman, which landed him back in Paddington at 2.43pm, 2min early, in 85min from Swindon. When it is recalled that it required a coke consumption of anything up to 38lb per mile to run the Dutchman of 1850, with a trailing load of about 60 tons, one cannot be surprised at anyone looking to means of saving coal when the regular load in the 1880s was around 140 tons, with the same engines. It is true that most of the Gooch eight-footers would have been pretty thoroughly rebuilt by then; but their basic dimensions were unchanged.

When he was a pupil in the locomotive works at Swindon, E. L. Ahrons made a number of journeys on the fast broad gauge expresses, which had then been augmented by the 3pm Zulu, on the same running times, and he

35

GREAT WESTERN RAILWAY.

"CONVERSION OF GAUGE."

This is the last Broad Gauge Train to travel over the line between Penzance and Exeter.

To the
Station Master

Traffic
Inspector.

Station.

May 20th, 1892.

One of the certificates issued to ensure that no broad gauge vehicles were left stranded in the West.

formed the impression that time could be kept on the 87min down journey when there was no contrary wind, no load more than about 130 tons, and with the engine 'thumped'. This was not surprising having regard to the vintage for the engine design. *Rover*, for example, with 170 tons, lost 3¾min on book time, with no speed exceeding 58mph. *Eupatoria*, with the same load, did slightly better, and would have clocked into Swindon in just under 90min but for one slight signal check. *Hirondelle*, with one coach less, made a comparably faster run, though even so not exceeding 60mph anywhere. In view of the impending conversion of the gauge there was no case for building larger engines, and so far as the men were concerned it seemed a point of honour to carry on as best they could. The average running speed of 50mph between Paddington and Bristol was much the same as that in operation when D. K. Clark carried out his fuel consumption tests in 1849, and the trailing loads were no more than 55 or 60 tons. It can well be imagined how those same engines had to be 'thumped' and at what cost in coal, in attempting to keep the same schedules when the loads were up to seven bogie coaches weighing 24 to 25 tons each.

As a Swindon pupil Ahrons was often on the footplate, though more frequently on standard than broad gauge engines. But there was one occasion when, at his instigation one would imagine, an attempt was made at a really high maximum speed. Gooch himself had clocked up 78mph down the Dauntsey bank, but the maximum Ahrons noted there was 66½mph. So he went farther afield, and anticipated the classic effort of *City of Truro* in 1904, by participating in an all-out descent of Wellington bank. The train was the up Zulu, allowed 38min for the 30¾ miles from Exeter to Taunton, start to stop, and the load was one of five eight-wheeled coaches, about 125 tons behind the tender. The engine, appropriately, was named *Lightning*, and descending Wellington bank they just topped 81mph. In the reverse direction a pilot was usually taken from Taunton up to Whiteball summit if the load exceeded five of the heaviest coaches.

Before the final conversion of the gauge, though many excellent standard gauge engines were already at work, particularly those based at Wolverhampton and running the Birmingham expresses, a brave attempt was made to sustain the legendary superiority of the broad gauge, and standard gauge expresses running over mixed gauge sections, such as the New Milford boat trains, were timed between Paddington and Swindon at slower average speeds than trains like the Flying Dutchman and the Zulu. The Sir Alexander class of 7ft 2-2-2s was used on these trains which had a time allowance of 97min from Paddington to Swindon. At times of exceptional traffic some odd things happened. One Easter the 3pm Zulu had to be run in two sections. As there was no extra broad gauge stock or engine available, the second part had to be standard gauge, and the 2-2-2 engine No 1123 *Salisbury*, set out with a load of no less than 195 tons. It began extremely well, passing Reading in a good minute quicker time than the broad gauge 4-2-2s did with their 140 ton loads, and apart from checks would have reached Swindon in little more than 88min. The legend of Great Western speed was beginning to take a different form by 1892.

36

THREE FAMOUS STATIONS

Paddington

Soon after the GWR was opened from London to Maidenhead a director of another railway travelled over the line and reported his impressions in a letter to the Editor of *The Railway Magazine* (only distantly related to the present publication of the same name). The Paddington station of those days impressed him favourably. He wrote:

I rode at a charge of sixpence in half an hour from the Bank of England to the London station of the railway at Paddington; which is approached from the end of Oxford Street, through the left-side of the Edgeware Road. The entrance gates and piers, with a gate-keeper's lodge in the centre, are substantial, and sufficient without any pretensions to splendour. An excellent road for carriages, with a broad pavement for foot passengers, leads to the centre of the station, on the right hand side of which is a capacious engine-house and carriage sheds, better designed than any I have before seen; on the left side a wide space is left, apparently for a merchandise station, and a further space near Paddington Canal, which is, I presume, intended for shipping docks for forwarding goods by canal to the Thames, and the London and other docks. There are some roads carried across the station at two or three points by arches of the best design and execution I ever witnessed; these arches are very roomy, and will be of service for carriages and merchandise.

Paddington station as seen by The Illustrated London News *on 8 July 1854. Light, airy, and spacious, this effect is more obvious with the lack of buildings to darken the area beyond the 'lawn'.*

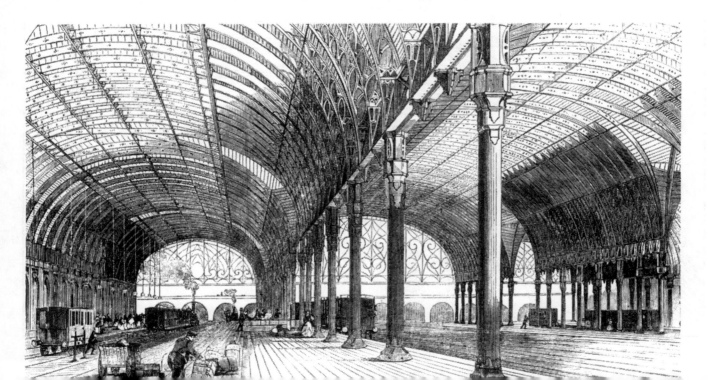

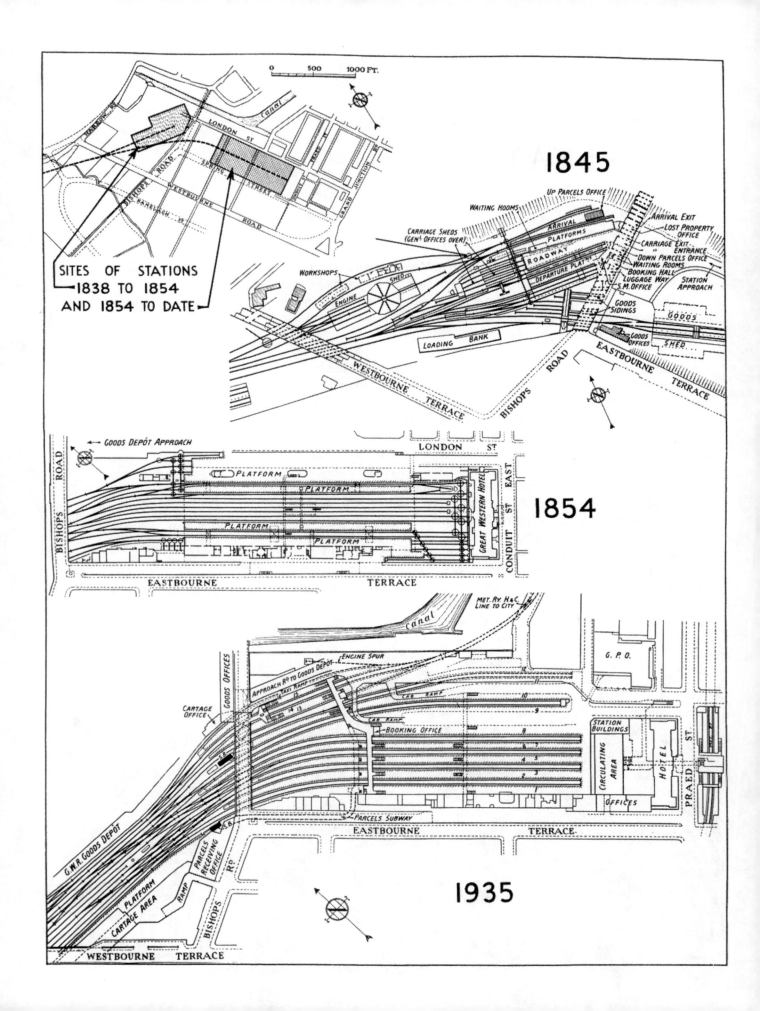

SITES OF STATIONS
1838 TO 1854
AND 1854 TO DATE

1845

1854

1935

The station described above, north of Bishop's Road, was the one at which Queen Victoria arrived from Slough on 13 June 1842 when making her first railway journey. Her train was driven by Daniel Gooch himself. This was a temporary terminus, and land was acquired south of Bishop's Road for a permanent station. First some temporary buildings on this site had to be demolished and replaced and it was not until 1853 that completion of the plan was sanctioned.

By 29 May 1854 the new Paddington was fully in service and what remained of the original station north of the bridge was demolished to make room for a new goods depot. The new station was designed by Brunel in conjunction with the architect Matthew Digby Wyatt. Its most impressive feature was the glass roof in three spans of 70ft, 102ft 6in, and 68ft with its wrought iron arched supports and elaborately traceried end screens. Two 50ft transepts broke up the main arcades, forming what Gordon Biddle has described in *Victorian Stations* as 'an intricate geometrical pattern which was unique'. It had been intended to install traversers here for moving carriages from track to track but this was never done, and what had been planned as a practical facility remained as a pleasing architectural feature.

Opposite: Stages in the development of Paddington

A view looking down Paddington's No 1 platform around World War I when the coaches were painted in maroon with white roofs. As the clock shows 10.30am the train is possibly the 10.55 to Penzance. The trolley on the platform adjacent to the porter with his luggage contains locomotive or carriage head/tail lamps and, judging by the number of schoolboys with caps, it is beginning of term time.

Paddington
Paddington itself is described by
Mistress Priscilla Wakefield, in
1814, as 'a village situated on the
Edgeware Road, about a mile from
London'. In 1801, when the Grand
Junction Canal was opened, and
the first barge, full of passengers,
arrived from Uxbridge at the
Paddington basin, bells were rung,
flags were hung, and cannon were
fired. But Charles Knight men-
tions that even so recently as that
time 'only one stage coach ran
from the then suburban village of
Paddington to the city, and it was
never filled', and that, to beguile
the travellers at the several resting
places on their journey 'Miles's
Boy' told tales and played on the
fiddle. How great the change from
all this when, in 1853, William
Robins, the historian of Paddington, wrote that 'a city of palaces
has sprung up in twenty years',
and that 'a road of iron with steeds
of steam' was in use. Between the
end of the passenger station and
the West London Junction – a distance of about a mile and a half –
there are twelve miles of running
lines and thirty-eight miles of
sidings. A staff of more than 3,000
officers and men is stationed at
Paddington, including the chiefs
of the service. Nearly 300 trains
pass in or out of the station every
day, and about 11,000,000 of passengers use it every year.
From *Our Iron Roads*,
F. S. Williams (1883).

Opposite:
*Shrewsbury station in 1938 with Star
class 4-6-0 No 4013* Knight Of St.
Patrick *(still attached to a 3,500
gallon tender) at the head of a
Bournemouth to Birkenhead train
of Southern Railway stock.*

Great Western hero, No 3440 City of
Truro *as running after its emergence
from York Museum in the late 1950s.
It was used in regular service over the
Didcot, Newbury & Southampton
route as well as on enthusiast
specials.*

To improve communication between Paddington and central London the GWR contributed to a scheme for a connection to the Metropolitan Railway. The alignment of the link prevented trains from calling at platforms in Paddington itself and so new platforms were built on the north side of the main lines at the 'country' end of the terminus. They formed the separate Bishops Road station. The line was mixed gauge, and GWR broad gauge trains began working to Farringdon Street on 10 January 1863.

The Hammersmith & City Railway built a line from Hammersmith to join the GWR at Westbourne Park and on 13 January 1864 Great Western trains began a service between Hammersmith and Farringdon Street via Bishops Road. From 1 April 1865, however, services through Bishops Road were worked with standard gauge stock by the Metropolitan. The Metropolitan was also extending westwards to form what was to become the Inner Circle. On 1 October 1868, when it reached Gloucester Road, Praed Street station was opened on the opposite side of the road to the Paddington terminus and hotel. Paddington station on the Bakerloo tube dates from 1 December 1913.

At first Metropolitan services through Bishops Road ran to and from Westbourne Park over the GWR main lines but separate suburban tracks were opened on 30 October 1871. Trains continued to cross the GWR on the level to reach the Hammersmith & City line until a subway from Royal Oak to a new Hammersmith & City station at Westbourne Park, on the south side of the main line, was opened on 12 May 1878.

Over the years platforms in Paddington main line station were added and extended, and the approaches improved. A major development authorised in 1906 was not completed until the years of World War I. Three new platforms were brought into use on the arrival side under a steel and glass roof 700ft long and with a span of 190ft, designed to match Brunel's original structure. By 1915 Paddington had 12 platforms, but Platform 12 dealt mainly with inwards milk, fish, mail and parcels traffic. Down milk trains left from an extension of the main departure platform, but in 1923 all milk traffic was transferred to Paddington Goods.

In further rebuilding in 1933 the platforms at Bishops Road were renumbered in the main sequence, becoming 13 to 16, and the Bishops Road name was dropped, the platforms being known as Paddington (Suburban). Another and more obvious feature of the 1933 improvements was the creation of a spacious circulating area at the platform ends. Generations had known the site as the 'Lawn' and it is thought that the name derives from a grass slope that existed there alongside the approach to the original temporary station on the north side of Bishops Road. When Brunel built his terminus on the other side of the road he encroached on the 'Lawn' by extending the tracks beyond the platforms and linking them with turnplates for transferring vehicles from track to track. But the name lived on, even surviving the years after removal of the turnplates when the 'Lawn' was a parking area for mailbags, parcels, and horse-drawn vans. The tidying up in the 1930s could not restore the verdure of the 1840s but it converted an eyesore and an inconvenience into an amenity worthy of a great terminus.

Reading: An up Plymouth express detaches a slip coach as it runs through the platform track, having slackened speed to take the crossovers at each end of the platform loop.

Reading in 1937 with an up express headed by Star class 4-6-0 No 4020 Knight Commander (small tender) and 4082 Windsor Castle. Both carried the GWR roundel on their tenders. Note the full lining on the locomotives and the clerestory stock on the centre tracks.

In its centenary year, 1935, the Great Western Railway reprinted a special centenary issue of *The Times* with the title *Great Western Progress*. A section on Paddington compared the traffic at the terminus over nearly one hundred years in the following words:

In 1842 the total number of trains in and out of London was 16 each way (including the two 'goods trains' for the unfortunate third class passengers) and 15 in and out of Bristol. About 140 trains are now despatched from Paddington main station and 255 from the suburban side (30 steam, 225 electric) every 24 hours, while the number leaving the main station on a busy Saturday in the holiday season is 190, and about the same number of trains arrive. The timetable has necessarily had to keep pace with this growth of traffic. There are now two issues yearly, and the summer timetable this year runs to upwards of 300 large pages (11½in by 7½in) of closely printed matter.

Traffic patterns change. Paddington in 1983 was handling 180 main line and 200 suburban and commuter trains daily. The daily flow of passengers through the terminus was 50,700. Busiest periods from Mondays to Fridays were from 08.00 to 09.00 when some 9,500 passengers arrived on 22 trains, and from 17.15 to 18.15 when over 9,000 passengers departed on 24 homegoing trains. Every day some 10,000 mailbags passed through the station, and the 220 tons of newspapers despatched on six days a week rose to 550 tons on Saturday nights. The station had a staff of 900. How long, one wonders, will the concourse be remembered as the 'Lawn'? The tradition is being kept alive, and on 11 July 1983 the 'Lawn' took on a garden party atmosphere with a buffet supper, fashion show, and live music to speed travellers by the first Night Riviera MkIII sleeping car service on their way to Penzance.

Bristol

Although the Great Western had its roots in Bristol, operations began at the London end of the line and the terminus at Bristol Temple Meads was not opened until 30 June 1841. A Tudor-style façade with tall, square-headed windows and heavy mullions, screened the train shed. Here, as at Paddington, the most notable feature was the train shed roof with a span of 74ft across the four broad-gauge tracks. At Bristol, however, Brunel used timber. The interior was late Gothic ecclesiastical with an arcade of flattened arches on each platform and hammerbeams supporting the ribs of the roof, of which there were 44 at 10ft intervals. It earned the approval of Pugin, the Gothic revivalist, who had designed the detail of Sir Charles Barry's new Houses of Parliament. Behind the façade, on upper floors extending over the buffer stops in the train shed, were the company's general offices. Stairs led from the booking hall to the platforms, which were 15ft above street level.

The Bristol & Exeter Railway had begun running trains between Bristol and Bridgwater a few weeks before the Great Western station was opened.

No Cheap Fares to Paddington
A friend on a pleasantly long holiday stay at Paignton, in the early 1920s, received a call to attend a brief business meeting in London. To lessen travelling expenses and having regard to the attractions of London as a tourist centre he enquired at the station about any cheap fare facilities. He was met with an implacable NO; when he asked politely why not, was met with the irrefutable statement: 'Paddington is not a seaside resort'!

Opposite:
Birmingham Snow Hill 1939. Saint class 4-6-0 No 2937 Clevedon Court *runs tender first towards the turntable and servicing area situated at the top left hand of the picture. To the right of the locomotive is a 'Toad' four-wheeled brake van carrying the inscription Bordesley Junction; behind this is a four-coach Birmingham Division local train set. Both the Saint and the coaches carry the GWR roundel.*

Swindon Works 1937. One of the large 2-8-0 tanks No 4283 in plain unlined green and GWR roundel stands outside A shop after a general repair.

Bristol Temple Meads station from the entrance road around the turn of the century. Since the drawing shown earlier the building has become more ornate with clock tower and Victorian Gothic pinnacles added. On the left are the Midland Railway offices and on the right those of the Great Western.

Opposite:
Stages in the development of Bristol Temple Meads

It had its own station close to the GWR establishment but at right angles to it. Vehicles had to be transferred between the two railways by turntables where the tracks intersected. Shifting a whole train one vehicle at a time was a long process and in 1845 the lines were joined by an 'express curve' with one narrow platform. All up trains stopped there, but those continuing beyond Bristol ran forward and then backed into the Great Western station before continuing their journey. Three down trains backed into the Bristol & Exeter station.

The Midland Railway gained access to Bristol by its acquisition of the broad gauge Bristol & Gloucester Railway and in 1854 standard gauge tracks were laid to accommodate its trains. The extra traffic in the Great Western station became a problem and various schemes for a joint station were put forward by the three railways involved. Finally it was decided to develop the accommodation on the 'express curve' and from that stems the impressive curved sweep of Temple Meads station today. Sanction for the new work was given by the Bristol Joint Station Act of 1865. It was stipulated that there should be no interruption of traffic and so operations were spread over several years. The down main platform was opened in 1874 and the remainder by the beginning of 1876. This was the year in which the Bristol & Exeter amalgamated with the Great Western and so the new station was joint Great Western and Midland only. Midland trains starting and terminating at Bristol used the original Great Western station, where the platforms were extended under a light iron roof to meet the up main platform of the new station.

Bristol Temple Meads was now roughly in the shape of a letter V, with a new entrance façade near the apex, the terminal platforms on the left of the approach, and the new through platforms on the right. The unpretentious wooden train shed of the Bristol & Exeter Railway was done away with. Once again a roof was the dominant architectural feature, this time the great curved sweep over the main line platforms. A writer in the *Great Western Railway Magazine* of December 1907 described it as follows:

46

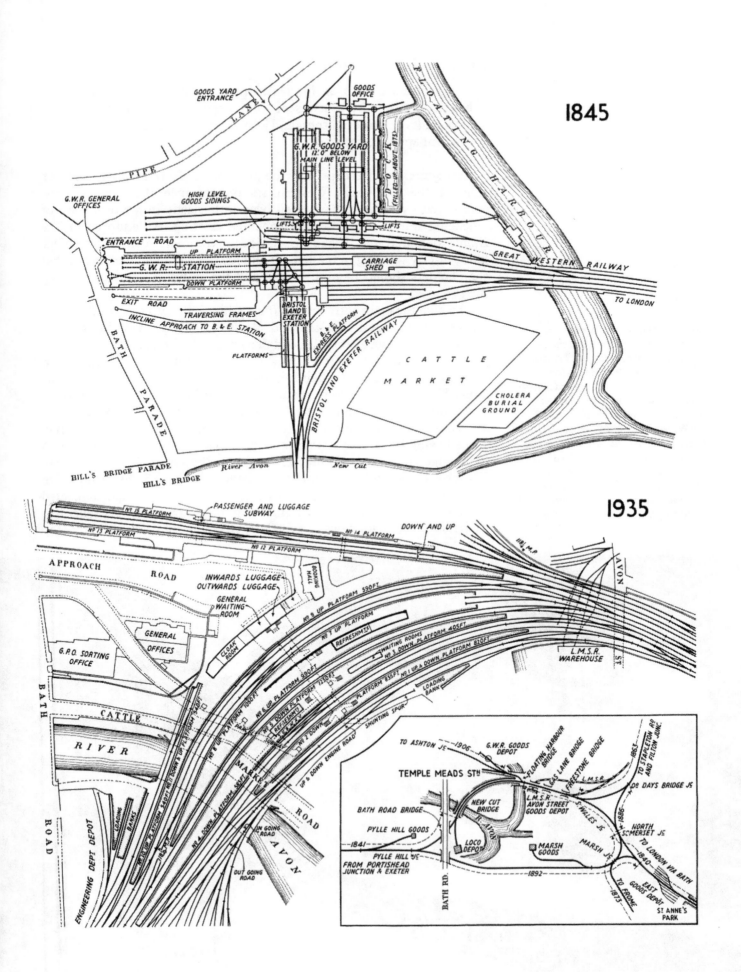

The roof consists of an immense span without a single column, braced together by a series of iron suspension rods and arched girders. Its extreme lightness and lofty curvilinear character gives it a graceful appearance.

Less successful, perhaps, was the new façade. In retaining the Tudor style of the old Great Western station entrance the designer was considered by some to have been over-enthusiastic in his profusion of crocketed spires, turrets and ornamented cresting. An editorial in *The Builder* deplored it as 'Pseudo-Gothic of the commonest and most vulgar kind, utterly wanting in refinement and knowledge', and demanded that shareholders should be told the name of the architect who was wasting their money.

Through the main entrance was the booking hall with separate booking offices for the Great Western and Midland railways. On the left was Platform 5, known as the Midland departure platform, and on the right Platform 4, the main Great Western up platform with waiting and refreshment rooms and a hairdressing saloon. Platforms 2 and 3 in the Great Western station were islands. Platform 2, some 350ft long, dealt with Midland arrivals and interchange traffic generally. The other island was added towards the end of the 1890s to cope with increasing traffic, space having become available with the abolition of the broad gauge. A footbridge connected the four platforms in the Great Western station. Platform 4 was contiguous with the Midland's Platform 5. A subway led to Platform 7 on the opposite side of the line while a footbridge connected Platforms 6 and 8 which ran through into the old train shed. A relief line by-passing the station was opened in 1892, in time for the non-stop

One of the main platforms at one of Britain's busiest stations at the height of the railway age. Bristol Temple Meads in 1906, two years after City of Truro *made its record run up from Plymouth with the London mails, now diverted in this year of 1906 via Castle Cary. But at busy times trains still had to queue outside the station for a platform, local comings and goings outnumbering long-distance ones. The curved roof remains but much else has changed, including the removal of the middle platform.*

running of the Cornishman between Paddington and Exeter.

The 1935 re-building scheme involved widening the bridge over the Floating Harbour on the London side and the River Avon on the Exeter side of the station, allowing platforms to be lengthened; the purchase of additional ground allowed the station to be widened by 230ft. A platform was constructed alongside the wall supporting the 1878 roof and two islands were also built; as the face of one was extensive, the platform was divided and provided with scissors crossovers giving the station an additional six platforms. With the additional use of a bay at the Exeter end of the main platform, the number of platforms was increased from eight to fifteen. The coverings of the new platforms were of the 'umbrella' and 'arcade' type and the buildings constructed of Carrara glazed blocks and a grey granite plinth. Under the old roof the original four platforms were entirely altered to give two very long platform faces, the running lines of which were divided centrally by scissors crossovers, allowing each platform to bear two numbers and for trains to depart independently through the central lines. The overbridge was demolished and the subway was constructed. A new signalling system was installed, being of the most modern design at that time, and operated by two new signalboxes – Bristol East and Bristol West. They were termed 'power boxes' as semaphore signals were replaced by colour lights and points were controlled by electric motors while the levers in the boxes were likened to 'beer pulls'.

The original GWR station, now with its two long platforms divided centrally, were numbered 12, 13, 14, 15 and were utilised for LMS express and local services and the Avonmouth lines. The platforms used by Great Western trains were numbered 1 to 11, the latter being the Portishead Bay at the west end of the main up platform. This platform was divided by a scissors and was numbered 9 (east end) and 10 (west end). The remaining three islands were numbered 7 (east end), 8 (west end) with intermediate scissors, and 6; 5, 3 (east end) and 4 (west end) with scissors; 2 and 1.

In 1966, platforms 12 to 15 were taken out of use and the track in the 'Old Station' (as it is now popularly known) was taken up and the portion nearest Victoria Street – under the Brunel roof – became a car park. The far end nearest London became the site for the new MAS signalbox and the intermediate area was ear-marked for use by the Post Office as a sorting and transfer area between road and rail. The new signalbox was started and a year's planning and preparation took place prior to 21 February 1970 which saw the start of the uplifting of track in the immediate Temple Meads area as part of the work entailed in the Bristol re-signalling scheme, one of the largest to be installed in Europe. An entirely new signalling system was installed which involved the alteration of junctions, cross-overs, etc. to permit a faster approach to the station and for trains in either direction to use any of the platforms. Hitherto, with the exception of the main platform, the signalling arrangements were for down through trains to be dealt with only on the down side and the others only on the up. With the second phase of the work on 8 March, the new box came into partial use and the platforms were re-numbered changing the main platform from

The Fire Fly Project 1984
When the first GWR passenger train left Bristol Temple Meads for Bath at 8.00pm on 31 August 1840 it was hauled by *Fire Ball* a Fire Fly locomotive, one of sixty-two similar locomotives of the class, including *Fire Fly*, which was the first to be delivered to the Paddington end of the line in March 1840.

The Fire Fly class was a great success, and together with its sister class of Sun locomotives, worked all of the early traffic. Queen Victoria made her first railway journey behind a Fire Fly locomotive. They made regular workings at speeds up to 60mph, and gave the new Great Western Railway a reputation for being the fastest railway in the world.

The project to build and run a replica was conceived in 1981 and began to take shape after discussion with British Rail and the Bristol City Museum led to sponsorship proposals from both these organisations. During late 1981 and 1982 a series of design studies and research was carried out and by 1983 the idea had gained support in many quarters.

The Fire Fly Trust itself was formed with charitable status in October 1982 and a public appeal for funds was opened in April 1983. Fund raising activities include steam workings by the Bristol Industrial Museum in association with British Rail, and production of silver and bronze medals by the Royal Mint.

It was hoped to start construction of the replica locomotive in 1984 and to set up a drawing office at Swindon to prepare specifications and drawings for the work. The replica will be built to 7/8ths full size in order to come within the standard British Rail loading gauge, and the frames will be arranged so that by / a wheel change, the running gear is adaptable from broad gauge to standard gauge.

49

9 and 10 to 3 and 4. The area controlled by the box is now bounded by Cogload (Taunton), Pilning, Charfield, Badminton, Bathampton (for the London route) and Bradford on Avon, covering 117 route miles.

Birmingham

For many years Birmingham Snow Hill seemed as permanent an entry in the timetable index as Bristol Temple Meads. Other composite titles might disappear as station closures made them unnecessary – Leeds and Sheffield need no suffixes now – but surely Birmingham would always have its Big Two. It was not to be. The end began for Snow Hill in 1967 with electrification of the Euston–Birmingham line and diversion of the Paddington services into New Street; Paddington–Banbury via High Wycombe and Shrewsbury–Birkenhead became thin red lines on the BR map.

There had been a station at Snow Hill since the Oxford & Birmingham line was opened in 1852 but at first it was a modest wooden structure. The building was later removed to Didcot, and a new and more solid station was completed in 1871. Events in the later years of the century pointed towards expansion and acceleration of the Birmingham service, the most important development being a cut-off route to Banbury via High Wycombe and Bicester, part of which was joint with the Great Central Railway. The Great Central had reached London in 1899 by running powers over the Metropolitan from Quainton Road, north of Aylesbury but sharing tracks with a busy suburban service would create problems. Collaboration with the Great Western in a joint line from Northolt Junction to Ashendon Junction enabled the GCR to by-pass the Metropolitan bottleneck. It also brought Great Western trains to within 18 miles of Aynho on the route to Birmingham via Didcot and Oxford. When that gap was closed the distance from Paddington to Birmingham via Bicester was 110½ miles compared with 129¼ miles by the old route, and actually 2½ miles shorter than Euston to Birmingham.

The development of Birmingham Snow Hill, below, as it was after the first rebuilding in the 1870s, and opposite after the enlargement carried out in the early years of the present century ready for trains by the new direct route through Bicester.

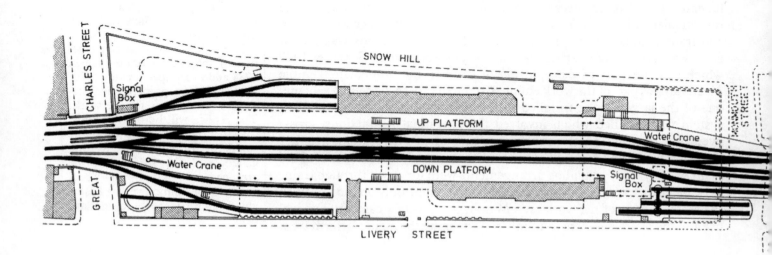

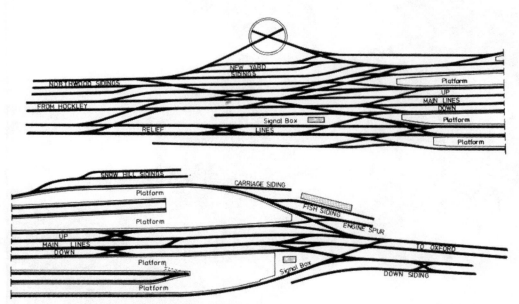

The new GWR route to Birmingham was opened to two-hour expresses in July 1910. Work on the remodelling and improvement of Snow Hill station had begun in 1906. The site was on the side of a hill, the parcels area on the up side being 24ft below the level of the tracks and platforms. Snow Hill itself was on the up side of the station, forming one boundary of the site. There was also a difference in the vertical level. Approaching from London, the railway passed in tunnel under Colmore Row, at the south end of the site, but at the other end of the original platforms it crossed over Great Charles Street.

In the original station there were two platform tracks and four short bay lines. Enlargement presented problems. The site, in the heart of the city, could not be widened because of the valuable property on both sides. It could only be lengthened, and that only towards Wolverhampton because of the tunnel at the London end. The new station, therefore, had two long island platforms, the longer being the up main (1,197ft). The down main was 1,188ft long. Both platforms had a main line on the inner face and a relief line on the outer. Two through lines ran through the centre of the station. Two trains could be handled at the same time on all platform faces, scissors crossovers with the through lines being provided for entry and exit when one half of the main platform was occupied. Each platform face therefore had two numbers, as follows:

Down Relief, Platforms 1 and 2   Up Main, Platforms 7 and 8
Down Main, Platforms 5 and 6   Up Relief, Platforms 11 and 12
Bay platforms at the Wolverhampton end of each island were numbered 3 and 4 (down side) and 9 and 10 (up side).

The six lines through the station converged into two on entering the south tunnel, but north of the station four tracks continued through Hockley to Soho and Winson Green. In spite of the restricted site, some siding accommodation was provided in the station area. At the north end this involved widening the bridge over Great Charles Street to take two extra tracks. There were platforms for fish and perishables traffic on each side of the main line at the south end of the station. The locomotive depot and carriage sidings were at Tyseley, some four miles to the south. In the

51

A 1929-built member of its class No 4964 Rodwell Hall alongside No 12 platform at Snow Hill station Birmingham in the early years of Nationalisation. The train is probably one from Hereford and Worcester via Stourbridge Junction terminating here, for the shed plate number, 84E, indicates a Tyseley engine; the headlamps show an empty stock working to Tyseley carriage sidings.

absence of bays for local services at the south end of Snow Hill, a separate terminus for suburban traffic south of the city was opened in 1909 at Moor Street, alongside the main line before it took the plunge under the Midland and LNW lines converging on New Street.

The Snow Hill of 1871 had an overall roof. In the rebuilt station a main roof 500ft long of the ridge and furrow type covered two-thirds of the station area, the remainder being covered by roofs of various designs. The central portion of the station, over the tracks, was left uncovered for a width of 22ft, providing for the escape of smoke and steam. In the old station the Great Western Hotel had a frontage on Colmore Row. This building was taken over and partly converted into offices which had been displaced from the platforms, but the ground floor was converted into a restaurant and altered to provide the main entrance to the station for foot passengers, leading to the main booking hall. A wide staircase from Snow Hill also gave access to the booking hall, described in a contemporary account as 'an imposing structure with a length of about 165ft and a width of about 93ft.' From here two inclined footways led to the footbridge connecting the platforms. There were other entrances, with their own booking offices, from Great Charles Street and from a subway communicating with Livery Street. In this part of the station the railway and platforms were above street level and several shops were built below them, both on the Snow Hill and Livery Street sides.

The platform buildings which most impressed a contributor to *Engineering* in 1914 were the two refreshment rooms on each platform. He described them as 'handsome and elaborately fitted' (although not entirely in favour of segregating first and third class passengers). A later writer found them 'resplendent with heavy oak panelling and *art nouveau* coloured glass over the doors'.

For many people Snow Hill was as much a symbol of the Great Western Railway as Paddington. Two-hour London–Birmingham expresses were only part of the story. Snow Hill was also a gateway to the West of England and the resorts of the South. Before the new station was completed the last link had been established in a route via Honeybourne and Cheltenham which reduced the distance by GWR from Birmingham to Bristol to 95 miles. Previously it had been 133 miles via Worcester, Hereford, and the Severn Tunnel; or 141 miles via Didcot and Banbury. South Wales services also used the new route, including the first 'inter-city' diesel railcars between Birmingham and Cardiff in the mid-1930s. Through trains and excursions to resorts in the South via Reading West and Basingstoke were another feature of the services from Snow Hill. These Great Western activities are often overlooked, cross-country travel from Birmingham being associated in many minds with the Midland's Derby–Birmingham–Bristol main line.

For a time the transfer of Snow Hill to the London Midland Region in 1963 seemed no more than a paper transaction but plans for a rebuilt New Street to accommodate the new electric services from Euston foretold the end. In their last years the Paddington–Birmingham–Birkenhead express-es were diesel-hauled but steam made a come-back before Snow Hill ceased to be served by main line traffic on 6 March 1967. Four steam-hauled specials were run on the fourth and fifth of the month using two restored Castles. The very last steam-hauled train (and the last through service from Birkenhead) was the return excursion on the fifth. As the empty stock pulled slowly into the tunnel behind No 7029 *Clun Castle* a curtain came down on Snow Hill. Some local services continued to use the station until 4 March 1972 when it closed completely. But all is not yet lost for it is likely to reopen as part of a West Midlands suburban railway renaissance.

Apart from the flat bottomed track Snow Hill station is virtually unaltered from the date of its reconstruction between 1908 and 1912. The photograph shows the end of an era as it was taken on 18 August 1962 only a month before the withdrawal of the Kings from the London services because of dieselisation. (Five Kings were, however, steamed every day at Wolverhampton Stafford Road shed for a period of several weeks to cover failures). The train is the 6.30am Birkenhead to Paddington and the engine No 6002 King William IV.

4
LOCOMOTIVE CONSTRUCTION

Swindon is so much a part of the Great Western image that the fact that the company's first locomotives came from outside builders is easily forgotten. For some years Swindon was the main workshops where locomotives were maintained and repaired. The first locomotive designed and built at the works was the broad gauge 2-2-2 tender locomotive *Great Western* of 1846. It was later converted into a 4-2-2, and this wheel arrangement was continued in the Iron Duke class which followed.

When Daniel Gooch retired from the post of Locomotive Superintendent in 1864 he was succeeded by Joseph Armstrong, who had been in charge of building locomotives for the GWR standard gauge lines at Stafford Road Works, Wolverhampton. As withdrawals of broad gauge engines gathered pace, Armstrong was faced with a heavy programme of building standard gauge replacements at Swindon. In this he was assisted by William Dean, whom he transferred from Wolverhampton to help him.

A very early photograph of Daniel Gooch alongside a model of one of his first broad gauge designs.

Dean became Locomotive, Carriage & Wagon Superintendent of the Great Western in 1877. The Dean Goods 0-6-0 is probably the design by which he is best remembered because of its long working life, but there are still coloured postcards to remind us of the elegance of his 4-2-2 singles, a development of his 2-2-2 design of 1891. In his book *Swindon Steam, 1921–1951* K. J. Cook describes them as 'probably the most graceful and handsome locomotives ever constructed'. He adds:

They may have tied, in this respect, with the Johnson singles of the Midland Railway, but with the Great Western embellishments of polished brass safety valve and steam dome covers and whistles, brass beading around the splashers and number plates, copper tops to the chimneys, the Dean Singles could claim to win.

By the turn of the century criticism of the gap between best and the slower Great Western services was reaching its target. Dean had now been joined by G. J. Churchward as his Chief Assistant. Express passenger 4-4-0s began to be turned out at Swindon and soon the Churchward influence could be seen. Churchward succeeded Dean as Locomotive, Carriage & Wagon Superintendent in 1902. To meet the continuing demand for more express engines ten new 4-4-0s with 6ft 8in coupled wheels were built by Churchward, although the design was evolved by the two men in collaboration while Dean was still the chief. These were the Cities, and the best known is *City of Truro*, now part of the National

54

collection preserved at Swindon to commemorate its high-speed run with an up Ocean Mail special on 9 May 1904. The actual maximum speed down Wellington bank was long accepted as 102.3mph but later opinion has put it within a whisker one side or the other of the 100mph mark.

Shortly before Dean's retirement a scheme for six standard locomotive classes had been drawn up, including two 4-6-0s with different wheel diameters. One of them, with 6ft 8½in coupled wheels was built in 1902 while Dean was still in office. Churchward named it *William Dean* after his old chief. He developed this prototype into his own characteristic type of two-cylinder 4-6-0, keeping the 18in by 30in stroke cylinders selected for the standard classes, but increasing the valve travel from 8½ to 10in. Churchward's piston valves were a hallmark of his design. The advantages to steam distribution of large-diameter valves was well understood but there were problems in making them steamtight. Churchward experimented extensively to find a solution. The construction eventually adopted was relatively complex but the valves could be mass-produced and so justified themselves economically as well as by performance.

A long valve travel allowed flexibility in planning valve events, a subject in which Churchward took personal interest and discussed in detail with his design team. With the Stephenson link motion the point in the piston stroke at which admission of steam begins (the lead) becomes earlier as the gear is notched up. The steam has a cushioning effect which is useful at high speed. Churchward adopted a negative lead of ⅛in in full gear (ie admission *after* the piston has begun its return stroke), when cushioning is not necessary, and a positive lead of the same amount in normal running cut-offs. His Saint class 4-6-0s with this arrangement were smooth runners at speed, and in hard pulling could sometimes perform better than the later Stars with Walschaerts gear and a fixed lead at any cut-off.

The two outside cylinders and link motion between the frames of the Saints reflected Churchward's interest in contemporary practice in the United States, and the same influence was seen in the integral construction of cylinders and saddle to accommodate the drumhead type smokebox. In later years the US changed to outside Walschaerts valve gear but, although changing to Walschaerts, the Great Western remained faithful to the inside arrangement. It was argued that connecting rod big ends needed attention more often than the valve gear, and if the gear was outside it had to be at least partly dismantled for big end maintenance. Churchward was not able to follow US practice in frame construction, the substantial bar frames being too heavy for British conditions. He compromised with plate main frames and forged steel extension frames bolted to them.

Commenting on cylinder dimensions, Churchward once said: 'The long stroke in relation to the bore is the only way we know of making the simple engine equal in efficiency to the compound engine'. His interest in compounding led him to order three compound locomotives of the type doing excellent work on the Northern Railway of France from French builders. These were four-cylinder Atlantics, and for comparison he converted the two-cylinder 4-6-0 No 171 *Albion* to the same wheel arrangement. Completion of a four-cylinder simple Atlantic at Swindon in

The other Great Man, George Jackson Churchward, CBE

Engine No 4700 – In 1921
Just after the end of World War I Churchward wanted to put a larger boiler on the Star class four-cylinder 4-6-0s, and a new design was worked out at Swindon; but it came out too heavy and the project was shelved. In 1919 however the prototype of a new type of heavy mixed traffic engine of the 2-8-0 type with 5ft 8in coupled wheels had been completed. This had the standard No 1 boiler, as used on the 4-6-0s and the 2-8-0 freight engines. Then it was found that the boiler designed for the proposed enlargement of the Star could be used on the 5ft 8in 2-8-0, without exceeding weight limits; and the re-boilered prototype, No 4700, came to Old Oak Common, and was immediately put into passenger work, in a strangely assorted link of four engines that included *The Great Bear*. For some time, in the autumn of 1921 No 4700 worked on such trains as the 10.45am from Paddington.

1906 allowed direct comparison between the French compounds and a British simple-expansion locomotive of the same wheel arrangement. Questions of compounding apart, it was decided that the 4-6-0 wheel arrangement was more suitable than the 4-4-2 for Great Western requirements, and ten four-cylinder simple 4-6-0s were put in hand at Swindon, appearing in 1907 as the Star class.

In the Stars Churchward changed from link motion to two sets of inside Walschaerts gear, with horizontal rocking levers transferring the drive to the spindles of the outside cylinder piston valves. While his two-cylinder and four-cylinder 4-6-0s were settling down to their work Churchward made a brief essay into the Pacific type. He once expressed the view that the principal locomotive problem was the boiler and in his one and only Pacific, No 111 The Great Bear, he went to a considerably larger one than he had yet used to supply four 15in diameter cylinders. With the introduction of superheating, however, it was found that a standard boiler as carried by the Star class could meet the demand. Later Stars were fitted with 15in cylinders, and the same size replaced the original 14¼in diameter cylinders when earlier locomotives required renewals. The axle load of The Great Bear restricted its use to the Paddington–Bristol main line. Until the advent of the Gresley Pacifics in 1922 it was the only locomotive of that wheel arrangement in Great Britain and was held in some esteem by the management for that reason. It was difficult, however, to fit a locomotive with such limited route availability into working diagrams and when The Great Bear required a new boiler in 1924 the CME, C. B. Collett, decided to rebuild it as a Castle.

In addition to his 4-6-0s Churchward introduced 4-4-0, 2-6-0 and 2-8-0

tender engines and 4-4-2, 2-6-2 and 2-8-0 tank engines, all with two cylinders. The 4-4-0 class were the Counties in which the two outside cylinders drove the leading coupled axle. Their performance was good, but they had the reputation of rough riders, perhaps because of the angle made by the short connecting rods in relation to the piston rods when the cranks were in their top and bottom positions. Churchward was keenly interested in valve events and would spend much time in the drawing office discussing them. His 10in diameter piston valves gave a free flow of exhaust steam and in his locomotives with link motion he adopted a valve setting which gave a negative lead in full gear, while for fast running with a normal 18 per cent cut-off the lead was ⅛in positive (ie the admission valve opened ⅛in before the piston reached the end of its stroke so that the incoming steam provided a cushioning effect). This was found just right for smooth running at 70–75mph. At low speeds and hard pulling no cushioning was necessary.

Perhaps the most characteristic feature of the Great Western locomotive

The Great Western's only Pacific, No 111 The Great Bear, *inside Old Oak Common shed. Built in February 1908, probably for prestige purposes, it was not a popular engine and Churchward's dislike of it was well known. As a publicity move it was probably a considerable success but because of its weight it was restricted to the main line from Paddington to Bristol. It was condemned on 7 January 1924 and nominally rebuilt as a Castle though little other than the numberplates and front end of the frames were used again.*

The erecting shop in the rebuilt (1932) Stafford Road Works, Wolverhampton, in 1939. This was one of the projects undertaken by the Great Western under the Government grant aid scheme during the depression years. In its final form the works only lasted just over thirty years. After the London Midland Region took over on 1 January 1963 the result was inevitable and the last engine to be repaired left on 11 February 1964. The last boiler repair was the spare acquired for the now preserved Dart Valley Railway 2-6-2 tank No 4555.

to the average observer was the taper boiler. Churchward tapered the upper part of the firebox from the backplate to the junction with the boiler tubes at the throatplate, and also the boiler barrel. This practice required considerable skill and a special type of press in the boiler shop but it paid off in boilers with the free-est possible circulation of water and a steaming capacity equal to all demands. Churchward's interest in water circulation led him to fit impellers in certain positions with their shafts extending through the boiler plates so that he could see what was going on inside.

A scene in A shop at Swindon in the late 1930s when locomotive construction was still in full swing with Castles, Halls, Granges and Manors under erection. In 1935 (the Great Western's centenary year) it was claimed that Swindon Works comprised one of the largest and most up to date establishments of its kind in the world for the construction of locomotives, carriages and wagons, and that A shop was one of the world's finest locomotive shops. About 100 new locomotives were then being built annually and 1,000 repaired. The works covered 323 acres of which 73 were roofed, but sadly the period of expansion was nearing its end.

One surprising fact he learned was that firing practice could reverse the direction of flow in some places.

The Great Western had used a bottom feed system for the boiler feedwater. Churchward changed to top feed which improved circulation and reduced corrosion and scale deposits. The feedwater passed through the steam in the steam space before merging with the boiler water so that there was a measure of feedwater heating as well as the other advantages. This was another improvement in thermal efficiency. In a report to the Board dated 2 January 1912 Churchward wrote: 'The improved method of boiler feed is doing all that was expected of it, and the reduction in the wear and tear and necessary repair of boiler tubes and fireboxes is very great.'

When Churchward retired in 1922 he was succeeded by his deputy, C. B. Collett, who had a long association with Swindon and the Churchward developments. Collett's first task was to design a new express passenger 4-6-0 with the instruction to keep within an axle load of 20 tons over the same 14ft 9in driving wheelbase as the Stars. Later versions of the Stars had gone up to 19.4 tons axle load and Collett might well have been given a freer hand had the progress made in upgrading bridges between London and Plymouth to take 22 tons been taken into account. It seems that there was what would now be called a 'failure of communication' between the civil and mechanical engineering departments.

Working to his 20 tons limit, Collett produced his Castle class 4-6-0. The Castles were distinguished alike by their performance and by the time span of 27 years over which the engines were built – a remarkable record for what with hindsight might almost be considered an interim design, for a new 4-6-0 with 22½ tons axle load was called for only three years after the first Castle appeared in 1923.

The Castle was an enlarged Star with some constructional modifications. Cylinder bore was enlarged from the 15in used in the later Stars to 16in, but boiler pressure remained at 225lb per sq in and wheel diameter at 6ft 8½in. The significant change was a firebox with 12 per cent more grate area and 6 per cent more heating surface. This required a 12in extension of the frames, giving the opportunity to provide a larger cab with side windows. When the first of the class, No 4073 *Caerphilly Castle*, was exhibited at the British Empire Exhibition at Wembley in 1924 it was claimed to be the most powerful passenger locomotive in Great Britain on the grounds of a tractive effort calculated at 31,625lb.

By 1926 only four bridges between Paddington and Plymouth remained unable to take an axle load of 22½ tons. The order went forth from Paddington that all were to be upgraded by the summer timetable of 1927, and Collett went to work again on a larger and still more powerful express engine. This time his product was the 4-6-0 King class. Again the Churchward precepts were applied but on a larger scale. The boiler was the biggest yet built at Swindon and was never used on any other class. With 250lb pressure and four 16in by 28in cylinders the tractive effort worked out at 39,700lb. Here management stepped in and requested over 40,000lb to substantiate another 'most powerful locomotive' claim by the Publicity Department. The cylinder diameter was therefore increased to

---

In a Class by Itself

The Great Bear was possibly built as a prestige symbol for the Great Western. It certainly looked the part and few, if any, of the hundreds of British Pacifics built in the subsequent fifty years can be said to have surpassed it in appearance. That Churchward never modified *The Great Bear* to the extent of out-performing the smaller Great Western engines is perhaps evidence that he had been persuaded beyond his real desires to build the engine, and saw no need to spend time and money in attempts to improve it. The eight-wheeled tender looked slightly ramshackle but, what was worse, on one occasion it directed excess water picked up from a trough so accurately on to the end of the adjoining coach as to break through and half-fill it with water. This is the kind of incident that every Chief Mechanical Engineer had to try to explain to the General Manager, or indeed to the Board of Directors, and no doubt Churchward took it in his stride.

From an article, *George Jackson Churchward*, by Dr W. A. Tuplin

The King George V on Test in the USA

In 1927 very soon after its completion at Swindon King class 4-6-0 No 6000 *King George V* was shipped to the USA to take part in the centenary celebrations of the Baltimore & Ohio Railroad; having been on exhibition from 24 September to 15 October that year, and taking part in a daily procession of locomotives past the viewing stands it was given a test run on the main line of the Baltimore & Ohio Railroad, with a heavy load, including a dynamometer car. The load was as great as the maximum hauled on the West of England trains at home, but instead of the progressive shedding of the load by slip coaches, as on the Cornish Riviera Express the full load had to be conveyed over a total of 272 miles. Moreover, instead of the familiar soft Welsh coal the crew had to burn a hard gas coal that formed large quantities of clinker, but nevertheless they adapted themselves very successfully to this unfamiliar stuff and put up a fine performance.

In the early stages of the test running the fireman had difficulty in keeping boiler pressure above 200lb/sq in; as he became accustomed to the fuel, he greatly impressed the American railwaymen who were riding in the dynamometer car by maintaining a steady 235 to 245lb/sq in. There was an almost complete absence of black smoke, in contrast to American locomotives generally, which usually smoked heavily for much of the time. At the request of the railroad officials speed did not exceed 74mph, and for much of the test it was limited to 65mph; but the general running with this heavy load of 544 tons was up to the standards normally maintained on the GWR at home. The Americans who travelled on the footplate were much impressed by the smooth riding of the engine. In all No 6000 proved a notable envoy indeed for the Great Western Railway.

16¼in, giving 40,300lb tractive effort by the formula, but when the engines were recylindered in the course of their service the extra quarter-inch was dropped. Other features were an increase of 1in in piston valve diameter to 9in, and 6ft 6in coupled wheels, this last being the first departure in a GW express engine from Churchward's 6ft 8½in.

The large cylinders brought a clearance problem between the inside pair and the leading bogie. It was overcome by shaping the bogie frame so that the rear axleboxes were inside the frames but the front ones were outside and became a very noticeable characteristic of the King class.

K. J. Cook has recorded that the first drawings for the King class were not received in the works at Swindon until the end of December 1926. It had been planned to complete the first engine by the end of the following October, but unknown at first to the works staff there had been negotiations to exhibit it at the Baltimore & Ohio Railroad's 'Fair of the Iron Horse' in Baltimore to celebrate its centenary. The engine, *King George V*, therefore had to be ready for shipment early in August. Swindon met the target, and *King George V* led the procession past the grandstand at the Fair. Cook recalls that 'Driver Young gave a few puffs from the siding, then shut off steam and coasted slowly past the stand. USA locomotives being grease lubricated did not become so free until they had run a few miles and when their drivers tried to emulate Young it was not successful; they stalled, starting off again amid clouds of smoke and steam'.

There were some important technical developments at Swindon in the 1920s and 1930s, sometimes minor in themselves but far-reaching in their effects. One of these was improved lubrication of connecting rod bearings. The established method of feeding oil to the bearing surfaces was through a worsted trimming in an oil pipe leading from an oil box machined in the connecting rod to a groove at the top of the bearing. The motion of the rod splashed oil on to the top of the trimming, which acted like a wick. Examination of overheated bearings in some locomotives showed, however, that oil was not being spread evenly over the bearing surface. A solution was found by substituting a felt pad lubricator of a type used successfully in some machine tools. The pad was at the bottom of the oil pipe and was kept lubricated by oil passing down the pipe. It both controlled the flow of oil and prevented leakage from the box. So long-established was the use of worsted trimmings that a plug with channels to allow oil to pass was screwed into the pipe to block any attempt to force a trimming up it.

A more sophisticated development was a method of seam welding copper fireboxes which greatly reduced the boiler maintenance required at running sheds. This was a Swindon speciality. The works also bought from the firm of Zeiss in Germany optical equipment which was adapted for lining up cylinders, frame and axlebox guides, replacing the stretched wire or cord used previously. The combination of very precise measurement and specialised machinery enabled adjustments to the horn guides to be specified to thousandths of an inch. O. S. Nock pays a tribute to the effectiveness of the method in his book *GWR Steam* with the comment: 'A newly repaired Star, Castle or King became the nearest thing to a railway Rolls-Royce that I have ever encountered'.

60

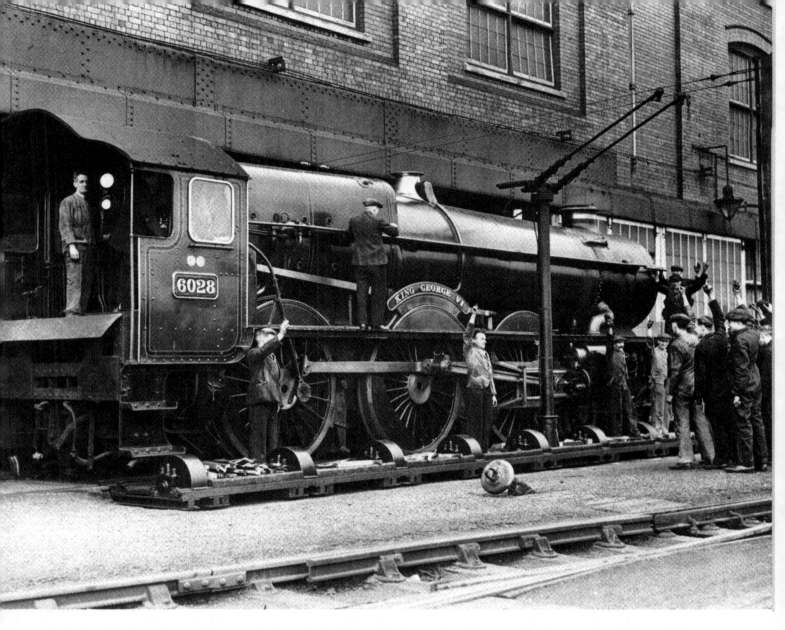

It is said that the semi-streamlining applied to a Castle and a King locomotive in 1935 was 'designed' by Collett on the spur of the moment by using Plasticine to smooth the outline of a model of the King class. This then fashionable refinement had been demanded by the Board to enhance the Great Western's modern image. The King chosen for the experiment was No 6014 *King Henry VII*, and the Castle was No 5005 *Manorbier Castle*, both receiving their streamlined fairings in March 1935. Each had a bullet nose on the smokebox, fairings behind the chimney and safety valve casing, curved and angled spectacle plates in front of the cab, and an extension piece at the top of the tender which aligned with a cab roof extension. These were the most immediately visible additions, but there was also 'air-smoothed' plating at the front end, and this caused problems of accessibility and overheating. The Castle relied on condensation of steam and oil from the hydrostatic lubricators for lubricating the inside cylinder valve guides. With natural cooling impaired by the fairings, the condensation of steam was reduced and the small amount of oil deposited

Keeping up to date. When the Kings were first built the monarch sitting on the British throne was HM King George V, hence the naming of the pioneer member of the class No 6000. On the accession of King Edward VIII No 6029 King Stephen was renamed and on 12 January 1937 No 6028 King Henry II given the name of the new King, George VI.

61

In March 1935 Castle class 4-6-0 No 5005 Manorbier Castle *and King class No 6014* King Henry VII *were partially streamlined at Swindon following the then current vogue. This consisted mainly of a bullet nose to the smokebox, coverings over the outside cylinders, chimney and safety valve cowling, a long splasher and a wedge front cab. Although this fad did not last for long No 6014 is seen here at the head of the Torbay Express near Frome on 3 February 1936.*

was dried out. The King had a two-feed oilbox for supplying oil to the inside valve guides, but it seems that the heat thinned the oil so much that the oilbox quickly emptied. Special four-feed oilboxes were fitted later to both engines, and being raised clear of the air-smoothed plating they were fitted with bullet noses in order to preserve aerodynamic conventions. By the end of 1935 the streamlining of both engines had been modified by removing the cab roof extensions and the front-end air-smoothing. Further removals took place during the war years, the longest survivals of the streamlining being the vee-fronted cabs. On the King this feature remained until the locomotive was withdrawn in 1962. The Castle received a normal square-fronted cab in 1947. It was withdrawn in 1960.

In 1941 Collett was succeeded as Chief Mechanical Engineer by F. W. Hawksworth. He took over at a difficult time, when constantly varying coal quality was showing up the drawback of moderate superheat in the Great Western boilers when coal, driving and firing were not all of the highest standard. Hawksworth raised the superheat in a batch of Hall class 4-6-0s built in 1944, increasing the heating surface of the superheater elements from 263sq ft in the standard boiler to 314.6sq ft in a superheater of new design. He also departed from the Churchward practice of carrying the cylinders on forged steel extensions bolted to the main frames, instead continuing the main frames through to the front buffer beam. Cylinders were cast separately from the saddle, and bar frame bogies gave place to a plate frame design.

Hawksworth had plans for a Pacific locomotive which did not materialise. In 1945, however, a further batch of 4-6-0 engines was authorised and Hawksworth produced a new design with 6ft 3in coupled wheels and 280lb boiler pressure – two features he had intended for his Pacific. These were the County class, the last GW express type before nationalisation. Building of more Castle class engines began in 1946. The Hawksworth Castles were again given more superheater surface the increase being from 263 to 313sq ft. Coal problems were now more serious than ever and the Great Western decided to experiment with oil firing, beginning with some 2-8-0s, Halls and Castles. Soon a national fuel crisis led the Government of the day to make funds available for widespread conversion to oil firing on the country's railways. Then it was realised that foreign exchange to buy oil was in short supply. The whole scheme collapsed and the Great Western's own plans went no further.

Hawksworth's other new design was an 0-6-0 shunter with outside cylinders and Walschaerts valve gear. With outside Walschaerts gear visible at Paddington, clearly anything might happen and in 1947 it was announced that the Great Western was to buy a gas turbine locomotive from Brown, Boveri of Switzerland. Hawksworth and the General Manager, Sir James Milne, had been looking at this form of traction during a visit to an International Railway Congress meeting in that country. The gas turbine interlude on Great Western metals belongs to British Railways history, as do the years after nationalisation during which Great Western steam still carried the imprint of Churchward and Collett.

5

LOCOMOTIVE SHEDS AND WORKSHOPS

Sheds, design and allocation

The first official depot was at Paddington, which formed part of the original terminus. It was timber-built with a slated roof, and composed of a central roundhouse with a small straight shed running off opposite sides. This engine shed was later replaced by a brick-built depot at Westbourne Park in 1855, when the terminus was rebuilt on its present site. The standard gauge shed building to this depot was added in 1869.

As the GWR expanded and absorbed other smaller railways, so the company built and acquired further engine sheds. Once the railway gained stature the sheds took on a permanent appearance, the timber construction giving way to brick. A form of similar depots appeared throughout the system, as some broad gauge sheds were identical in pattern. Truro, Southall, Basingstoke, Salisbury, Swindon, Exeter, and Whitland, were all straight road sheds with a turntable virtually outside the shed entrance. Straight road sheds were favoured, but from the layout of sheds plus their building dates, it can be said that other layouts were put into operation.

The first depot to change was at Swindon in 1871 when the original broad gauge shed had to make way for factory development within the railway works. This new depot comprised a straight road shed with a turntable at the rear, all under the same roof. Five years later, Neath (Court Sart) was built, consisting of two turntables all under a twin-pitched roof. Another five years elapsed before the Reading shed

One of the Great Western's through type sheds was Landore (LDR) in the Neath Division. This type of shed was adopted where a large number of locomotives were not required, as it was relatively cheap to build in contrast to a roundhouse. In view in this 1930s photograph are three typical South Wales classes – a 72XX 2-8-2 tank, a 43XX 2-6-0 and a 56XX 0-6-2 tank.

Exeter (St Davids) shed as seen in the mid-1920s. On the turntable road is a Saint class 4-6-0 while a 43XX class Churchward 2-6-0 blows off to the left of the steam railcar which is being washed out over a pit road. Exeter had a number of these units which worked the services to Dulverton and Heathfield and, sometimes, over the main line to and from Dawlish Warren.

replacement was erected. This was similar in construction to Swindon, and the layout was a straight road shed with a turntable centrally placed, rather like the smaller depot it replaced. During this decade Pontypool Road engine shed was built, being similar to the one at Reading. Pontypool Road was built in two sections, the turntable unit in 1865 and four years later the straight road section.

In 1882, Cardiff Canton shed was opened and comprised a straight road shed with a turntable shed built eccentrically on the gable end of the straight road shed. Both sides had independent entrances and the long shed even possessed a turntable located in the front before the coaling stage. The sheds had no separating wall and both had a northlight pattern roof instead of the conventional pitched roof. Two years later a standard gauge shed replaced the small broad gauge shed at Southall. This new shed was a straight road type with a northlight pattern roof. A repair shop and offices were along one side, and the boiler house, sand and turntable were sited along the other side. Similar depots were built over the next 16 years replacing the earlier broad gauge sheds. The depots were:

Southall 1884; Weymouth 1885; Newton Abbot 1893; Exeter 1894; Salisbury 1899; Truro and Llantrisant 1900.

The turntable depots had their share of similarity as well. All were single unit types and had the northlight pattern roof just as the straight road depots. The repair shop was merely an extended radiating road and the offices conveniently placed along one of the walls. The depots were:

Tondu 1884; Taunton 1896; Laira 1901; Croes Newydd 1902.

Thus, at the end of Dean's reign as Locomotive, Carriage, and Works Superintendent, a large measure of standardisation of locomotive sheds had taken place. In G. J. Churchward's term of office, 1902–21, the types of depots were maintained although a more complete attempt of standardisation was adopted.

Commencing with Old Oak Common, which was completed in 1906,

64

this depot formed the nucleus for all other turntable sheds constructed. This size of engine shed was actually never repeated (four turntables under one roof), but was nonetheless catered for in similar single and double turntable sheds, built later, should the opportunity for extension arise. Churchward's standard straight road depots were also built to enable further covered accommodation to be provided. Two depots were opened in 1906. Both types of shed had the conventional pitched roof outline, the northlight style being abandoned.

CHURCHWARD STANDARD DEPOTS:

Turntable Units

	Shed	Built	No of Turntables	Repair shop
1	Old Oak Common	1906	4	Traverser type
2	Oxley	1907	2	2 road
3	Aberdare	1908	1	2 road
4	Tyseley	1908	2	Traverser type
5	St Philip's Marsh (Bristol)	1910	2	2 road
6	Ebbw	1915	2	Traverser type
7	Llanelly	1925	2	2 road
8	Stourbridge	1926	1	1 road

Straight Road Units

	Shed	Built	No of Roads	Repair shop
1	Leamington Spa	1906	4	—
2	Fishguard	1906	4	—
3	Cheltenham	1907	2	—
4	Carmarthen	1907	6	2 road
5	Severn Tunnel Junction	1908	4	—
6	Banbury	1908	4	—
7	Penzance	1914	4	1 road
8	Westbury	1915	4	1 road
9	Aberbeeg	1919	4	—

The layout of Tyseley shed, one of the standard Churchward units built around turntables in 1908.

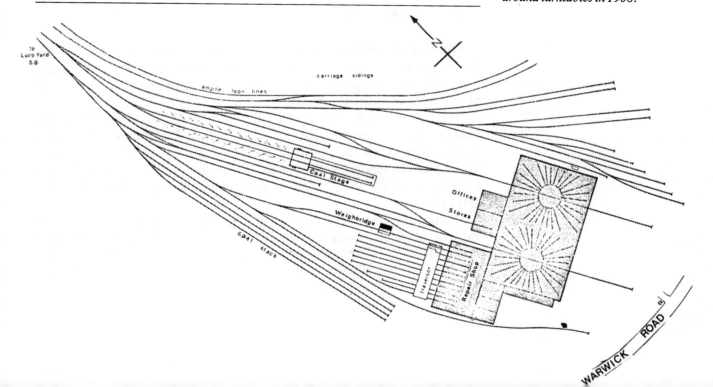

Early methods of engine cleaning. (*From* Railway Ribaldry, *see page 154*)

The First World War interrupted several new and redevelopment schemes. It was during this period, in July 1916, that the responsibilities of the depots and works came under the new office of Chief Mechanical Engineer, and all remaining civil engineering work came under the jurisdiction of the Chief Engineer.

The 1922 amalgamation brought extra depots into the network. During the 1920 decade only two new depots, replacing much older inadequate sheds, were built. The opportunity to replace outdated depots was taken under the Government's Loans & Guarantees Act (1929). Due to high unemployment at that time the government aided companies which wished to expand, therefore creating work for many. For the GWR this Act not only promoted long awaited new depots, but other permanent way and railway structures too. Many absorbed depots were updated to suit modern needs. Examples were standard coaling stages and repair shops added, electric lighting installed, headroom increased, and extra covered accommodation provided.

All the new depots built were straight road types having virtually the same dimensions as the Churchward predecessors, varying only in construction. They were built to enable further extensions to be added if and when required.

Shed	Built	No of Roads	Separate Repair Shop
Abercynon	1929	2	—
Cardiff East Dock	1931	8	1 road★
Pantyffynon	1931	4	—
Radyr	1931	4	—
Treherbert	1931	4	—
Didcot	1932	4	1 road
Landore	1932	4	1 road
Kidderminster	1932	2	—
Bristol, Bath Road	1934	8	2 road

★*one wall attached to shed*

While these sheds were being built some further rationalisation was taking place. Some absorbed sheds near GWR sheds were closed, and a few sheds were relegated to sub-sheds but still managed to retain separate allocations.

Aberystwyth was completely rebuilt in 1938. It replaced the ex-Cambrian depot on the same site and the main construction reverted to brick. Once again the outbreak of World War cancelled many depots earmarked for modification. In fact, some construction for the new depot at Whitland had taken place, in particular a turntable laid, plus some trackwork.

During the Second World War, with the increased demand by the railway network, some depots actually received much-needed lifting shops. This enabled engines to be repaired more quickly and pressed into traffic again. Ash shelters appeared at several depots. They were merely a

light steel-framed structure clad in asbestos with 6ft 0in high brick walls, and were to prevent the glow of firebox ash waste from being seen by enemy aircraft.

Once hostilities had ceased the postponed modifications and modernisation were put into operation. The timber built depot at Neath (N & B) was totally rebuilt and took on a different appearance from previous depots. This depot was the last built by the GWR before it became the Western Region of the nationalised British Railways network on 1 January 1948.

However, rebuilding still took place. During 1953/4 Southall shed was rebuilt. The new spacious steel-framed shed possessed only a bucket and hoist system for coaling locomotives, perhaps indicating a predetermined thought for a different motive power to come. Moat Lane received a

Not a shed but an important turn round and servicing point – Ranelagh Bridge, Paddington. A Wolverhampton (Stafford Road) King is being turned ready for the return journey. Note the two headlamps of differing pattern, GWR and BR.

replacement shed in 1957 and in 1959 Pwllheli acquired a modern steel and glass depot, to last only seven years.

With the onrush of diesel power in the 1960s, few depots survived and they were converted to suit. With the alteration of regional boundaries some depots changed hands, only to be abandoned. It appears that Weymouth and Shrewsbury were the last GWR depots to see steam service. Oxford, the running shed unaltered since broad gauge days, closed a month earlier than Weymouth and gave nearly 120 years of service to the steam locomotive, with Shrewsbury a very close second.

Great Western Railway Locomotive Allocation

This list shows the allocation of all locomotives on the GWR as at 15 June, 1947, the last year before Nationalisation. The allocations refer ónly to main sheds against which code letters appear with the exception of Crewe (included under Wellington) and Aberystwyth (included under Machynlleth). Engines allocated to sub sheds are included in the main sheds.

The list was originally published in *The Railway Observer* which commented at the time that although compiled from official sources, a few allocations did not agree with other GWR records.

London Division
PDN. Old Oak Common:—2, 100A1/111, 1000/3/8/10/2/5/21/6, 1912, 2276/82, 2826/7/40/3/50/5/6/68/75/81, 3600/18/9/35/44/6/8/58/9/69/72/85/8, 3710/23/34/8/54/66, 3823/51-3, 3903/52/4, 4037/73/5/6/91, 4606/9/15/42/4/65/6/7/80/91/8/9, 4700-2/5/7, 4800/53/4, 4900/35/43/51/8/61/2/78/85/98, 5000/4/8/14/22/3/7/9/35-40/3-5/55/6/65/69/81/5/7/99, 5717/64, 5922/31/2/6-41/50/2/62/87/96, 6001/3/7/9/13-5/21/5, 6111/2/7/20/1/9/32/4/5/7/41/2/4/9/55/8/9/66/8, 6865/9, 6900/10/59-62/8, 7713/34/8/54/60/91, 8707/35/8/50/1/3/4/6/7/9-63/5/7-73/80, 9302/6/8/10, 9401-7/9, 9658/9/61, 9700-10/25/6/51/4/8/84, W.D. 77005/15, 77130/84, 78632, 79234, L.M.S. 8477. (**232**).
SHL. Southall:—1443/62, 1925/69, 2285, 2845/58, 3562, 3620, 3704/27/50/99, 3854-60, 4604/8/10/63/73/95, 5119, 5360, 5401/5/9-11/3-8/20/1, 5727/50/3/5/99, 6102/10/8/25/8/39/47/8/56/65/9, 6325/88, 6407, 6809/26, 7709/30-2, 8752/8/64/74, 9300/1/11. 9641, 9755. (**75**).
SLO. Slough:—1426/37/42, 2055, 2112, 2757/90, 3652/77/81, 3769/98, 4617/50, 5715/37/83, 6100/1/4-8/13/4/6/9/23/4/6/7/33/43/5/6/50-3/7/60/1/4/7, 9640/53, 9781/9. (**49**).
RDG. Reading:—1335/6, 1407/44/7, 2076, 2208/45/64/99, 2573, 3025/47, 3386, 3418/26, 3663/97, 3736/70/83, 3840/1/3-6, 3953, 4085, 4649/61/70/88/90/2, 4914/20/31/89/94/5, 5320/56/75/85, 5751/61-3/6/72, 5901/33/48/56/9/73, 6109/15/30/1/6/40/54/62/3, 6302/12/3/34/63/6/83/93, 6802/64, 7318/20, 7708/77/88, 9303-5/7/9/13/5/8/9, 9722/49/63/91, W.D. 77378, 782522. (**96**).
DID. Didcot:—907, 1334, 1861, 2202/21/2/6/7/40/52/89, 2532, 2783, 3376/96, 3408/19/48, 3622, 3709/21, 4318/26, 4601, 5330/80/1/97, 5710/35/44/52, 5903/35, 6329/59/79, 6923/52, 7204/14/28/52, 7710, 9006/15/83, W.D. 70843. (**48**).
OXF. Oxford:—1159, 1448/50, 1531, 1742, 1935, 2249, 2579, 2861, 3583/5/8/9, 3608/87, 3715/22/41, 3835/6/8/47/8/62/6, 4004/21/49/52, 4645/76, 4902/3/21/8/38/73, 5323, 5616, 5904/60, 6103/22/38, 6300, 6682, 6925/33/7, 7404/11/2, 9316/7, 9611/54, W.D. 77058. (**57**).

Bristol Division
BRD. Bristol, Bath Road:—1002/5/7/11/3/4/28, 1415/30/63, 2072, 2322, 2462,

2929/31/9/42/50, 3950, 4019/20/30/3–5/41–3/7/80/4/9/93/6, 4142/3/51/2, 4535/6/9/63/77/80/95, 4942, 5019/24/5/48/74/6/82–4/91/6, 5169, 5325/7/43, 5506/11/2/4/23/7/8/35/6/9/46–8/53/5/8/9/61/4/72, 5803/9/13, 5949, 6958, 7809/12/4, W.D. 79226. (**90**).

SPM. Bristol, St. Philip's Marsh:—5, 6, 1538, 2031/64/70, 2135, 2203/6/20/5/51/3/8/65/9/93, 2340, 2426/44, 2534/78, 2702/9/86, 2812/44/6/59, 3013/7/22/34/41/5/6, 3604/14/23/32/43/76, 3720/46/59/63–5/73/84/95, 3900/2/51, 4603/7/12/9/24/6/47/55, 4804, 4965/9/86/90, 5241, 5351/8/74, 5784, 5964/79/84, 6601/56/70/1, 6830/6/42/6/50/2/61/3/7/76, 6909/12/22/44/54, 7208/15/34/7, 7711/8/9/26/8/9/49/79/80/2/3/90/3/5, 7801/4, 8105, 8702/3/13/4/22/30/7/41/6/7/66/90/3/5, 9604–6/20/6, 9729/32/64, W.D. 70801/36/76, 77116/42, 77200/47/55/89, 77325/6, 77421, 77508, 79261, 79301/9. (**153**).

SDN. Swindon:—992, 1366/9/71, 1400/33/6/46/53, 1542, 1731/58, 2014/7/60, 2195, 2224/50, 2568, 2908/13/27/34/5/45/7/9/54, 3421/52, 3561, 3645/66/82/4, 3724/37/9/48/80, 4015/7/22/36/55/7/62, 4381, 4502/7/10/21/38/43/4/50/1/85/90/2, 4651/97, 4905/25/45/56, 5067/8, 5322/67/71/96, 5510/34/63/6, 5800/2/4/5, 5934/43/78, 6320/2/40/57/8/60/74/84/7, 6716/37/9/41, 6902/35/65, 7321, 7415/8/24, 7792/4, 8733/79, 9011/8/23, 9400, 9600, 9720/1/72/3/90/5. (**118**).

WES. Westbury:—1027, 2023/53, 2445, 2803/18, 2928/41/6, 3014/9/32/5, 3363/4, 3438, 3696, 3731/5/58, 3842/9/50/63, 4028/38/45, 4365/77, 4508/20/72/3, 4636, 4926/7/63, 5306/11/26, 5402/3/6/19/22/3, 5508/9/54, 5689, 5718/57/71/81/5, 5900/24/5/61/71/4/85, 6314/51/61/8/9/75/99, 6690/9, 6804/45, 6955/66, 7300/2/9, 7727/84, 8744/5, 9612/2/5/28, 9762. (**86**).

WEY. Weymouth:—1367/8/70, 1403/54/67, 1789, 2912/55, 4527/62, 4660, 4988, 5305/14/28/37/8/40/59/84, 5968/9, 6945, 7408, 9642. (**26**).

YEO. Yeovil:—1767, 3671, 3733, 4689, 5529/65, 5767, 9601, 9771. (**9**).

Newton Abbot Division

EXE. Exeter:—1020, 1405/29/35/40/9/51/68/9, 2088, 2230, 2814/34/73, 3335/95, 3451, 3603/6, 3794, 3815/34, 4054, 4410, 4530, 4706, 5012/59/98, 5321, 5525, 5760, 6301/97, 7316, 7716/61, 9646/7, W.D. 77288. (**40**).

LA. Laira:—1004/6/9, 1361/3–5, 1799, 1973/90, 2776, 2809/35/57/67, 3186/7, 3391, 3401/31/41/5/6, 3629/39/75/86, 3705/87/90, 3811/64, 3901/4/55, 4032/87/8/90, 4402/7, 4517/24/8/31/42/83/91, 4653/6/8/79/93, 4703, 4807/52, 4908/37/66/91, 5009/26/41/50/7/60/79/90/5, 5148, 5318/76, 5412, 5540/67/9, 5998, 6000/2/4/10/2/6/7/9/20/2/6/9, 6319, 6406/14/7/9/21, 6907/13, 7762, 8709/19, 9711/6/65/70, W.D. 77161/96, 77294, 78671, 78717, L.M.S. 8427. (**110**).

NA. Newton Abbot:—1001/18, 1362, 1427/39/66/70, 2097, 2785, 3341/75/83, 3400/7/30, 4012/6/77/98/9, 4109/33, 4405, 4516/26/47/82/7, 4983, 5011/28/34/47/58/62/71/8/94, 5108/13/32/42/50/3/7, 5350/91, 5505/30/51/2/7, 5798, 6018/23/4/7/8, 6345, 6813/4/22/9, 6934, 7000, 7200/20/50, 7427, 9623/33, 9717, W.D. 77001, 77210/4/41, 77388. (**77**).

Weymouth shed with locomotives from three railways, an SR Lord Nelson 4-6-0, LMS Class 4F 0-6-0 No 4169 (off the Somerset & Dorset Joint line) and GWR Star class 4-6-0 No 4042 Prince Albert. The new coaling plant installed in 1930 is being served by steel sided loco coal wagons. Weymouth shed was of standard straight road construction.

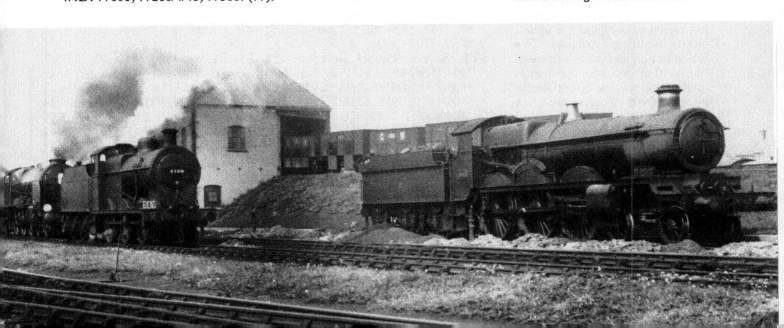

The Birthplace of Kings

On a bright spring morning in 1933 a large part of Lendrick School, Teignmouth, assembled on the up platform of Teignmouth station together with contingents from the Grammar School and others awaiting a Schools' Special to Swindon Works. For the Great Western believed strongly that to make its propaganda felt you should instil it into the young. But they had no malice aforethought in this and were very much bent on giving the school populations on their system a good day out. Indeed, when No. 4975 *Umberslade Hall* hove round the corner at the head of a long train, whose carriages all bore little window-stickers "SWINDON WORKS SCHOOLS' EXCURSION". Jutting out of the windows, were not only school caps but pigtails as well, for there were boys *and* girls. With an echoing whistle from our *Hall*, we rumbled alongside the great range of buildings which was Swindon Works, from countless vantage points of which green locomotives galore enticingly peeped. The vast throng was soon marshalled into tidy groups, each under the care of a kindly Great Western man and so began the long trek round the Works. We stood in awe, watching the furnace men pouring molten lead into moulds, listening to blacksmiths clouting ringing metal on anvils, which somehow beat into the shape of springs, following the activities of panel beaters preparing carriage doors and the upholsterers stuffing cushions. We walked miles and miles and miles but neither we nor the female contingent from the Bishop Blackall just ahead of us showed any signs of wilting. Of course we had already been provided with descriptive leaflets – the GWR never let its protégés go short of guidebooks – and a new Chapman book on Swindon Works was on sale, of which needless to say those who had not spent all their pelf on their

PZ. Penzance:—1019/22, 2148, 2737/52, 4097, 4500/9/25/37/40/5/8/66/74, 4946/7/9/70, 5915, 6318/54, 6801/8/25/38, 6911. (**27**).

SBZ. St. Blazey:—1900/30, 2050, 2181/2, 2768/80, 3582, 4215/98, 4503/5/29/52/9/65/8/70/98, 4940, 5140/58, 5502/19/31, 5926, 6330/56, 7715, 8783, 9655. (**31**).

TN. Taunton:—1338, 1760, 1909, 2038, 2127/94, 2211–5/61/6–8/75, 2708/48/55, 3361, 3443/4, 4026/56, 4113/7/36, 4954, 5003/77, 5172, 5501/3/4/21/2/33/42/3/71, 5812, 5902/82/99, 6305/23/8/64/72/98, 6420, 7304/14, 7421, 9718/57. (**56**).

TR. Truro:—1023, 1753/82, 4523/32/54/61/9/81/8/9, 4906/29/36, 5500/26/37/62, 5779, 6373, 6931, 7422. (**22**).

Newport Division

ABEEG. Aberbeeg:—3616/70/80/3, 3729/76/9, 4217/22/31/43/67/87, 4522/41, 4682/5/6, 5259, 5532, 5733/56/86/8/9, 6621, 7703/40/89/98, 8723/4/39/76/7/94, 9723. (**37**).

CDF. Cardiff:—200/9/38, 310/3/7/35/57/81, 410/20, 1889/91, 2484, 2537/8/70, 2667, 2820/1/37/60/4/77/89/90/1, 2905/6/36/40/3/52, 3038/42/4, 3708/16/55, 3809/12–4/7/23/4, 4083/94, 4200/27/36/90, 4622/33/7/52/77, 4901/13/52/3/74/5, 5001/5/7/10/20/30/46/9/52/4/80, 5200/5/36/49/62, 5307/35/78/82/8, 5628/79/85, 5749, 5910/46/58/70/7, 6343/53/94, 6622/91, 6805/10/1/7/27, 6928/46/8/69, 7001, 7201/19, 8728/40, 9629/48, 9713/59/96, W.D. 77053, 77380, L.M.S. 8464. (**121**).

ABDR. Aberdare:—65, 282/4, 311/4/62/74, 1769, 2117, 2801/6/8/10/1/22/3/8/31/6/41/70/80, 3036, 3605/10/55, 3747/53, 4228/57/64/85/97, 5237/45/58/63, 5520, 5770/87/96, 6410/3/37, 6605/28/52/92/3, 7205/13/21/42, 7423, 7748/73, 9607/9, 9712. (**59**).

NPT. Newport, Ebbw Junction:—1372/3, 1421, 1668/70, 1713/20, 1800/62/83/94, 2063/73, 2122, 2218/39/80, 2407, 2726/94/5, 2842/51/65/6/76/9/94/6, 2979, 3634/6/47/62, 3700/12/4/26/96, 3800/1/4/5/7/10/6/30/3, 4145, 4203/6/24/5/30/42/7/8/60/3/8/70/1/6/89/94, 4518/93/9, 4671, 4941, 5201/6/8/17/8/22/4/9/33/4/8/43/51/5/6/64, 5364, 5516/45/50, 5602/3/38, 5709/32/41, 5906/11, 6409/15/26/8/39, 6612/49/54/63/72, 6821/37/68/70/4, 6926/7, 7203/12/7/31/41/5/7/9/53, 7712/36/53/68/71/81, 8710/1/78/86/96, 9632/7/44, 9731, W.D. 77123. (**140**).

LTS. Llantrisant:—247, 1471, 3586, 3617/56/91, 3703, 4208/61, 4674, 5708/77, 7721, 9616, 9746/80. (**16**).

PILL. Newport, Pill:—11, 62, 190, 426, 504, 666/7/98, 1084, 1113, 1205, 1709/26/64, 1896, 2033, 2113/36/54, 2731/4/8/64/93, 4201/11/26/9/33/5/7/46/53/8/9/80/91, 4662, 5235/44, 5740/7/76, 6710/1/25–32/5/43, 7774, 9660. (**58**).

PPRD. Pontypool Road:—349/85, 1422, 1730, 2021/35/94, 2159, 2385, 2669, 2728/39/49, 2800/2/13/47/93, 3002/12/8/23/37/40, 3406/53, 3628/51/90/2, 3711/7/30, 3822/6/8, 4131/5/8, 4238/75, 4303, 4514/33/97, 4611/39/68, 4912/32/3, 5355, 5649, 5728/68/92, 5818, 5975, 6333/70, 6400/3/24/9/30/2/8, 6634/6/51/87, 6742, 6820/40/75, 7206/30/2/3/5, 7426, 7720/4, 8716/55/88, 9650, 9787, W.D. 77099. (**89**).

STJ. Severn Tunnel Junction:—21, 332, 1752, 1870, 2414/60, 2635/7, 2804/15/9/24/9/38/84/7/92, 3150/4/7/9/61/3/5/7/8/70/2/4/6–8/82–5/8–90, 3575, 3806/8/31, 4119/30/7/44/8, 4262, 4801/3/51, 4979, 5183, 5362, 5620/5/6/45, 5706/14/29, 5953, 6317/77/86, 6639/66/73/6/89, 6815/34/71/3, 7202/9/10/6/23/4/9/39/46/51, 7429, 7764, 8799, 9745/78, W.D. 77106, L.M.S. 8466/7. (**93**).

TDU. Tondu:—2735/61/7/9, 3100/3, 3612/27/40/68/74/95/9, 3772, 4214/8/41/51/73, 4404/8, 4557, 4634/43/69/75, 5202/52, 5556, 5633, 5707/97, 6642/75/85, 7725/46/52/70/5/8, 8712/21/48, 9649. (**45**).

Neath Division

CARM. Carmarthen:—1472, 1903/41, 2047/56/69, 2111, 2216/7/36/54/71/2/84/91, 2409/11/31/74, 3592, 4223/66, 4910/5/22/81/4, 5207/31, 5339, 5819,

5963/72, 6310/31/44/67, 6818/24, 6919, 7400/1/7/129/25. (**45**).

DG. Danygraig:—60, 71, 359, 779, 803, 929/42/3/68, 1085/6/98, 1101–6, 1358, 1945, 2082, 2134, 2798, 3661, 3781, 4299, 4694, 5730/75, 6713/34, 8720. (**32**).

DYD. Port Talbot, Duffryn Yard:—69, 70, 184/8, 291/4/6, 1768, 1867, 2079, 2715/21/92, 3011, 3718/91, 4255/77/86/92, 4640/81/4, 5216/50/7/60, 5606/12/ 29/39/56, 5713/31/4/73, 6616/29/86/8, 6715/7–20/49, 7733/44, 9617/34, 9735– 7/66/85/99. (**57**).

FGD. Fishguard, Goodwick:—1419/23/31/52, 3577, 5395, 5716, 5905/8/28, 6823, 7413, 7747, 9602/3, 9760. (**16**).

LDR. Landore:—2273, 3678, 3701/13/68/85/97, 4003/23/39/48/50/74/8/81/95, 4134, 4212/50/6/95, 4982, 5002/6/13/6/51/72/89/93, 5211/9, 5341, 5400/8, 5604/31, 5759, 5913, 6304, 6412/25/31, 6604/6/38/44/67/78/9/83, 6800/6/28/57/ 72, 6903/18, 7002/3, 7787, 8789, 9738/61/75/7. (**66**).

LLY. Llanelly:—1907/57/67/91, 2002/12/9/27/42/59/81/3/5/98, 2126/37/62/5/7/8/ 76/93/6–8, 2707/30/6/46/51/87, 3004/6/10/5, 3642/98, 3719/52/61/71/7, 4213/ 54/78/81, 4802/5/6/50, 5203/4/9/12/3/5/20/3/6/8/30/40/7/8/61, 5675, 5702/5/22/ 82, 6674, 7225/44, 7745/55/65/76/85, 8706/8/32/49/85, 9743/87/8, W.D. 77429/89. (**88**).

NEA. Neath:—75, 906, 1715, 1855/8, 2192, 2722/97, 3455, 3611/21, 3757/74, 4132, 4221/32/52/9/72/4/9/84/8/93, 4621, 5225/39/42/54, 5703/20/46/78, 6613/ 50/80, 7701/37/9/42/3/57/67/9/86/99, 8104, 8715/75/82, 9627, 9734/50/6/79/83/ 6/92, W.D. 77310, 77407. (**60**).

NEY. Neyland:—3009, 3447, 3654, 4358, 4654, 4957/97, 5310/53/7/68/72/92, 5929, 6347/55/71/89, 7306, 7816, 9652. (**21**).

SED. Swansea East Dock:—289, 408/38, 696, 701, 935/74, 1754, 2166, 2789, 3633/41/79, 4207/65/82/3/96, 5210/4/21/7/32/46/53, 5704/43, 6695, 6714, 7211, 7704/56, 9625/45, 9744. (**35**).

WTD. Whitland:—1964/79/96, 2010/1/3/8, 2288, 3637, 4506/15/9/53/6/76/9, 5513/49/68, 7417, 8102/7. (**22**).

Wolverhampton Division
BAN. Banbury:—1428/58/73, 2256/95, 2408, 2612/43, 2805/16/7/69/71/4/8/82/5/ 95/8/9, 2981, 3630/94, 3751, 3802/3/19–21/5/7/9/61, 4118, 4631/46, 4909, 5302/17/24/49/61/73, 5404/7/24, 5724/36, 5930/54/67/91/2, 6390, 6696, 6803/ 16/32/5/9/41/9/54, 7763, 7800/5/6/11, 8729/87, 9782. (**73**).

BHD. Birkenhead:—1917/49/68, 2004/6/52/89, 2104/6/8/29, 2833, 3169, 3926, 3742, 4120–9, 4337/53/86, 5316, 6346/60/76, 6404/5, 6819/78, 7714, 8393, 8725, 9651. (**40**).

CHR. Chester:—1434, 2262, 2513, 2662, 2778, 2853/83/6, 2915/26/30/53/89, 3003, 3366/99, 3665, 3762/86, 4013, 4918/76, 5137/74/6/9/81/4/6, 5344/99, 5647/90, 5723/91, 5912/23/66, 6308/11/37/9/80/92, 6624, 6859, 6941, 7313, 9728/74/94, W.D. 77115, L.M.S. 8428. (**54**).

CNYD. Croes Newydd:—1401/11/6/57, 1532, 1706/47/73/80, 2183/4/8/90, 2259/87, 2704/13/6/7, 3026/8, 3203/6, 5315/9/34/65, 5810/1, 6303/16/27, 6694/8, 7305/10, 7403/9/14, 7817, 9656, W.D. 70808. (**43**).

LMTN. Leamington Spa:—2772, 2902/33, 3631, 4102/12, 5104/9/30/44/61/3/ 85/7/92/4, 6625/30/57/97, 7218, 7702, 7810, 8100/9, 9740. (**26**).

OXY. Wolverhampton, Oxley:—1762, 2623/65, 2825/30, 3016/24/31/3/9, 3102/ 4, 3744/5/92/3, 4708, 4904/16/23/44/50/5/64/87/96, 5300/13/31/3/79/86/90, 5657/70/84, 5748/80, 5916/8/20/1/45/7/57/89, 6332/5/42/61/2, 6600/9/10/40/5, 6862/79, 6915/32/9/42/56/67/70, 7207/22/6/7/36/8/40/3/8, 7307/11/7, 7759/96/ 7, 7813, 8798, 9312/4, 9408, 9714/5/30/9/42/7/52/68/9, W.D. 77012/4/36/8/40/ 9/64/77/9/97, 77102/51/65, 77202/34/57/97, 77408, 78604/95, 78714, 79219/24/ 5, L.M.S. 8478. (**119**).

SRD. Wolverhampton, Stafford Road:—1016/7/24/5/9, 1863, 2061/7/95, 2109/ 10/56, 2231/2, 2791, 3008/20/43, 3160, 3615, 3756/60/78, 4000/18/25/31/53/60, 4101/3/5/8/10/5, 4960, 5015/8/31/3/53/70/5/88, 5111/43/51, 5739, 5909/19/27/

inner men bought a copy. And so at last we came to the *pièce de résistance* – the Machine Shop.

You could hear the concentrated cry of delight which broke from scores of teenage throats as each party was ushered in, for here were engines in every stage of construction, dress and undress. There were skeletons of engines, fireboxes covered with something that looked like lignite standing in rows, hundreds of pairs of wheels and of course the huge transporter crane which (for our benefit, we thought) picked up *Rougemont Castle* and walked across the shop, holding her above our heads. Then there was the static testing plant, on which another *Castle* was standing, with her wheels racing round at sixty miles an hour but getting nowhere. There were *Kings, Castles, Stars, Saints, Halls* – many of the latter still under construction and arguments were breaking out as to whether you could claim to have seen an engine when only its cab and firebox had been assembled! There were "Dean Goods" engines, tanks without number, Moguls and even one of the big-boilered 47XX 2-8-0s, while in the corner stood the cream of them all, specially ready for us with driver and fireman to show us round the cab, her bell gleaming, her two plaques from the Baltimore & Ohio polished up to the nines – our own, gorgeous, magnificent, famous No. 6000 *King George V*.

But all was not over; our kindly guide led us outside and there, in the multiple sidings between the Works and the main line, stood lines of engines which had just been or were about to be "shopped". Here were countless more new ones for our books and we had, of course, "The GWR Engine Book – Names, Numbers, Types & Classes" while for those who did not aspire to such stuff there was always the little notebook with a red shiny cover which an indulgent parent had bought that very morning! Here were two very rare birds indeed, the crane engines *Hercules* and *Cyclops*, Nos 16 and 17, which appeared on page 52 of the book, the last page before the Index, and looked like a Chief Mechanical Engineer's nightmare.

Alas! All good things come to an end and in the early evening we bade farewell to our guide and took the long trail back to the Junction Station where we fell with ravenous force upon the tea and currant buns of the refreshment rooms. A South Wales express tore through behind a *Castle* and then a whistle and a steady exhaust announced our faithful *Umberslade Hall*, fed and watered again, advancing out of a siding with our train. So in the golden evening we headed westward.

From *More Great Westernry* by T. W. E. Roche

The interior of Tyseley shed in July 1959 with 0-6-0 pannier tank No 3673 on the left hand side and 2-6-2 tank No 4111 on the right. Although full of atmosphere this photograph clearly shows the gloom and poor working conditions applying to most steam locomotive sheds.

42/4/95, 6005/6/8/11, 6321/91, 6418/22, 6844/8/56, 6901/8/24/64, 7007, 7315, 8705/26/34, 9621. (**75**).

SALOP. Shrewsbury:—2228/9/33–5, 2744/5, 2897, 3377, 3442, 3602, 3702/82/8, 4040/4/6/61, 4602/23/72, 4704, 4919, 5021/32/61/4/73/86/97, 5154/68, 5642/73, 5774, 5981/94, 6307/38/48, 6633, 6963, 7006, 7319, 9024/73/6, 9657, 9719. (**49**).

WLN. Wellington:—2030, 3417, 3732/49/75, 4400/1/3/6/9, 5127/35/9/46/78, 5309/32, 5758, 9624/30/9. (**21**).

STB. Stourbridge:—1410/4/38, 1745/9, 1835, 2092, 2107/85/6/7/9, 2246/70/9/81, 2620/55, 2706/12/71, 2852, 3450, 3649/67, 3740, 4104/46/9/50, 4638/87/96, 5101/5/7/22/31/4/6/8/41/7/55/60/5/7/70/80/9/91/3/6/7, 5712/9/26/54/94/5, 6617/46/65/77/84, 6812, 7428, 7705/6, 8704/42/91/2/7, 9613/36, 9741/67. (**79**).

TYS. Tyseley:—2065/71/90, 2152, 2209/38/57/92/6/7, 2719/33, 2903/16/88, 3005/49, 3101/51/8/80, 3613/24/5/50/3/7/60/4/73/89/93, 3743, 4058, 4106/7/11/6/47, 5605/20/48/83, 4917/24/30/4/9/59/67/92/3/9, 5102/3/6/17/21/5/9/52/6/62/4/6/71/5/82/8/90/8/9, 5346/69/70, 5634, 5700/1/38/42/5/90, 5907/93/7, 6336, 6611, 6831/3/43/7/53/5/8/60/6, 6904/14, 7402, 7735/58, 8108, 8700/84, 9007/8/10/9, 9608/10/35, 9724/33/48/53/93/8. (**118**).

Worcester Division
CHEL. Cheltenham:—1402, 3449, 4141, 4320, 4564/7/78, 5345, 5515/38/74, 6326/41, 7303/12, 7818. (**16**).

GLO. Gloucester:—1406/13/24/41/64, 1943/89, 2009, 2248, 2515, 2656, 2756, 2938/80, 3153/64/71/5, 3204/5, 3379, 3440, 3609, 4059/82, 4140, 4627/8/59, 4977, 5042, 5312/36/47/94/8, 5697, 5793, 5951/65/80/8/90, 6309/81, 6623/81, 6917/40, 7004, 7723/41, 7815, 8701/17/31/81, 9064/89, 9727/76, W.D. 79232, L.M.S. 8451. (**63**).

HFD. Hereford:—1404/45/55/60, 2026/9/40/96/9, 2102/38, 2243/86, 2349, 2541, 2651/80, 2714, 2807, 2920/4/32/7/44/8/51/87, 3209, 3432/54, 3601, 3725/8/89, 4079, 4534, 4600/57/78, 5348/77, 5765, 5807/8/14/7, 6349/52/95, 6631, 6905/20/43, 7420, 7707, 9619. (**56**).

KDR. Kidderminster:—28/9, 1206, 2093, 4584/6/94, 4625/41, 5110/2, 5303, 5518/73, 7700, 8101, 8718/27. (**18**).

LYD. Lydney:—1409/56, 2025/34/9/43–5/80/91, 2114/21/31/2/44/6/53/5/60, 2350. (**20**).

WOS. Worcester:—1408/18, 1919, 2001/7/16/37/51, 2100/1/15, 2205/7/37/41/2/7/63/74/7/8/90/4, 2339, 2458, 2551, 2631, 2743/74/99, 3007/21/7/9/30/48, 3382/93, 3574, 3607, 4007/51/86/92, 4100/14/39, 4504/46/58/96, 4613/4/29/64, 4980, 5017/63/92, 5114/73, 5544, 5815/6, 5914/7/83, 6306/24/78/82/5/96, 6807/51/77, 6916/21/30/6/8/47/50/1, 7005, 7301/8, 7416, 7750, 8106, W.D. 77203. (**91**).

Cardiff Valleys Division
CV.AYN. Abercynon:—236/81/7/8/95, 337/51/6/80/97/8, 402/14, 2000, 2140, 3599, 5618/9/30/7/41/3/4/69/82/6, 6401/11. (**28**).

CV.BRY. Barry:—212/3/24/31/48/58/9/61–3/5/7–72/4–7/80/3/6, 322/45/61/72/7/9/82/6–9/94, 404/39/40, 783/4, 1993, 5195, 3609/21/2/7/32/48/62/4/5/7/93/9, 6602/14/9/20/37/41/3/7/53/8/62/8/9, 6712/22–4/33/6/8/40/5–8, 9631. (**81**).

CH. Dowlais, Cae Harris:—83, 292, 320, 5652/3/66/71/4/94. (**9**).

CED. Cardiff East Dock:—31/3/6/7, 46/7, 51–5/7–9, 61/6–8, 72–4, 92/4, 155, 285/97, 319, 604/5/8/10/1/81–4, 1705/7, 1884/8/97, 2008/22/48/86, 2123/4/30/41/7/50, 2754/81, 3707, 4616/8/30, 6700–9/21/44, 7751, 8743. (**71**).

CHYS. Cardiff, Cathays:—301/5/43/4/6–8/60/4/7/70/1/5/6/83/4/90/1/3, 406, 1375, 1420/5/61, 2066, 2724, 3597, 5605/14/7/23/4/46/51/8/9/61/72/81/7, 6402/16/23/33/5/6, 6615/26/7/35/48/55/9–61. (**55**).

CV.FDL. Ferndale:—278/90/8/9, 315/21/4, 5600/10/68. (**10**).

MTHR. Merthyr:—333, 1878, 2760, 4632/5, 5654/77/8/98, 5711/21/69, 6408/27/

34, 7717/66/72, 8736, 9618/22/38/43. **(23)**.
RYR. Radyr:—30/2/4/5/8, 40–4, 56, 63/4, 198, 214/40/6/50/93, 433, 5640/55, 6603/7/8/18/64. **(27)**.
RHY. Rhymney:—39, 76–82, 5128, 5635/60/83/92/6. **(14)**.
THT. Treherbert:—279, 302/3/52/65/6/8/73/8/99, 409, 792–4, 5159, 5601/7/8/ 11/3/5/36/50/63/76/80/8/91/5, 7722. **(30)**.

Central Wales Division
BCN. Brecon:—2343/51, 2401/68, 2523/69, 3638, 3706/67, 5801, 9614. **(11)**.
MCH. Machynlleth:—3, 4, 7, 8, 864/94, 1213, 1465/74, 1965, 2151, 2200/4/19/ 23/60/83/98, 2323/56, 2464, 2572, 3200/1/7, 4501/11–3/49/55/60/71/5, 5507/17/ 24/41/60/70, 7406, 7802/3, 9000/2/4/5/9/12–4/7/21/5/7/54/72/87/91. **(59)**.
OSW. Oswestry:—680, 822/3/44/9/55/73/84/7/92/3/5/6/8, 1196/7, 1308/31, 1412/ 7/32/59, 2032/54/68/75, 2201/10/44/55, 2327/54/82/6, 2449/52/82/3, 2516/43/ 56, 3202/8, 5806, 7405/10, 7807/8/19, 8103, 9001/3/16/20/2/6/8/65. **(58)**.

Diesel Rail Cars
Southall: Parcels Cars 17 and 34.
Reading: 1, 12/9, 35/6.
Oxford: 10/1.
Bristol, St. Philip's Marsh: 21/4, 37/8.
Weymouth: 20.
Leamington Spa: 26/9.
Stourbridge Town: 8, 14, 33.
Gloucester: 32.
Worcester: 5, 6, 7, 22/5/7/8.

Newport, Ebbw Junction: 3, 23.
Llantrisant: 18, 31.
Pontypool Road: 30.
Carmarthen: 15/6.
Landore: 2, 4, 13.

Service Locomotives
Reading Signal Works: 27.
Didcot Stores: 26.
Taunton, Engineering Department: 23/4.

GREAT WESTERN RAILWAY

Locomotive Stock, 31 December, 1947
4-6-0 (675). County: 1000–29 (30). Saint: 2902/3/5/6/8/12/3/5/6/20/4/6–55/79– 81/7–9 (47). Star: 4003/4/7/12/3/5/7–23/5/6/8/30/1/3–6/8–62 (47). Castle: 100A1, 111, 4000/16/32/7/73–99, 5000–99, 7000–7 (141) (Nos. 100A1, 5039/79/83/91 are oil burning). Hall (oil burning): 3900–4/50–5 (11). Hall (coal burning): 4900–6/8–10/2–47/9–67/70/3–99, 5900–54/6–75/7–85/7–99, 6900–48/50–2/4–6/8 (247). Modified Hall (coal burning): 6959–80 (22). King: 6000–29 (30). Grange: 6800–79 (80). Manor: 7800–19 (20).
4-4-0 (85). Bulldog: 3335/41/63/4/6/76/7/9/82/3/6/91/3/5/6, 3400/1/6/7/8/17/8/9/ 21/6/30/1/2/8/40–55 (45). 9000: 9000–28 (29). Duke: 9054/64/5/72/3/6/83/4/7/9/91 (11).
2-8-0 (221). 28XX (coal burning): 2800–31/3/5–8/40–4/6/50–2/5–61/4–71/3–87/ 9–99, 3800–12/4–7/9/21–30/2–6/8/40–64/6 (147). 28XX (oil burning): 4800–11/ 50–7 (20). ROD: 3002/4–6/8–44/6–9 (45). Mixed Traffic: 4700–8 (9).
2-6-0 (253). Aberdare: 2612/20/3/43/51/5/6/62/5/7/9/80 (12). Mixed Traffic: 4303/18/20/6/37/53/8/65/75/7/81/6, 5300/2/3/5–7/9–28/30–41/3–51/3/5–62/4/5/7– 82/4–6/8/90–2/4–9, 6300–14/6–99, 7300–21, 8393, 9300–19 (241) (No 6320 is oil burning).
2-4-0 (3). MSWJ: 1334–6 (3).
0-6-0 (183). Cambrian Railways Class 15: 844/9/55/64/73/87/92–6 (11). 2251: 2200–99, 3200–17 (118). Dean Goods: 2322/3/7/39/40/3/9–51/4/6/82/5/6, 2401/7– 9/11/4/26/31/44/9/52/8/60/2/4/8/74/82–4, 2513/5/6/23/32/4/7/8/41/3/51/6/68–70/ 2/3/8/9 (54).
2-8-2T (54). 72XX: 7200–53 (54).
2-8-0T (151). 42XX: 4200/1/3/6–8/11–5/7/8/11–5/7/8/21–33/5–8/41–3/6–8/50– 99, 5200–64 (151).
2-6-2T (458). Vale of Rheidol: 7, 8, 1213 (3). AD: 1205/6 (2). 3100: 3100–4 (5).

Line up of GWR locomotives, from top to bottom: Dean 4-4-0 No 7 Armstrong *nominally a rebuild from a 2-4-0, which with three rebuilds from broad gauge 2-4-0s formed the first GWR standard gauge express passenger 4-4-0 type; Dean/ Churchward City class 4-4-0 No 3434* City of Birmingham; *the pioneer Churchward four-cylinder locomotive, originally built as a 4-4-2 No 40 but later rebuilt as a 4-6-0 and named* North Star; *one of the first of Churchward's two-cylinder 4-6-0s of modern style, No 98, later named* Ernest Cunard *and numbered 2998, of the Saint class; one of the odd-looking outside framed Aberdare 2-6-0s, No 33.*

31XX: 3150/1/3/4/7–61/3/4/5/7–72/4–8/80/2–90 (33). 44XX: 4400–10 (11). 45XX: 4500–99, 5500–74 (175). 51XX: 4100–59, 5101–14/7/9/21/2/5/7–32/4–44/6–8/50–99 (149). 61XX: 6100–69 (70). 81XX: 8100–9 (10).

2-4-0T (13). Cambrian Railways: 1196/7 (2). Liskeard & Looe: 1308 (1). GW: 3561/2/82/5/6/8/9/92/7/9 (10).

0-8-2T (1). PT: 1358 (1).

0-6-2T (391). BM 4ft 6in: 11, 332, 422/5/6/8, 504 (7). BM 5ft: 433, 1372/3/5, 1668/70 (6). RR R: 30–2/4, 46 (5). RR A: 52–75 (24). RR M: 33, 47, 51 (3). RR R1: 35–44 (10). RR P: 76/7/82/3 (4). RR P1: 78–81 (4). Cardiff Railway: 155 (1). PT: 184 (1). AD: 190 (1). BR B: 198, 212/3/31/8/40/6/8/58/9/61–3/5/7–72–4–7 (24). TV O4: 200/4/5/7/9/10/36/78–99, 301/2/10/4/7/20/1/4/33, 409/14/20 (41). TV A: 303/5/22/35/7/43–9/51/2/6/7/60–2/4–8/70–91/3/4/7–9, 402/4/6/8/38–40 (58). TV O3: 410/1 (2). 56XX: 5600–99, 6600–99 (200).

0-6-0T (1251). WCP: 5, 6 (2). CMDP: 28/9 (2). RR S1: 90/2, 605 (3). RR S: 93/4, 610/1 (4). LMM: 359, 803 (2). AD: 666/7/80 (3). Cardiff Railway: 681–4 (4). BR D: 783/4 (2). TV H: 792–4 (3). Welshpool & Llanfair: 822/3 (2). SHT 1085/6 (2). Whitland & Cardigan Saddle Tank: 1331 (1). 1361 Dock Shunter: 1361–5 (5). 1366 Pannier Tank: 1366–71 (6). NB (GW 1854): 1715 (1). 1501: 1531/2/8/42 (4). 1854: 906/7, 1705/6/9/13/20/6/30/1/52–4/8/60/2/4/9/99, 1855/8/61–3/7/70/8/84/8/9/91/4/6/7, 1900 (35). 655: 1742/5/7/9/73/80/2/9, 2702/4/6–9/12–7/9 (21). 1813: 1835 (1). 1901: 992, 1903/7/9/12/7/9/25/30/5/41/3/5/9/57/64/5/7–9/73/9/89–912/3/6, 2000–2/4/6–14/6–9 (44) (Nos 1925 and 2007 saddle tanks). 2021: 2021–3/5–7/9–35/7–40/2–5/7/8/50–6/9–61/3–73/5/6/9–83/5/6/8–99, 2100–2/4/6–15/7/21–4/6/7/9–32/4–8/40/1/4/6–8/50–6/9/60 (110) (No 2048 saddle tank). BPGV: 2162/5–8/76/92–8 (13). 2181: 2181–90 (10). 2721: 2721/2/4/8/30/4/8/9/43–6/8/9/51/2/4/5/7/60/1/4/7/9/71/2/4/6/80/1/5–7/9–95/7–9 (43). RSB (GW 2721): 2756 (1). 57XX: 3600–99, 3700–99, 4600–99, 5700–99, 7700–99, 8700–99, 9600–61, 9711–99 (751). 54XX: 5400–24 (25). 64XX: 6400–39 (40). 67XX: 6700–59 (60). 74XX: 7400–29 (30). 94XX: 9400–9 (10). 9700 Condenser fitted: 9700–10 (11).

0-4-2T (100). Corris Railway: 3, 4 (2). 14XX: 1400–74 (75). GW: 3574/5/7 (3). 58XX: 5800–19 (20).

0-4-0T (17). PM 696, 779, 935/42 (4). SHT: 701, 929/43/68/74, 1098 (6). Dock Shunter: 1101–6 (6). Cardiff Railway: 1338 (1).

Total Steam Locomotives—3,856.

Diesel-Electric Locomotive (1) **0-6-0**: 2.   Total Locomotives—3,857.

Rail Motor Vehicles (37).

Diesel (37). AEC Railcars: 1–8, 10–38.

Service Locomotives (4).

Petrol (4). Simplex Shunters: 23/4/6/7.

Miscellaneous Locomotive. (Not included in Locomotive Stock).

Engineer's Department, Simplex Petrol Shunter: 15.

Locomotives on Loan, 31 December, 1947

2-8-0 (89). From Ministry of Supply: WD 70801/8/36/43/76, 77000/1/5/12/4/5/26/8/40/9/53/8/64/77/9/97/9, 77102/6/15/6/23/30/42/51/61/5/84/96, 77200/2/3/10/4/34/41/7/55/7/88/9/91/4/7, 77310/25/6/68/78/80/8/93, 77407/8/21/9/43/89, 77508, 78510/2/21/2/42/3, 78604/32/71/95, 78714/7, 79219/24–6/32/4/5/61/74/8, 79301/3/9 (89). **Total Locomotives Held on Loan—89.**

The Workshops

A much-quoted passage in Gooch's diary records: 'Mr Brunel and I went down to look at the ground, then only green fields, and he agreed with me to its being the best place'. The 'green fields' were soon to see the first buildings of Swindon Works, for in Gooch's words the site had the advantage of being 'the junction with the Cheltenham branch and also a

From top to bottom: The first of Churchward's large boiler 2-8-0s No 4700; County tank, 4-4-2T No 2221; mainstay of London suburban services, one of the 61XX 2-6-2Ts No 6110; the archetypal GWR branch engine which lasted to the end of steam, 48XX class 0-4-2T No 4866, later 1466 and today preserved by the Great Western Society at Didcot.

convenient division of the Great Western line for engine working'.

The works site was west of Swindon station and on the north side of the line. As the works would be some two miles from the town of Swindon, the railway arranged with builders to erect cottages for its workmen. Funds were short at the time, and the company rented the property and sub-let it to its employees. This was the genesis of 'New Swindon', and soon it was extended until it linked up with the old town. The two were officially merged in 1900, with G. J. Churchward as the first Mayor.

On 2 January 1843 the establishment was brought into use as an engine depot and repair shop. There were three buildings: a running shed, 490ft by 72ft, with accommodation for 48 locomotives and tenders was built parallel to the line; the engine house, 290ft by 140ft, was at right angles to it and used for light repairs; the erecting shop at the north end of the engine house could accommodate 18 locomotives undergoing heavy repair. Engine building at Swindon began in 1846 with the Great Western class 4-2-2s.

Amalgamation of the Great Western with the two standard gauge companies based on Shrewsbury made extensions necessary so that Swindon could build standard as well as broad gauge locomotives. Construction of a carriage & wagon works was authorised in October 1867 and the first vehicles from the new shops were turned out during 1869. Expansion continued as the workload increased and by the end of the century a new and much larger erecting shop was taking shape. This was the 'A' shop, brought into use in stages between 1900 and 1903. It was visited in its early days by the Editor of *The Railway Magazine*, G. A. Sekon, who said of it: 'Its vastness appals one; we have a fairly good eye for measurements and standing at one end gave us our opinion that it was 500ft long and of similar width. The exact measurements are 498ft 6in long by 466ft 6in wide, so we were not very far out'. He then proceeded to find a

Also in A shop was the locomotive testing plant consisting of a bedplate carrying five pairs of water cooled bearings; they were arranged to slide longitudinally so that they could be aligned to suit the wheelbases of different engines. The drawbar was coupled to a steelyard holding the engine in position and at the same time registering the pull on the drawbar at various speeds. It was on this machine that LMS Class 2 2-6-0 No 46413, a 1946 design, was tested; tests of a Dean Goods 0-6-0, a design of the last century in many ways proved it to be the superior locomotive, and front end arrangements for the modern engines were then redesigned! The photograph taken in the late 1930s shows Saint class No 2931 Arlington Court on the test plant.

*Reading 1947. No 9303, a late
43XX class 2-6-0 as fitted with a side
window cab, takes water at the
platform column. Note the fireman in
his proper position on the tender, and
the post war green livery with the
letters GWR on the tender.*

Chippenham 1949. A typical GWR steel post metal arm lower quadrant bracket signal. Note the white diamond on the post indicating a track circuit so that the fireman would not immediately need to report to the signalbox if the train was detained.

Pilning, Severn Tunnel in October 1958. A Manchester to Plymouth express emerges from the southern portal behind County class 4-6-0 No 1016. County of Hants *fitted with a double chimney.*

Newbury in 1939 with Duke class 4-4-0 No 3256 nearing the end of its days on a Southampton stopping train. Note the full lettering Great Western on its tender. No scene could have more GWR atmosphere, with the train of clerestory stock, typical station island awnings and diesel railcar No 18 in the background on the Lambourn branch service.

*Pilning, Severn Tunnel. A coal train
from South Wales behind a 72XX
2-8-2 tank piloted by 51XX class
2-6-2 tank No 4152, both in dirty
condition externally. Severn Tunnel
Junction shed had a number of
31XX and later 51XX tanks
specially for this duty. No 4152 was
one of the last of its class to be built in
GWR days though the Western
Region continued to build further
examples.*

parallel that would enable the dimensions to be grasped, and after sundry calculations estimated that the roof of the shed would be 'big enough to cover 120 suburban residences, gardens, roads and all'.

Dean was still the chief at Swindon at the time of this visit, described in *The Railway Magazine* of October 1901. Sekon enlarged on the size and ingenuity of the machine tools he saw in action, and he was particularly impressed by the fact that:

> Mr Dean has taken advantage of the latest scientific development of gas and electric power. A mammoth three-cylinder Westinghouse gas engine of 250 brake horsepower has been erected, and this will drive a dynamo that will generate sufficient electric current to work about one-third of the machinery in this large shop.

Not all that he saw was equally pleasing to him, and he commented:

> In the erecting shop we were introduced to the newest specimens of Mr Dean's designs in locomotive construction. Here we saw colossal engines of the 2602 type in various degrees of completion. Monsters such engines are and powerful without doubt, but it is sad to find that even on the Great Western Railway beauty of outline has succumbed at last to power and utility. Swindon has ever been the stronghold of graceful outlines in locomotive construction, but with the advent of the 'Camel' type of locomotives, and the later inelegant monsters that have been evolved from the design, all traces of beauty have of necessity been eliminated.

After this lament, Sekon wistfully hoped that coming years might again produce a design that had all the advantages of the latest engineering mammoths and yet had toned down their ungainly features. He was not to be disappointed.

The end of Dean's years at Swindon saw the beginnings of plans for the locomotive testing plant that was to be installed and put into operation by Churchward. Sekon described the idea:

> Mr Dean is trying an important experiment and to carry out the same is providing a species of friction rollers on which the new engines will stand and work through machinery for a certain period at full speed instead of running over the line for a distance of several hundred miles. The revolution of the driving wheels of the locomotives thus on trial will supply power to work several of the tools etc in the shop, so that instead of the trials being an actual waste of effort they will in future economically supply the force that will perform useful work in the Swindon Locomotive Works.

Visitors were certainly impressed by the machinery. One wrote of multiple drilling machines ranging up to fifty spindles, two forging presses of 200 tons, a firebox drilling machine in which almost all the holes in a

The change over from Broad to Narrow Gauge.
(*From* Railway Ribaldry, *see page 154*)

firebox could be drilled at one setting, and 'the hydraulic flanging press of 600 tons with ten rams pressing the large fireboxes into shape in two heats and the smaller fireboxes in one'. An interesting comment on Swindon boiler practice was made by H. Simpson, Vice-President of the GWR Mechanics' Institution, in a paper read to the Institution in 1906. Referring to a practice at one time of crowding as many tubes as possible into the tube plate to obtain maximum heating surface, he pointed out that this caused the plate to become overheated and to result in leaky tubes and cracked meshes. In Churchward's large boilers the area of the firebox tubeplate had been enlarged to the limit and the true secret of efficiency had been exploited, namely free circulation. If only it were possible to carry the sides of the firebox down straight instead of curving them inwards to clear the frames, they would have a boiler perfect in every respect as a steam generator.

The same speaker mentioned problems with hard water in the Swindon Division, making it necessary to take out and replace a large number of tubes annually. In 1903, when there were about 490 engines in the Division, 14,871 tubes had been renewed at an approximate cost of £3,718. Thanks to water softening plant these figures had been reduced to 8,309 tubes and £2,077 in 1905, and said the speaker, 'If Mr Churchward continues his present policy of providing softening plants at the various watering stations the expenditure under this head will almost reach vanishing point'.

A graphic account of Swindon Works and workmen was given by Alfred Williams in his book, *Life in a Railway Factory*, published in 1915. He worked for 22 years as a hammerman in the stamping shop, sometimes astonishing the foreman by chalking Latin or Greek words on the wall to help him memorise the classical vocabulary he was acquiring as part of his continuous efforts at self-improvement. Some of his descriptions give the impression of a scene from Dante's inferno illustrated by Hogarth, but he was a poet and found some aspects of his dramatic environment emotionally stimulating. He says:

To stand in the midst of it and view the whole scene when everything is in active operation is a wonderful experience, thrilling and impressive. You see the lines of furnaces and steam hammers – there are fifteen altogether – with the monkeys travelling up and down continually and beating on the metal one against the other in utter disorder and confusion, the blazing white light cast out from the furnace door or the duller glow of the half-finished forging, the flames leaping and shooting from the oil forges, the clouds of yellow cinders blown out from the smiths' fires, the whirling wheels of the shafting and machinery between the lines and the half-naked workmen, black and bareheaded, in every conceivable attitude, full of quick life and exertion and all in a desperate hurry as if they had but a few more minutes to live.

The passage continues with some more powerfully vivid descriptions of

Opposite:
The interior of Tyseley shed factory sometime in 1910, containing a fascinating selection of locomotives including Nos 3279 Exmoor *(Duke class), 7 (Armstrong 7ft 0in coupled 4-4-0 later renumbered 4171: at this time all the members of the class had just been sent to the Wolverhampton Division), a Dean Goods 0-6-0 (still with copper capped chimney), two 31XX 2-6-2 tanks one being 3168, and two 3901 class 2-6-2 tanks Nos 3908 and 3911 (this class was converted from Dean Goods 2301 class 0-6-0s in the early 1900s in response to a demand for more powerful suburban tanks in the Birmingham area). Major repairs finished in 1931-3 but the works remained open for intermediate repairs until the London Midland Region take over of the area; all work ceased in 1964.*

sounds and sights and then suddenly slackens to the comparative calm of the press shop with the comment: 'The hydraulic work, on the other hand, though interesting, is not engrossing. There is a lack of life and animation in it; it is not stirring or dramatic'.

Swindon Works continued to expand. In 1921 the Erecting Shop was almost doubled in size to cover 11½ acres. Against 36 pits in the older section there were 60 in the new, each 100ft long, and four overhead electric cranes of 100 tons capacity and 75ft span. This was double the capacity of the four cranes in the older part of the shop.

In the centenary year 1935 Swindon was building about 100 new engines annually, and repairing 1,000. The works covered 323 acres, of which 73 were roofed. In 1939 Swindon again turned some of its resources to war production, as it had done in the first world war, but whereas the years between the wars had seen the steam railway reaching its zenith, the aftermath of the Second World War saw a completely changed situation with the role of the railway in national transport progressively diminishing. At the same time the town of Swindon was developing industrially and its life was no longer centred on the railway. In March 1960 Swindon

turned out its last steam locomotive, the Class 9F 2-10-0 No 92220. A competition was held to choose a name for it. Three entrants proposed *Evening Star*, which was adopted and the prize shared between T. M. Phillips, driver, of Aberystwyth, J. S. Sathi, boiler washer, Old Oak Common, and F. L. Pugh, general manager's office, Paddington. The naming ceremony was performed by Keith Grand, then a Member of the British Railways Board and a former Western Region General Manager.

Largest and longest-lived of the other Great Western works were Stafford Road Works, Wolverhampton. They had their origin in the locomotive shed and repair shops of the standard gauge Shrewsbury & Birmingham Railway which reached Wolverhampton in 1849 and built its depot on the west side of Stafford Road. The premises later became the locomotive headquarters of the Shrewsbury & Birmingham and Shrewsbury & Chester Railways. They were presided over by Joseph Armstrong, who continued there as Locomotive Superintendent when the two companies were amalgamated with the Great Western in 1854. In that year, too, the Great Western broad gauge reached Wolverhampton and established a locomotive depot on the opposite side of Stafford Road. The Great Western reorganised and extended the works of the Shrewsbury companies so that they could undertake new construction as well as repair work. Stafford Road thus became the locomotive centre for the standard gauge Northern Division of the GWR. Its first new locomotive was produced in 1859.

Pressure of work following amalgamation with the West Midland Railway in 1863 made further expansion at Stafford Road necessary. The site was restricted, and a new erecting shop was built on available space in the broad gauge yard on the opposite side of the road, with a footbridge connecting the two sections of the works. Joseph Armstrong remained in charge until 1864 when Gooch retired as Locomotive Superintendent of

The then new Tyseley (Birmingham) locomotive shed and works in 1908 showing the two roundhouses (passenger and freight) with the factory in front. The shed was re-located here during the general modernisation and reconstruction of the area in 1905-12. It was adjacent to the junction for the new North Warwick line. Note the huge coal stocks and loco coal wagons. Like all GWR sheds the depot marked its resident locomotives with a letter code on the front of the frames (or in the case of some tank engines the top of the front step). In this case the letters were TYS. This was one of the last large sheds to house ex GWR engines, the final three being 0-6-0 panniers for work in Halesowen yard; they lasted into 1966.

the GWR and Armstrong succeeded him. He moved to Swindon, where the company built the family a residence, Newburn, beside the line. It was in walking from Newburn to the works on a misty December morning in 1933 that G. J. Churchward, then living there in retirement, was struck by an express and killed.

At Stafford Road Joseph Armstrong was succeeded by his brother George who remained there as Divisional Locomotive, Carriage & Wagon Superintendent until 1897. During that time the numbers employed at the works doubled. Throughout the period the Stafford Road products, mainly 0-4-2 and 0-6-0 tank engines and numerous rebuilds of varying degrees of thoroughness, maintained a distinct individuality. After George's retirement there was conformity with Swindon practice.

With their layout on both sides of Stafford Road, the works were not convenient and reconstruction was planned in the early 1900s but not put into effect. Instead, manufacture of locomotives at Stafford Road was discontinued in 1908.

Some 20 years later reconstruction of the works was at last undertaken under a Government scheme to relieve unemployment. The new factory was built on the west side of the old Shrewsbury & Birmingham line and opened in 1932. The main shop, 450ft by 196ft, was in three bays, two forming the erecting shop and the third the machine and wheel shop. With two 50 ton overhead electric cranes in the erecting shop and two of 6 tons capacity in the machine bay the works could deal with the heaviest engines and were useful in taking the load off Swindon.

The new Stafford Road served the GWR and the Western Region for some 30 years but on 1 January 1963 it was transferred to the London Midland Region. Little over a year of life remained. The last locomotive repaired left the works on 11 February 1964 and a few months later the works was finally closed.

The need for a works closer than Swindon to maintain Great Western locomotives in South Wales became pressing at Grouping. It was decided to develop Caerphilly, which had been opened for locomotive repair and rebuilding by the Rhymney Railway in 1901 and was now in the Great Western Group. The older shops were remodelled and a new erecting shop built of about 60,000sq ft area. With a central traverser and two repair bays, each with two 40 ton hoists on a gantry, the shop had a capacity for 60 locomotives. It was opened in March 1926. As the number of locomotives belonging to GWR constituent companies in South Wales dwindled, most Great Western types passed through the shop. The works survived until the end of June 1963.

Other heavy repair shops at Newton Abbot, Barry and Worcester lasted until the 1960s and the run-down of BR steam. A whole group of shops including Old Oak Common, Tyseley, and Bristol Bath Road ceased heavy repairs in 1931–2. Wartime reorganisation in 1941 saw the grouping of eleven shops as repair depots but four of them closed in the following year. While Newton Abbot, Barry and Worcester were upgraded as 'factories' in 1949, Tyseley did not resume major repairs and from that date was classified as a motive power depot.

The cover of one of the most popular publications ever produced by a railway company, The GWR Engine Book. *This superb book priced at one shilling (5p) was printed throughout on art paper and not only contained lists of all names, numbers and classes extant on the GWR at the date of each issue, but also had photographs and line drawings. There was in addition a thirteen page introduction describing general history of the company's locomotive development over the years. One of the remarkable facts about this book is that it was first produced before the first world war. The cover illustrated is from the 1932 edition and is a boyhood memory.*

85

6
A RECORDER REMEMBERS

Expectations of the kind of running one could expect on the Great Western were aroused in the late autumn of 1921 when Cecil J. Allen described his first post-war trip on the Cornish Riviera Express, in *The Railway Magazine,* and in the following July he recalled the record runs between Paddington and Plymouth that had been made in 1903–4. The last of the Dean 4-2-2 singles had been withdrawn in December 1915, but they were well remembered from days in Reading before the war. The very last one to go, No 3050 *Royal Sovereign,* looked magnificent when seen at Paddington one day about 1913. She was one of those rebuilt with a domeless boiler and high raised Belpaire firebox, and everything about her had been lovingly polished. Those that retained domed boilers were not so ornate in their later years, because the domes were painted over in green. No 3006 *Courier* seen on an up express in Reading station at that time must have been in her last days, for she was withdrawn in February 1914. But of course the Cities, which figured so prominently in Allen's article of July 1922 were all at work at the end of 1921.

The writer's first experience of real brilliance in Great Western running came in September 1924, on the up Limited. The train had the usual summer load of only eight coaches from Plymouth, and engine No 4066, then *Malvern Abbey.* That last series of Star class engines was originally turned out in 1922 in plain green, with cast iron tapered chimneys, but in 1924 No 4066 had evidently been through the shops, for she was indeed 'in glorious Technicolor', and positively glittered. The run began well enough, but approaching Exeter it was evident that the heavy 1.25pm up, running late, was still in the station, and it checked the Limited on every adverse stretch until it was about 12min late before Savernake. Then the preceding train also must have run very hard, for the crew of the Limited were able to make an undelayed, and truly thrilling finish, covering the 70.1 miles from Savernake to Paddington in 61¾min pass to stop, regaining 9¼min of lost time, and arriving in only 3min over the level 3 hr from Exeter.

For sheer brilliance, however, one cannot think, with all subsequent experience of Castles and Kings, that two runs recorded within a fortnight of each other in 1925 on the down Torbay Limited, as it was then called, and on the 6.28pm up from Taunton have ever been surpassed. On both occasions it was at first disappointing not to have Castles, but that disappointment did not last long once the train was under way. On the Torbay there was a load of 13 of the latest 70ft stock, 469 tons tare, and a gross load of just 500 tons. At that time the down Limited often took '14'

Opposite:
Latterday Star. No 4066 Malvern Abbey *heads a Birmingham to Paddington express the Great Way Round, via Oxford on 9 June 1930. The sun is out in Sonning Cutting showing off the gleam of the dark green paint and polished brass. Note that 4066 still has a 3,500 gallon tender; the two leading coaches are clerestory dining cars of turn of the century years. Although designated an express the train will probably have made five stops over the 126 miles – Warwick, Leamington, Banbury, Oxford and Reading, passengers changing at Leamington from Stratford-on-Avon.*

out of Paddington, but this would be reduced with slip portions to 12 from Westbury, and 10 from Taunton, but on this trip the full load had to be taken through to Exeter, where the five coaches comprising the Cornish part of the train were detached.

This run was made in the last week of the winter service; during the height of the summer the train ran non-stop to Torquay, with a considerably lighter load. Engine No 4042 *Prince Albert* was wisely not pressed from the start with this tremendous load, but was going finely up the Kennet Valley when the train was stopped dead by signals at Hungerford. In consequence Bedwyn was passed 9¾min late, and thereafter the performance was magnificent. The remaining 112.2 miles

Briefing for the Ocean Mail Runs
In 1904 when competition with the London & South Western Railway in running the ocean liner specials from Plymouth to London was working up to a new intensity, Churchward, responsible for locomotive running, became aware that his redoubtable contemporary on the LSWR, none other than the great Dugald Drummond, was taking an intense personal interest. So he selected a young running inspector then based at Newton Abbot, G. H. Flewellyn by name, summoned him to Swindon, and put him in charge of all the running with the ocean specials, to ride on the footplate on each occasion, and see that nothing less than top class performance was put up. On no account was the LSWR to be allowed to show any advantage, even though their route was then nearly 12 miles the shorter. After a most thorough briefing on his duties, Churchward summed up his instructions characteristically: 'Withhold all attempt at a maximum speed until I give you the word; then you can go and break your bloody neck!'

from Hungerford to Exeter were run in exactly 2hr, start to stop, and this included the severe slowings through Westbury and Frome and a relaying slack near Keinton Mandeville. Splendidly as the train had done as far as Taunton, it was to be expected that with such a load a stop might be made to take a pilot up to Whiteball summit, but to the accompaniment of a truly thunderous exhaust beat the engine was pounded up on its own. Speed was still 30mph at the tunnel entrance, but had fallen to 25½ on breasting the summit. A fast run down to Exeter at 75–76mph concluded a notable run. That net start-to-stop average speed of 57.4mph from Hungerford to Exeter remains a classic in Great Western annals.

A fortnight later, with engine No 4026 *King Richard*, a 13-coach train, brought up from Newton Abbot, was augmented at Taunton by through carriages from Minehead and Ilfracombe, and the slip coach that was detached at Newbury – no fewer than 16 coaches in all but most of them, although 70 footers, of the 'toplight' variety. Even so the load was a somewhat staggering 514 tons tare, and at least 550 tons full. The train had no sooner started from Taunton than it was pulled up by signals; but from the restart the 137.9 miles to Acton were covered in 146min, making a running average of 58¼mph over the 130.6 miles from Athelney, and this again included the hampering speed restrictions through Frome and Westbury stations, which would be worth at least 5min compared to an unchecked run over the by-pass lines. The Newbury slip coach reduced the load by about 35 tons, and the outstanding quality of the performance can be judged by the sustained maximum speed of 69mph on level track at Slough, with the reduced load of 515 tons.

With the introduction of the Kings in 1927 the stay of the Castles as the top-line express passenger engines on the West of England main line was relatively short; but with the acceleration of the Cheltenham Flyer to a 70min run from Swindon to Paddington in the summer of 1929 the Castles came into their own in a different way – not that they had that famous train entirely to themselves in the first few months of its acceleration. There was, for example, an outstanding run by No 4017 *Knight of Liége*, on which Ealing Broadway, 71.6 miles from Swindon, was passed in 56min 51sec having averaged 80.7mph for nearly 61 miles continuously. It seemed that the GWR was anxious that everyone should join in the enjoyment of high speed because the Company issued cheap excursions to Swindon, outward by the 1.19pm from Paddington to return on the 'Flyer' for no more than 5s (25p). Railway enthusiasts were not so thick on the ground as they are today, and although the writer availed himself of this remarkable facility on many occasions a fellow railfan was never encountered, not even on Saturdays.

The first trip, in October 1929, was one of the best of all. The driver was one of the best Old Oak men of the day, C. Wasley; and after a gentle start out of Swindon he made a thrilling display, with an average speed of 83.8mph over the 27.9 miles from Challow to Reading, and a maximum of 86½mph on level track. The load was 275 tons and the engine No 5003 *Lulworth Castle*. By Slough the train was getting so far ahead of time that the engine was eased down, and even with a signal check that reduced speed to walking pace at Westbourne Park the arrival in Paddington was still 3min early.

Two other runs, when the train was running to its 70min schedule, did not compare with the foregoing. No 4090 *Dorchester Castle*, with a completely clear road, made the journey in 69¼min, eased at one point to such an extent that speed fell to 59mph, but on a winter evening No 5001 *Llandovery Castle* ran so poorly as to lose 6¼min, of which not more than 2½ could be debited to a permanent way check near Wantage Road.

Log of Cheltenham Flyer, 6 June, 1932
3.48pm Express Swindon to Paddington
(2.30pm ex Cheltenham)
Engine 5006 *Tregenna Castle*. Type 4-cyl 4-6-0.
Engine Crew: Driver Ruddock and Fireman Thorp.
Load: 6 coaches=186 tons tare, 195 tons full.

miles				min	sec	mph	miles				min	sec	mph
0.0	SWINDON	..	start	0	00	—	35.8	Pangbourne	..	pass	26	33	
1.0	*Milepost* 76¼	..	pass	2	10	—	37.3	*Milepost* 40	..	pass	27	34	90.5
2.0	,, 75¼	..	pass	3	15	64.3	38.7	Tilehurst	..	pass	28	28	
3.0	,, 74¼	..	pass	4	09	69.2	41.3	READING	..	pass	30	12	
4.0	,, 73¼	..	pass	4	58	75.0	42.3	*Milepost* 35	..	pass	30	51	91.4
5.0	,, 72¼	..	pass	5	45	78.9	46.3	Twyford	..	pass	33	31	
5.7	Shrivenham	..	pass	6	15		47.3	*Milepost* 30	..	pass	34	12	89.5
7.3	*Milepost* 70	..	pass	7	24	81.8	52.3	*Milepost* 25	..	pass	37	38	87.4
10.8	Uffington	..	pass	9	51		53.1	Maidenhead	..	pass	38	08	
12.3	*Milepost* 65	..	pass	10	56	84.9	57.3	*Milepost* 20	..	pass	41	06	86.5
13.4	Challow	..	pass	11	42		58.8	SLOUGH	..	pass	42	10	
16.9	Wantage Road	..	pass	14	05		62.3	*Milepost* 15	..	pass	44	36	85.7
17.3	*Milepost* 60	..	pass	14	21	87.8	64.1	West Drayton	..	pass	45	51	
20.8	Steventon	..	pass	16	40		67.3	*Milepost* 10	..	pass	48	13	82.9
22.3	*Milepost* 55	..	pass	17	41	90.0	68.2	SOUTHALL	..	pass	48	51	
24.2	DIDCOT	..	pass	18	55		71.6	Ealing Broadway		pass	51	17	
27.3	*Milepost* 50	..	pass	20	55	91.4	72.3	*Milepost* 5	..	pass	51	48	83.7
28.8	Cholsey	..	pass	21	59		75.3	*Milepost* 2	..	pass	53	56	84.4
32.3	*Milepost* 45	..	pass	24	15	91.4	76.0	Westbourne Park		pass	54	40	—
32.6	Goring	..	pass	24	25		77.3	PADDINGTON		stop	56	47	—

After the schedule had been cut to 65min, five runs were recorded, all of them good, with the Castles *St Mawes*, *Windsor*, *Kingswear* and *Chirk*, and the erstwhile 4-6-2 No 111 *Viscount Churchill*. Net times over the 60.8 miles from Uffington to Ealing Broadway varied between 44 and 47min, averages of 83 to 77¾mph. The last mentioned was just enough to keep time, and so slow a time was only once noted, with *Windsor Castle* on a busy summer Saturday when one or two slight checks were enough to show that faster running would only have involved worse checks. Strangely enough the fastest run noted was on a raw winter's afternoon in mid-December when the writer was travelling through from Gloucester, and despite an easterly wind and driving sleet the train ran up from Swindon, completely unchecked, in 62½min, with *Chirk Castle* and a load

The Cheltenham Flyer. *Making its debut behind Churchward's Saint 4-6-0 No 2915* Saint Bartholomew *on 9 July 1923 the Flyer was to reach even further heights in the next decade with Collett's Castles. On 8 July 1928 No 5000* Launceston Castle *took nine coaches of 280 tons from Swindon to London in 70 minutes, a 68.2mph start to stop average, while in 1932 the September timetable saw an acceleration to 71.4mph, making it the fastest train in the world – a legend proudly acclaimed with a locomotive headboard. This timing was preceded by a run with No 5006* Tregenna Castle *on 6 June when the average speed was 71.3mph.*

of 270 tons. After attaining 80mph by Uffington, apart from an almost momentary drop to 79½mph on taking water at Goring, the speed did not fall below 80mph until nearing Ealing, and the maximum was 86½mph near Maidenhead.

After the vintage years 1932–4, including the 'Record of Records' of 6 June 1932 when, by special arrangement, the Cheltenham Flyer was run from Swindon to Paddington in 56min 47sec by No 5006 *Tregenna Castle*, the Great Western speed supremacy began to slip away, and the northern lines came into the picture. After the Bristolian was introduced, in 1935, King class engines were used for a time, and the writer had no occasion to travel on it; but from 1937 onwards there were opportunities of using it in the up direction. But after earlier experiences on the Cheltenham Flyer one cannot say that any of these experiences was very exhilarating. Occasionally there was a maximum of 90mph descending from Badminton to Little Somerford, but the running east of Swindon, even when earlier checks had put the train a minute or so behind time, did not seem to have quite the dashing enterprise of old.

On the first run, with No 5066 *Wardour Castle* and the seven-coach 225 ton load, the train was badly checked by signals before Swindon, after which the driver kept precisely to the booked point-to-point times, averaging 78mph from Shrivenham to Ealing and arriving 3½min late. Then came No 5070 *Sir Daniel Gooch*. This began well with a 90mph at Little Somerford, but a permanent way slowing to 20mph at Reading put the train 3½min behind time, and none of this was recovered afterwards. On the third run No 5019 *Treago Castle* got a clear road throughout, and finished 1½min early, though not averaging more than 76.7mph from Shrivenham to Ealing; and on the last trip before the war, in July 1939, No 5080 *Ogmore Castle* did not do more than slightly better. But for a final signal check the train should have been in Paddington in 104min from Bristol. Compared to the brilliant efforts of the Bristol drivers when the 105min timing was restored in 1954 these were pedestrian performances.

Although it is passing beyond strictly Great Western days, three post-nationalisation runs must be mentioned, all with gross trailing loads of 260 tons. First there was 5067 *St Fagans Castle*, which began so well that it was 3min early by Didcot, and with no subsequent checks ran quite easily. Then came 5076 *Gladiator*, which not only reached 92mph at Little Somerford, but was also doing 92 on almost level track at Didcot, while with the double-chimney No 7018 *Drysllwyn Castle*, and speeds of 94mph at Little Somerford, and 91½mph near Didcot, the crew went on in such style as to arrive in Paddington 8min early! Those were halcyon days on the Western.

Reverting to pre-war years, most of the runs noted with Kings were made on the Birmingham route, but without any of the exceptional loads that made the work so outstanding at times. It was the same on the West of England line, on two occasions at Easter when division of the Cornish Riviera Express gave loads of well under 500 tons. Nevertheless, a run in 1935 had its moments. Engine No 6016 *King Edward V*, with a gross trailing load of 440 tons, covered the first 94.6 miles to Heywood Road Junction in 88¾min, and with no checks of any kind afterwards it was a mere 'doddle' afterwards to reach Exeter 1¼min inside the 170min timing. Things became more exciting afterwards because after leaving one coach at Exeter there was a load of 16 tons over the statutory limit of 360 to take over the 'mountain' gradients of the South Devon line. The driver would have been fully entitled to stop at Newton Abbot and claim the assistance of a banking engine, but any such help was disdained and the Dainton and Rattery inclines were tackled with the utmost resolution and success. The roar of *King Edward V* from Aller Junction onwards, and later from Totnes, was reminiscent of No 4042 *Prince Albert* pounding up the last miles to Whiteball Tunnel, with the 500-ton Torbay Limited in 1925. Thrilling as running at high maximum speed can be, and since 1946 plenty has been noted with Great Western engines, both on and off footplate, there is a 'something' about a blasting cannonade at slow speed that fairly stirs the blood; and *King Edward V* certainly stirred the blood on that run by the down Limited in 1935.

A down Wolverhampton to Kingswear express (via the North Warwick line, Cheltenham and Gloucester) passing through Exeter (St Thomas) in the 1930s headed by No 5020 Trematon Castle. *The date is probably near the beginning of the decade (5020 was new in 1932) as the tender still carries the full Great Western lettering plus coat of arms.*

The Western way to the North. No 6003 King George IV *with the down Birmingham and Birkenhead express on Rowington troughs, north of Warwick, in 1933. Obviously a 'top up' situation as the engine is still over the trough and the passengers in the front coach are feeling the 'Niagara Falls' effect.*

Railway Speed

The Great Western Railway's Record of Records.

Records crowd upon records in this remarkable year of railway history. But the Great Western Railway's latest feat really does look something like a climax which may be expected to remain unassailed for a long time to come. Indeed, under existing conditions it could not easily be beaten, except by the removal of the three adverse conditions of Monday, May 9th, viz., the permanent way slow near Starcross, the accidental check at Wellington, and the severe slacking over the Cricklade Bridge under repairs. These certainly represented an aggregate abnormal hindrance of 5 minutes. The normal hindrances, viz., the slowings through Exeter and Bath and around the Bristol avoiding line, must, I fear, be deemed virtually permanent. The present Great Western Railway speed record has its solid practical side in the fact that it was attempted and achieved for purely business reasons of wide importance. And its success meant that the mails from America and also from Australia and New Zealand, *viá* San Francisco, as well as the bullion representing the American payment to France on account of the price of the Panama Canal, all reached London from New York in the shortest transit time ever effected, viz., 5 days 21 hours 58 minutes, including all delays by land and sea. *That* is a record of which everybody concerned may reasonably be proud.

The North German Lloyd steamer *Kronprinz Wilhelm* left New York on 3 May, at 3.10 pm and reached Plymouth Sound on 9 May, at 8am. It was a perfect morning, clear and bright, and the Devonian and Cornish scenery was a veritable dream of verdant beauty. But we had little time to admire after the big steamer had dropped anchor. She had made the Atlantic crossing in 5 days 21 hours, averaging 22.6 knots, or 26 miles, an hour. Our function now was to get her very heavy mails up to Bristol and London with all possible celerity. The transfer of some 1,300 big bags was effected with admirable smartness, the bags being sorted as they were put into the tender, those for Bristol, Wales, the Midlands, and the North being kept separate, so that when we reached the Millbay Pier they could at once be loaded into the rear van which was to be dropped outside Bristol. At 9.19am our 'Ocean Mail Special' was ready, and it was duly taken to the main line at Millbay Dock Crossing whence we were to take our formal departure.

The train comprised five heavily-laden double-bogie eight-wheeled postal vans, one being still a larger sorting van; the total weight, including mails and specie, was estimated at 148 tons exclusive of engine and tender. Our engine was No. 3440, "City of Truro," one of Mr. Churchward's fine "City" class, with 6 foot 8 inch four-coupled wheels, inside cylinders 18 by 26 inches, extended wagon-top boiler, and Belpaire firebox. The driver was Clements, a very smart man, who has given me some capital runs with "Herschell" of the "Atbara" type. We made our definite start at 9.23.10am. It took us 3 minutes 7 seconds to clear North Road, 70 chains, and then we began to "go." The terrific climb from Plympton to Hemerdon, 2¼ miles out of the 3¼ being on a continuous rise at 1 in 41, was accomplished in 3 minutes 55 seconds, and Wrangaton summit was breasted in 16 minutes 41 seconds from Plymouth North Road, a climb of 14 miles 10 chains, while the later ascent for 4 miles 65 chains from Totnes to Dainton, some being at 1 in 40, occupied only 5 minutes 1 second. Then came the service slack past Newton Abbot, the easing for the Teignmouth curves, the severe slowing for the 1½ mile of single line through the five tunnels near Dawlish, a still worse slackening for permanent-way works near Starcross, and a dead slow to walking pace in Exeter station. Yet we passed Exeter in 59 minutes 2 seconds from the Millbay start, and 55 minutes 55 seconds from Plymouth North Road, the latter being a distance of 52 miles 3 chains over the hardest road in the Kingdom.

Then came the climb of 20 miles to Whiteball summit, the last 2½ miles at 1 in 115, up which our speed never fell below 62 miles an hour – followed by a "hurricane descent" of the Wellington bank, nearly spoiled, however, by a check near the station through some foolish platelayers calmly staying on the "four-foot" when the "lightning special" was close on them; and a steady persistence of high even speed along the level length which virtually extends from Taunton to Bristol. We stopped at Pylle Hill Junction on the avoiding line, having made the run of 75¼ miles from Exeter in the astonishing time of 64 minutes 17 seconds, and having covered the 128½ miles from Millbay in 123 minutes 9 seconds, while our time for the 128 miles from Plymouth North Road was 120 minutes 12 seconds. At Pylle Hill Junction we cut off the Bristol mail van and also changed engines, it being doubtful whether our coal would carry us on to London at such speed as was contemplated. So No. 3065, "Duke of Connaught," a 7 foot 8 inch single, with leading bogie, driver Underhill, came on, and we started again, after a stay of 3 minutes 43 seconds, with a load of four eight-wheelers, or about 120 tons behind the tender. What with the long slow round Bristol by the avoiding line – we took 3 minutes 39 seconds to clear Bristol East Box – and the service slow to 10 miles an hour through Bath station, we spent 39 minutes 37 seconds on the 41¼ miles to Swindon. We slackened badly through the station so as to be able to cross the Cricklade Bridge – undergoing heavy repairs – at walking pace, but then we blazed forth in full glory, experiencing no further hindrances save the slight one of picking up water near Goring, until we arrived at Paddington, after a run of 3 hours 46 minutes 48 seconds from Millbay Dock Crossing to the final stop: 3 hours 46 minutes 28 seconds to the spot inside of Paddington station where we had stopped two days previously; 3 hours 43 minutes 21 seconds – i.e., 223 minutes 21 seconds – from Plymouth North Road to Paddington. The run from Bristol, 118½ miles, was done in 99 minutes 18 seconds to the Paddington platform, 99 minutes 26 seconds to the inside of the station, 99 minutes 46 seconds to the stop. From Bath, passing dead slow, we came to London in 85 minutes 40 seconds, platform to platform. But the Swindon–London run was the climax. Notwithstanding the slack almost to a walking pace at Cricklade Bridge, which cost us more than a minute, we actually ran from Swindon platform to Paddington platform in 59 minutes 41 seconds – 19 seconds under the hour – for 77¼ miles. From Didcot into Paddington station we took 40 minutes 18 seconds, from Reading 27 minutes 17 seconds, from Slough 14 minutes 23 seconds. Also we ran from Reading to Slough, 17½ miles, in 12 minutes 54 seconds, and from Wootton Bassett to Westbourne Park, 81¾ miles, in 62 minutes 55 seconds. Such figures simply make one gasp.

The following is the condensed log of this wonderful run:—

Millbay Dock Crossing	dep.	9.23.10
Plymouth (North Road)	pass	9.26.17
Newton Abbot ...	,,	9.59.52
Exeter	,,	10.22.12
Whiteball Summit ...	,,	10.41.41
Taunton	,,	10.50.1
Bristol (Pylle Hill) ... {	arr.	11.26.29
	dep.	11.30.12
Bath	pass	11.43.50
Chippenham ...	,,	11.56.0
Swindon	,,	12.9.49
Didcot	,,	12.29.20
Reading	,,	12.42.21
Slough	,,	12.55.15
Paddington,		
platform end ...	arr.	1.9.30
in station ...	,,	1.9.38
final stop	,,	1.9.58

I may add that I travelled at the courteous invitation of the Superintendent of the Line whose assistant superintendent, Mr Aldington, took able charge throughout, and Inspector Llewellyn efficiently superintended operations on the footplate. The respective drivers, Clements and Underhill, handled their fine engines splendidly. The road was kept absolutely clear from first to last and the travelling was perfect in its smoothness and steadiness.

Charles Rous-Marten.

Probably when Charles Rous-Marten wrote the above article for *The Railway Magazine* of June 1904 the 'record of records' in his own mind was the maximum speed he had timed during the 'hurricane descent' of Wellington bank. But high speeds when railways were racing each other, as the Great Western and the London & South Western were doing for the ocean mails traffic, had been a sensitive subject since the derailment of a night tourist train at Preston in the aftermath of the Race to Aberdeen. At the request of the Great Western, Rous-Marten confined himself in this article to reporting point-to-point times. The only speed mentioned specifically is the minimum of 62mph in the final stage of the climb to Whiteball summit. In his regular 'British Locomotive Practice and Performance' article in the same issue of the magazine,

Rous-Marten commented: 'Before such figures one can only stand astounded with one's hat carefully removed in reverence and recognition of such redoubtable achievements'.

Readers of *The Railway Magazine* were clearly probing for more details, for in the July 1904 issue Rous-Marten wrote: 'It is not desirable at present to publish the actual maximum rate that was reached on this memorable occasion and readers must be content with my statement that the case was as I have said!' In a later analysis of the figures he stated: 'I find that we covered not only 32 miles, but 73 (*seventy-three*) consecutive miles at the average rate of exactly 80 miles an hour, and that for a distance of 65 miles continuously our rate was 80.4 miles an hour'.

In 1906 he seems to be on the verge of telling all when he remarks: 'So, too, on the Wellington bank of the Great Western Railway. . . . In these days rates of 80 and even 90 are not seldom met with the travelling, as in the other cases instanced, is smoother and safer than ever'.

At last, in *The Railway Magazine* of December 1907, the figure of 102.3mph appears in a table of maximum speeds recorded with locomotives of various wheel diameters, but without being attributed to a particular occasion or engine. It is simply stated that 'even at the exceptional rate of 102.3 miles an hour the 6ft 8in coupled engine had not 'shot her bolt', for her steadier progress towards the higher rates was only interrupted by a special check, up to which point the pace for each quarter mile had been successively 90, 91.8, 95.7, 97.8 and 102.3 miles an hour; we were running with perfect ease and smoothness and there was nothing to indicate that we had reached our *maximum possible* when we were checked.

Identification of the record run appeared in Rous-Marten's article in the April 1908 issue of *The Railway Magazine*. Here he compares the performance of the 7ft 8in single *Duke of Connaught* from Bristol to London with that of the 6ft 8in *City of Truro* from Exeter to Bristol. The passage is as follows:

'For, while the single-wheeler undoubtedly did then establish a world's record by running from Bristol to London, 118½ miles, start-to-stop, in 99¾min, averaging 71.4 miles an hour, the coupled engine averaged only – a big only! 70.5 from Exeter to Bristol, 75½ miles in 64¼min – the single, moreover several times touching 90 miles an hour, and once or twice 91.8, the maximum of the coupled engine was more than 10 miles an hour faster, the unprecedented rate of 102.3 miles an hour being attained over a single quarter mile and exactly 100 miles an hour for half a mile, and, if the delay on the Wellington Bank be allowed for, the coupled engine's *net* average from Exeter to Bristol was really 71.9 with a load 20 tons heavier'.

Rous-Marten's last article appeared in The Railway Magazine *of May 1908.*

In the next issue of The Railway Magazine *the 'British Locomotive Practice and Performance' feature was taken over by R. E. Charlewood. Rous-Marten had died suddenly on 20 April 1908 as a result of a heart attack following influenza.*

7

THE LIMITED AND OTHERS

By the time the Great Western celebrated its centenary in 1935 its birthplace had been by-passed by its best known trains for nearly 30 years. For thousands who travelled between Paddington and the West Country the Great Western main line was the Westbury route, and the old main line through Bristol seemed secondary. The Ocean Specials were history, and the Flying Dutchman as much a legend as that unfortunate seaman, doomed to sail the oceans non-stop. Great Western and Cornish Riviera were names that went together, and the Cornish Riviera was a Westbury line train.

None the less the Cornish Riviera (and the name survives today) has its roots in the Bristol line. A train called (unofficially) the Cornishman introduced in June 1890 improved by 10min on the Dutchman's best time to Exeter, reaching that city in 4hr 5min from Paddington after stops at Swindon and Bristol. The times to Plymouth were 5hr 35min, and to

In BR days, the down Cornish Riviera Express near Twyford on 19 April 1954 headed by No 6017 King Edward IV. *The stock seems pure Great Western though painted in the new crimson lake and cream livery of early Nationalisation years.*

Penzance 8hr 42min (the up journey was 7min shorter). On 28 July 1896 the first portion of the Cornishman inaugurated what was then the longest regular non-stop run in the world – Paddington to Exeter (193½ miles via Bristol) in 3¾hr. In passing Bristol the train avoided Temple Meads station by taking the relief line – the East Depot-Pylle Hill avoiding line – which had been opened on 10 April 1892.

In the summer of 1904 the Cornishman extended its non-stop run to Plymouth, again a world record at 245½ miles. Named trains had been proved to catch public interest, and the GW General Manager looked for a new and official name for the Cornishman. A competition launched with the co-operation of *The Railway Magazine* produced the winning entry Riviera Express, which was accepted under the more specific form Cornish Riviera Express. The train was officially named in 1905 as the Cornish Riviera Limited.

The new name heralded a new route and new timings. The Westbury line was opened as a through route in 1906 and the Riviera was diverted to it, the journey to Plymouth being reduced to 225¼ miles and the time cut from 4hr 25min to 4hr 10min. Departure from Paddington was put back from 10.10am to 10.30am at which it remained until 1972. Originally a summer service, the train now ran all the year round. It was the first GWR service on which seats could be reserved in advance, and from 1905 it had been formed of a seven-coach set of Dreadnought stock with first and third class accommodation only, the GWR having decided in that year to withdraw second class from its principal London–Penzance services.

In later years the opening of cut-off lines at Westbury and Frome avoided the service slacks through those stations and the London–Plymouth timing was reduced to 4hr 7min, but the level 4hr long associated with the train was not attained until the King class locomotives became available in 1927. The London–Plymouth non-stop run was a feature of the summer timetables but in the course of years changing traffic demands made a stop at Exeter necessary in the summer. Previously important intermediate points and branches had been served by slip coaches. When this type of service was at its height on the GWR in 1908 the Limited carried slip portions for Weymouth, detached at Westbury; for Ilfracombe, dropped at Taunton; and for Exeter, this last continuing all stations to Newton Abbot. When the Westbury station cut-off was opened the Weymouth slip had to be dropped approaching Heywood Road Junction and after stopping at the junction was brought into the station by a shunting locomotive.

By the time the train was equipped with new 60ft coaches in 1929 it had acquired through coaches for St Ives and Falmouth in a formation of some 13 vehicles which included a separate kitchen car and two dining cars. The centenary year, 1935, saw the introduction of two new sets of coaches for the service. Access was by recessed doors at the ends only, and there was one wide window per compartment – a new feature for GWR compartment stock. In the summer timetable of that year a new phase began. The 10.30am departure from Paddington, still called Cornish Riviera Limited, carried reserved seat passengers only and served Truro, Falmouth, St Ives

The Cornish Riviera
The Cornish Riviera Express is the real live fairy tale of millions of holiday makers, conveying them speedily and smoothly from the roar and bustle of the metropolis to the delightful shores of the Cornish Riviera. It has brought Plymouth within four hours and Penzance within 6hr 20min, the fastest regular booked time ever achieved between that town and the London terminus, and given a world-wide prominence to some of the finest holiday resorts in the country.
From a GWR publicity handout issued for the 25th anniversary of the train.

Penzance, the Up 'Riviera'
At the far end of the line in the 1920s no one referred to the 10am up from Penzance as 'The Limited' or even the 'Cornish Riviera Express'; to all and sundry it was the 'Riviera'. It had a very special place in the hearts of the people of West Cornwall. Artists consigned their submissions to the London exhibitions by it; the business folk of Penzance, when the holiday season was over, travelled by it for a leisurely break before the winter, and Stanhope Forbes the famous artist who painted so many scenes of Cornish life, had a picture of it in Penzance station. As holidays ended visitors were always asked, 'Are you going back by the Riviera?' There would be many trains leaving Penzance on a summer Saturday, but in those far-off days none had the local prestige of the 'Riviera'.

The Great Western TPO

The first night mail train formed exclusively of postal vehicles was inaugurated by the Great Western Railway on 4 February 1840, conveying mail for Bristol, Bath, Gloucester and Stroud. The service of 1840 did not become a true Travelling Post Office, or TPO, until it was extended to Exeter. It was then named the London & Exeter Railway Post Office and mails were sorted en route between Bristol and Exeter. Accelerated from February 1855, it connected at Bristol with a passenger train which had left Paddington at 8.10pm. The trains were combined at Bristol, and reached Exeter at 3.20am. Sorting was now carried out between Paddington and Bristol, as well as between Bristol and Exeter.

Mails were first picked up and dropped at speed on the GWR in 1859, when apparatus was in service at West Drayton, Slough, Maidenhead, Wallingford Road and Farringdon Road. On 14 May 1869 the postal train lost its Special Mail status by the addition of one first class carriage, becoming a Limited Mail – so limited, in fact, that even Directors' passes were not valid unless a special permit had been applied for.

On 26 November 1895 the Post Office announced that the Night Mail between Paddington and Penzance would be called the Great Western Travelling Post Office. On 1 May 1896 the first direct letter-sorting carriage ran through from London to Penzance. The Great Western TPO had not yet resumed its original Special Mail status, but it did so on 1 January 1902. Over the years the name and status survived, and in 1983 the Down and Up Great Western TPOs, and the Down and Up Specials between Euston and Aberdeen were the only all-postal trains still running.

From *Great Western Society Journal.*

and Penzance. There was no advertised stop before Truro, although in fact the train halted at Devonport to change engines, the King which had brought it from Paddington not being allowed on the Royal Albert Bridge. On Saturdays the first booked stop was St Erth and only passengers for St Ives and Penzance were carried, those for Falmouth and Helston travelling by a relief express leaving Paddington at 10.25am. The other traditional Limited destinations were now served by a new train leaving Paddington at 10.35am for which the Great Western revived the name Cornishman. It carried passengers for Weymouth, Plymouth (reached in one minute over the four hours), Newquay, St Erth, Helston, Penzance and other Cornish stations. In the up direction the Limited left Penzance at 10.00am and made no advertised stop after Truro. The up Cornishman started from St Erth at 10.20am, called at Gwinear Road, Truro, Par and Plymouth, and then ran non-stop to Paddington.

By 1939 the Limited consisted of eight portions except at the height of the summer. These were: the main train with the restaurant cars for Penzance; then in order behind the main portion a through coach for St Ives, detached at St Erth; one for Falmouth, detached at Truro; one for Newquay, detached at Par; one for Kingsbridge, detached at Exeter and worked forward by stopping train; the Taunton slip, consisting of through coaches for Ilfracombe and Minehead; and the two Weymouth coaches slipped at Westbury. The early war years brought a diversion via Bath and Bristol, followed by a return to the Westbury route but now conveying a Torbay portion as well. Later, the Torbay service ran as a separate train leaving Paddington at 10.40 while the Limited continued as a Penzance train, usually formed of 14 coaches as far as Plymouth to cater for service travellers. True to tradition, it continued to carry its name on the carriage headboards – one of the very few former named trains to do so.

From 1945 there was a gradual return to pre-war timings but big changes were ahead under Western Region auspices. In the late 1950s diesel-hydraulic locomotives were taking over from steam and in 1961 the Western Region timetable was completely recast. In common with other West of England expresses the Limited now found itself again with a Torbay portion and a stop at Taunton as well as Exeter. At first this required an allowance of 4¼hr from London to Plymouth but when the more powerful Western class Diesels took over from the Warships the run was made in 4hr with the two stops, and from Paddington to Taunton the average speed was 69mph. During the summer peak period the Torbay portion ran as a separate train and the Limited omitted the Taunton stop. Its load in those conditions might amount to 525 tons.

There were important accelerations of the train in 1968 and 1969, the latter bringing the time to Penzance down to 5hr 35min. At this period the Limited was double-headed by two Warship diesels, providing 4,400hp compared with 2,700hp from a single Western class diesel. Diesel-electric locomotives were already being built for the Western Region and a report published by British Railways in 1965 had found in favour of electric transmission. Soon locomotives of Classes 47 and 50 were seen on the Limited. That name remained in popular use although compulsory seat

Torquay Pullman. *One of the Great Western's very rare Pullman trains was the Torquay Pullman from Paddington which ran for barely two seasons in 1929 and 1930. Generally speaking the GWR considered that it served its passengers well enough with its own trains and dining facilities but its special 'Super Saloons' introduced in 1929 for Plymouth–London Atlantic liner trains mirrored Pullman practice internally. These wide bodied vehicles lasted into the 1960s although they were confined to former broad gauge routes and were out of gauge for the rest of the railway system. Several have been preserved. A Castle 4-6-0 heads the Torquay Pullman at Newton Abbot in 1930.*

The South Wales Pullman. *Forerunner of the Blue Pullman dmu, The South Wales Pullman between Paddington and Cardiff had mixed fortunes. Castle-hauled in 1956 it is seen here passing through Stoke Gifford Yard, now the site of Bristol Parkway station. Note the quantity of van freight as well as the train load of coal to the left of the photograph. Times were to change very quickly.*

Capitals United. *One of the Western's Britannia Pacifics No 70020 Mercury storms out of Patchway tunnel with the up Capitals United Express from Cardiff to Paddington in May 1959.*

reservation was dropped in 1977 and timetable columns simply showed Cornish Riviera. Moreover by then splitting of Torbay portions from Plymouth and Penzance trains had ceased so that Limited had just one destination. Now it made its fastest run yet to Plymouth – 3hr 40min, with the up journey in 3hr 33min. But the traditional 10.30am down departure had gone in 1972, the new time of 11.30am being the prelude to further changes later. The biggest transformation was in October 1979 when the Riviera became an HST working, whirling its passengers to Plymouth in 3hr 13min and to Penzance in 5hr 8min, and further acceleration was in the pipeline. By 1983 the time to Plymouth had come down to 3hr flat, while for Penzance the 'five hour barrier' had been broken and the Cornish Riviera reached the end of its journey in 4hr 55min from Paddington.

The Torbay resorts had a named train in the Torbay Express, which originated before the First World War and at that time included a slip portion for Ilfracombe, dropped at Taunton while the train continued non-stop to Exeter. The four-coach slip portion was unique in including a restaurant car. Great Western slip portions did not have vestibule connections with the main train and except in this instance passengers were without refreshment service during their journey. Starting originally at 11.50am, the Torbay Express departure was changed to 12 noon shortly before the First World War and this time was maintained throughout the

100mph Bristolian. *Pride of the Western Region and as usual Mondays to Thursdays Castle hauled, (on a Friday a King would often substitute because of heavier loadings) the express roars along the embankment at Westerleigh in November 1959.*

inter-war years, and again when the service was restored after the Second World War in the summer of 1946.

The Taunton slip was not resumed after the 1914–18 war. By 1938 the non-stop run to Exeter was made in 2hr 49min at an average speed of 61.6mph. In those days as much importance was attached to mile-a-minute speeds as to 100mph and upwards today. Sir James Milne, General Manager of the GWR, had written in a foreword to a special centenary issue of *The Railway Gazette*: 'we run the largest number of steam services operated at over-all speeds exceeding 60 miles an hour', but the pre-eminence was soon to be lost in the tide of accelerations on other lines that began in that very year. The Torbay Express arrived at Torquay at 3.30pm. It was a through locomotive working and so usually brought a King on to the single-track section from Goodrington Sands to Kingswear. After Torquay the train called at Paignton, Goodrington Sands (to pick up the single line staff), and Churston. Passengers for Dartmouth took the GWR ferry from Kingswear and arrived at what was to all intents and purposes a GWR station except that it never saw a train nearer than the other side of the River Dart.

After its post-war restoration in 1946 the Torbay Express continued to run as a separate train until in 1961 it was combined with a Plymouth portion and left Paddington at 12.30pm. Four years later the name was dropped except in summer when a Torbay Express ran as a separate train leaving Paddington at 10.50am, non-stop over the 142.7 miles to Taunton in 124min, arriving at Torquay at 2.22pm and Paignton at 2.30pm. On Saturdays it ran through to Kingswear. The up timing was easier. From the early 1970s the name did not appear in the timetables but in 1983 it crept back almost unnoticed. A note in the first amendment list to the May timetable gave the instruction to insert the name Torbay Express in the column of the 9.20am Paddington to Paignton and the 12.55pm Paignton to Paddington an HST service.

The history of the Torquay Pullman was much shorter, the train being put on in the summer of 1929 and withdrawn in the following year. This was an all-Pullman train of six third class and two first class cars with a time of 3hr 40min to Torquay and 3hr 50min to Paignton. Leaving Paddington at 11.00am, it ran non-stop to Newton Abbot, reached at 2.25pm. The return train left Paignton at 4.30pm and was into Paddington at 8.30pm. The approximate weight of the train without engine was 310 tons and it had a total capacity of 260 passengers. In spite of a contemporary comment that 'the seating in the third class cars and the chairs in the first class cars are of a much improved type and afford extreme comfort' the service failed to attract sufficient traffic. In the same year the GWR ran an all-Pullman Ocean Express from Plymouth to London in connection with the *Mauretania*. Pullman cars were also included in other ocean liner specials to and from Plymouth.

The South Wales service had a named train in the Tenby & Carmarthen Bay Express introduced in 1928. With a departure from Paddington at 9.55am, keeping to the 55min past the hour tradition for South Wales destinations, the train ran non-stop to Newport in 2hr 24min. Subsequent

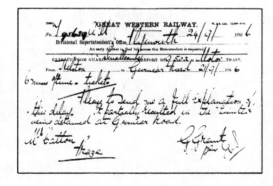

A 'please explain' memorandum from the Divisional Superintendent at Plymouth to the Stationmaster at Praze asking for details of a 6min delay to the 9.50am motor train from Helston to Gwinear Road on 21 September 1906 which in turn delayed the 'Limited'.

The Merchant Venturer. *This train was another of the named services on the Paddington to Bristol route and always Castle worked. Cumulo nimbus clouds tower in a late afternoon azure sky over the eastbound train near Thingley Junction, Chippenham in April 1954.*

stops were at Cardiff, Swansea, Carmarthen, and a string of local stations and resorts from there to Pembroke Dock. Tenby arrival was at 3.50pm, Pembroke 4.17, and Pembroke Dock at 4.23pm. The return service was at 9.20am from Pembroke Dock, following the same pattern of stops with the addition of Neath and arriving in Paddington at 4.10pm.

Bristol had to wait until 1935 for a named train of its own. The Bristolian in that year celebrated one hundred years of association between the city of Bristol and the Great Western Railway. For the first time the Paddington–Bristol time was brought below 2hr, the Bristolian taking 1¾hr in each direction, outward at 10.00am from Paddington via Bath and returning from Bristol at 4.30pm via Badminton. Both journeys averaged over 67mph, with the down trip by the slightly longer Bath route in the lead at 67.6mph. The 75.5 miles from passing Slough to passing Chippenham were allowed 61min, requiring an average speed of 74.3mph. This was exceeded on the up run with an average of all but 77mph over the 91 miles from Badminton to Southall.

After wartime withdrawal of the service the Bristolian name did not appear in the timetables until 1951. The 105min timing between Paddington and Bristol was restored in 1954, and in 1959, now with diesel haulage, the train embarked on a short-lived 100min schedule. From 1960, however, the star turn of the Bristol line was the Bristol Pullman diesel-electric set, although several minutes slower than the Bristolian at its best. The Bristolian name was omitted from the 1959 timetables but it reappeared in 1972 when one train in each direction serving the new Bristol (now Bristol Parkway) station was given a 105min timing between Paddington and Bristol. In the autumn of 1976 HSTs appeared on the London–Bristol run and the city finally lost its named train although gaining greatly in the overall service speed and frequency.

The Great Western services to Worcester and Hereford went largely unsung, and except by those who had occasion to use them regularly they are probably best remembered for the lengthy destination boards carried by the coaches detached at Worcester to serve Droitwich Spa, Kidderminster and Stourbridge Junction. The route had its moment of glory on 31 July 1939, however, when No 4086 *Builth Castle* attained 100mph down the 1 in 100 past Honeybourne with the 12.45pm from Paddington to Worcester. The run was timed by R. E. Charlewood, and in reporting it in *The Railway Magazine* of February 1940 the late Cecil J. Allen described it as embodying 'the first properly authenticated record of the attainment by a Great Western Railway express train, in normal everyday service, of a maximum speed of 100mph'. Some of the semi-fast trains on the route had sharp station-to-station timings between Oxford and Worcester. On another occasion Allen records 'a joyous sprint from Campden down to Evesham, 9.8 miles covered in the remarkable time of 9min 48sec start-to-stop, with a top speed of 90½mph at Honeybourne'. The engine was No 4004 *Morning Star* on the 10.15am from Paddington, which had been 5¾min late on starting from Oxford and regained 4½min on the schedule from there to Worcester. At that time Oxford was enjoying far brisker train services than its sister university at Cambridge. Allen considered that in view of the slack at Didcot and loads of between nine and eleven coaches the 60min schedule from Oxford to Paddington called for locomotive work which was little, if at all, inferior to that required by the 65min schedule of the Cheltenham Flyer from Swindon to Paddington.

The Cheltenham Flyer was a phenomenon. It was said that the motive for this dramatic exception to an otherwise run-of-the-mill train service between Cheltenham, Gloucester and Paddington was the desire of GWR officers visiting Swindon to be able to slip away not too long before 4pm and be in London at 5.00. On its final and best schedule the Flyer left Swindon at 3.55pm and with a 65min run over the 77.3 miles to Paddington averaged 71.3mph.

At first, from July 1923, the train simply made the fastest start-to-stop run in the British Isles with an average speed from Swindon to Paddington of 61.8mph. In July 1929 the time was cut by five minutes and with an average speed of 66.2mph the Flyer became the 'fastest train in the world'. This distinction was often misunderstood by the general public, who pointed to higher maximum speeds attained from time to time elsewhere. The staff of a railway periodical in the 1930s received frequent lunchtime telephone calls, usually with a background recognisable as public house noise, asking for arguments to be settled. The explanation that the record applied to regularly scheduled runs usually seemed to be beyond the comprehension of the disputants.

The 'fastest train' title was lost to the Canadian Pacific Railway in April 1931 but regained in July with an acceleration of the Flyer to a 69.2mph average. In September the GWR speeded the train further to an average speed of 71.3mph, the first regular schedule at over 70mph in the history of railways. The fact was proclaimed by a headboard attached to the locomotive smokebox reading 'World's Fastest Train'. A less flamboyant

Naming the Cheltenham Flyer
The Flyer was the subject of *A New Railway Book for Boys of all Ages* by W. G. Chapman in the series published by the GWR. Chapman discussed the origin of the name:

That name 'Cheltenham Flyer', by the way, seems to have been given to the train spontaneously by the press and public. 'Why not Swindon Flyer' you may ask, and why not? Although the train does a good turn of speed throughout its journey from Cheltenham to London, it is, after all, on its run from Swindon to London that it makes its world record speeding.

I think the name is explained by the fact that trains from and to London get called after their destination and starting stations respectively – thus the 2.30pm from Cheltenham (now 2.40pm) would be known as the 'Cheltenham' and when she earned her title by a special speed performance it was perhaps natural to add 'Flyer' to the name. Anyway, 'Cheltenham Flyer' she is and probably will remain.

Cheltenham Flyer headboard was used later but the title never appeared in the GWR timetables. By 1939 the train had been surpassed by streamliners elsewhere and it was lost in the first wartime timetables, never to return.

The train service from Paddington to Birmingham and the North via Bicester was best known for the two-hour schedules of the principal trains between Paddington and Birmingham (Snow Hill) and the standardised departure times from London at ten minutes past the hour. This was very much a businessman's service and was advertised at one time by a poster showing a typical executive of the day congratulating the driver on arrival with the words 'A splendid run; thank you!' The Great Western examined a 1¾hr Paddington–Birmingham schedule but took no action, and maintained the level at 2hr after the LMS had reduced the best Euston–New Street time to 1hr 55min.

From Shrewsbury on the Birkenhead line there was a connection via a GW&LNW joint line with Buttington on the Cambrian Railways, and from there a route to the resorts on Cardigan Bay. In July 1921 a through restaurant car train from Paddington to Aberystwyth, Barmouth and Pwllheli was introduced by this route and was the forerunner of the Cambrian Coast Express. Its departure from Paddington was changed from 9.50am to 10.15 in 1922, and a year later to 10.20, but in 1924 it became 10.10am in line with the other two-hour trains on the Birmingham via Bicester service. The name Cambrian Coast Express was given in 1927. This had always been a summer service, but by 1927 the train ran on Fridays and Saturdays only. In 1928 the departure was put back to 10.20 but it was still a 2hr train to Birmingham Snow Hill. Engines were changed at Wolverhampton, the usual Castle giving place to classes with lighter axleloads for the journey over the Cambrian – often one or a pair of Duke class 4-4-0s or in later years a Manor 4-6-0. Avoiding Shrewsbury station by the Abbey Foregate curve, the train called at Moat Lane and Machynlleth to Dovey Junction, where the Barmouth coaches were detached. The Aberystwyth portion continued to Borth and Aberystwyth, arriving at 3.55pm, while the Barmouth coaches reached their destination at 4.20pm after calling at Aberdovey and Towyn. The return train, leaving Aberystwyth at 10.00am and Barmouth at 9.20, was allowed six hours from Aberystwyth to Paddington but again made a two-hour run in from Birmingham.

An unnamed through service to Aberystwyth was resumed after the Second World War but in 1951 it became the Cambrian Coast Express again. At this time it again left Paddington at 10.10am but the schedule was altered to serve Shrewsbury, where the train reversed. After the Blue Pullmans appeared on the Birmingham line the through Aberystwyth service took up the 11.10am departure from Paddington, still as a named train. Name and train both succumbed in the changes in the Paddington–Birmingham service on the electrification of the Euston–Birmingham New Street route.

Stratford-on-Avon was awkwardly placed for services for London and was usually reached by through slip coach or by changing at Leamington.

The Great Western Railway was very much alive to its tourist possibilities however, particularly for visitors from the United States. Booklet No 3 in the company's *Handy Aids* series was entitled *Shakespeare-Land*.

In 1928 Stratford-on-Avon was given its own named train, the Shakespeare Express. The down train left Paddington at 9.25am, called at High Wycombe, Leamington and Warwick, and arrived at Stratford at 11.33. A carriage was slipped at Banbury at 10.41. Visitors could enjoy the best part of a day at the 'shrine' and return by the up Shakespeare Express at 5.30pm. The same stops were made, except High Wycombe, and arrival was at 7.35pm. A conducted road tour was run in conjunction with these trains. Passengers alighting at Leamington on the outward trip were taken by coach to Guy's Cliff, Kenilworth and Warwick, with a visit to the castle and time for lunch. The tour continued to Stratford-on-Avon, looped through Shottery for Anne Hathaway's cottage, and returned the passengers to Leamington to join the up Shakespeare Express.

Although off the main London line, Stratford-on-Avon was on the GWR's new and shortened route from the Midlands to the West via Honeybourne, Cheltenham, and Gloucester which was opened throughout in 1906. Various cross-country services used the line, among them a through service between Wolverhampton and Penzance which outlived the rest and was still operating in 1939. In those days it was unnamed, and so remained until Western Region days when in 1952 the time-honoured title of Cornishman was revived for it. In later years, as passenger traffic was gradually withdrawn from the Honeybourne–Cheltenham line, it was decided to re-route the train over the former Midland line between Birmingham and Cheltenham, and to extend it from Birmingham to Derby and Sheffield, omitting Wolverhampton. Finally the service was extended northwards again to Leeds and Bradford. More changes of route occurred before the Cornishman name was discarded in 1975.

The words North to West Express and vice versa often appeared in the columns of the Great Western timetables. At Shrewsbury these trains might combine portions coming from Manchester or Liverpool via Crewe

The Cathedrals Express. *This picturesquely named train was another Western Region innovation. It ran from Paddington to Worcester and Hereford and was the last express to be regularly hauled by Castles, with engines stationed at Old Oak Common and Worcester. The locomotives under shedmaster Harry Cureton were always spotlessly clean as is No 5037* Monmouth Castle *approaching No 10 platform at Paddington on a frosty morning in January 1959.*

THE TIMES ON THIS PAGE APPLY SATURDAYS ONLY.

For Service MONDAYS to FRIDAYS see pages 94 to 96A.

	a.m.	a.m.	a.m.	a.m.	a.m.	a.m.	a.m.	a.m.	a.m.	a.m.	a.m.	p.m.	p.m.	a.m.	a.m.	a.m.	a.m.		a.m.
... (Natl. Bus) dep.																			7 45 / 49
... dep.																			7 40
... dep.																			7 57
The Lizard (W. Natl. Bus) dep.																			8 1
Helston ... dep.																			6 30
...ear Road ... dep.																			8 10
...borne ... "																			8 16
...n Brea ... "																			8 24
...druth ... "																			8 28
...orrier ... "																			8 33
Chacewater ... arr.																			8 43
Truro ...								6 50											8 15
FALMOUTH ... dep.								7 30											8 47
Truro ... dep.								7 44											
Probus and Ladock Platform ... "								7 57											9 12
Grampound Road ... "																			8 0
St. Austell ... "								8 6								8 25			9 20
Newquay ... dep.								8 0											
Par ... dep.								8 17								8 34			
Fowey (M) ... dep.																			
Lostwithiel ... dep.								8 0											9 20
Padstow (Southern Rly.) dep.								8 25							8 42				9 34
Wadebridge ... "								8 30							9 0				
Bodmin ... "								8 15											
Bodmin Road ... "								8 45							9 12				9 53
Doublebois ... "															9 20				
Looe ... dep.										9 0			9 30		9 30				
Liskeard ... dep.										9 4	9 30				9 40	9 55			
Menheniot ... "										9 7	9 34					9 58			
St. Germans ... "										9 9	9 37				9 46	10 2			
Saltash (for Callington) ... "					8 35					9 11	9 39					10 4			
St. Budeaux Platform ... "					8 40						9 41								
Keyham ... "					8 44					9 13	9 43								
Ford Halt ... "					8 47										9 52	10 9			
Dockyard Halt ... "																10 13	10 25		
Devonport ...					8 50			9 18		9 25	9 43								
PLYMOUTH { North Rd. arr. / Millbay }			8 45		8 55			STOP	9 20	STOP	STOP		9 55		9 55	10 0			
{ Millbay dep. / North Rd. " }			8 52		9 0				9 23		10 0					STOP	10 35		
Plympton ...									9 33										
Cornwood ...									9 45										
Ivybridge ...									9 36										
Bittaford Platform ...									9 55										
Wrangaton ...									9 59										
Salcombe (W. Natl. Bus) dep.									8 30										9T25
Kingsbridge ...			7T55						9 20										9T50
Brent ... dep.									10 7										
Totnes ... "			9 26						10 19										11 10
Newton Abbot ... arr.			9 40	9 35					10 34			10 48		10 48		a.m. 11 24			11 4
Dartmouth ... dep.					8 50		8 50								10 5				10 5
Kingswear ... "					9 5		9 5					9 40		9 40	10 20				10 20
Brixham (M) ... "					9 20		9 0					9 55		9 55	10 20				10 20
Paignton ... "					9 26		9 40					9 52		9 52	10 30				11 10
Torquay ... "				9 32	9 40		9 50					10 20		10 48	11 0				11 20
Torre ... "					9 45				10 8			10 30		10 40	11 5				
Moretonhampstead (M) dep.			8 40					9 50	10 12 a.m.										
Bovey ... "			8 54					10 9	10 9								10 37		10 55
Newton Abbot ... dep.			9 46	9 55	10 0		10 10	10 28	10 40		10 55				11 18	11 30		
Teignmouth ... "			9 55	10 5	10 15		10 10	10 40	10 50		11 6		11 15			11 40		
Dawlish ... "			10 4	10 15	10 25		10 35	10 47	10 57		11 15		11 24		11 35	11 49		
Dawlish Warren ... "										Via Christow.								
Starcross (for Exmouth) ... "										10 40								
Exminster ... "										11 1								
EXETER { St. Thomas arr. / St. David's dep. }			10 21 / 10 25	1032 / 1037	1041 / 1047		10 55	11 10	11 25	11 35	11 36 / 11 38		11 43 / 11 50		11 55 / 12 0	12 6 / 12 12			12 15 / 12 20
Stoke Canon ... "								11 1		11 41								
Silverton ... "								11 8										
Hele and Bradninch ... "								11 12										
Cullompton ... "								11 20										
Tiverton (M) ... dep.											a.m. 11 10							
Tiverton Junction ... dep.							11 26				11 27							
Sampford Peverell ... "											11 32							
Burlescombe ... "											11 38							
Wellington ... "											11 47							
Norton Fitzwarren ... "											11 56							
TAUNTON ... arr.			11 4	1116	1123		11 46	11 50		12 2	12 10	12 4	12 10	12 36				2 22
Taunton ...			11 7				11 50	12 0			12 10		12 20	12 35	12 45			2 37
BRISTOL (T'ple M'ds) arr.			12 13					1 3			1 30		1 50	2 0				3 21
Bristol (Temple Meads) dep.			12b20												2 10			3 41
Newport ... arr.			1 35												2 16			5c20
Cardiff (General) ... "			1 54												3 1			9M1
Swansea (High Street) ... "			3Y20												3 26			
Fishguard Harbour ... "			6 38															
Bristol (Temple Meads) dep.															2 15			
Birmingham (Snow Hill) arr.												2 0	2 10		4 25	4 32		
Wolverhampton (L. L'vl) "												5 50	6 12		6 6	6 2		
Bristol (Temple Meads) dep.			12 20															
Crewe ... arr.			4 10									6 12						
Chester ... "			4 55								5 35	6 41						
Birkenhead (Woodside) ... "			5 33								6 16	7 20						
Liverpool (Lime Street) "			5 21									7 9						
{ Landing Stage "			5 47								6 27	7 37						
...chester (London Rd.) "			5 30								5 40		7 6					
...(Temple Meads) dep.			12 28				1 10				1 45				2 45		
... arr.			12 53				1 35				2 1				3 10		
... "											5a25						
... "											3 25						
...addington) arr.							1 55				4 5						

Column headings (vertical):
- Through Carriages Plymouth to Birkenhead, Liverpool (Lime St.) and Manchester; also (on Sept. 16th and 23rd) Plymouth to Glasgow and Paignton to Manchester. Restaurant Car Weston-super-Mare to Shrewsbury.
- Torquay to Leeds and Bradford Express. Restaurant Car Train.
- Kingswear, Paignton and Torquay to Leeds and Bradford Express. Restaurant Car Train.
- Through Train Saltash and Plymouth to Torquay and Paignton.
- Runs on August 12th, 19th and 26th only.
- Paignton and Torquay to London Express.
- Paignton, Torquay and Exeter to Bristol Express.
- M
- Plymouth and Kingswear to Manchester Express. Restaurant Car Train.
- Through Train from Minehead (depart 11.0 a.m.)
- Through Train Ilfracombe (depart 9.50 a.m.) to Manchester. Restaurant Car from Barnstaple.
- Plymouth and Paignton to Liverpool (Lime Street) Express. Restaurant Car Train.
- Kingswear and Torquay to Birmingham (G.W.) Express. Restaurant Car Train.
- Penzance and Plymouth to Birmingham (G.W.) and Wolverhampton Express.
- Paignton and Torquay to South Wales Express.
- Through Train Saltash and Plymouth to Torquay and Paignton.
- Runs July 29th to August 26th (inclusive) only.

Notes:
- Will not run after Sept. 16th.
- Arrive Torre 10.12, Torquay 10.15 a.m.
- Arrive Torre 10.12, Torquay 10.23 a.m. and Paignton 10.23 a.m.
- For continuation see 11.27 a.m. from Tiverton Junction.
- Will not run after September 9th.
- Arrive Torre 11.54 a.m., Torquay 11.59 a.m. and Paignton 12.5 p.m.

...ember 2nd, arr. Swansea 3.59 p.m.
h (inclusive) arr. 4.25 p.m. via Reading. Road.
...23rd arr. 6.10 p.m.

d—Will not run after September 2nd.
q—Will not run after September 9th. ...hampton arr. 2.22 p.m.

Commencing Jul...

with coaches from Birkenhead. They continued over the GW&LNW joint line to Hereford, and thence over the GWR again to Abergavenny, Pontypool Road and the junctions with the South Wales main line at Maindy (Newport). Trains for the West of England continued through the Severn Tunnel and then to Bristol via Stapleton Road. An overnight service by this route with coaches from both Manchester and Liverpool divided at Pontypool Road, one portion continuing to Plymouth and another to Fishguard.

Some sonorous descriptions can be read in the timetable pages: Breakfast, Luncheon and Tea Car, Liverpool to Plymouth; Luncheon, Tea and Dining Car, Liverpool to Newton Abbot; Luncheon and Tea Car, Manchester to Plymouth; and so on. The modern timetable with its pictograms representing different forms of catering reduces eating in trains to a convenience rather than a ceremony.

In these trains the present writer had his first experience of long-distance rail travel on the way from Wrexham to visit grandparents living near Wellington (Somerset). At that time no train journey could be too long, and the growing impatience of parents as the day wore on was noted with surprise. Pontypool Road is always associated with adult spirits reaching their lowest ebb, but with deplorable chauvinism they seemed to revive when the train was burrowing under the River Severn and well and truly into England. It has since been learned that this cross-country service was not remarkable for speed, but its trains are still remembered with reverence by at least one traveller. The route through Shrewsbury and Hereford today carries a service between Crewe and Cardiff, the trains between the West of England and the North having been switched to the old Midland main line from Bristol to Birmingham.

Another cross-country route in which the Great Western played a part has disappeared from the map. This was by the connection from Banbury to the one-time Great Central main line at Woodford & Hinton (later Woodford Halse). Trains and through coaches by this route ran between the Midlands and North, South Wales, and the South and West of England. In the closing paragraphs of *The 10.30 Limited* W. G. Chapman draws his young companion's attention as they arrive at Penzance to the longest journey via the Banbury–Woodford & Hinton link in these words:

Just one word more. You may be surprised to see coaches labelled 'Penzance to Aberdeen'. The Great Western Railway bids fair to break another record with a non-change run of 800 miles between these points. How fine it is to think that we can practically travel in one train from Land's End to John o' Groats and vice versa! What an interesting journey to be sure! Leaving Aberdeen at, say 9.45 on a Friday morning, it is possible to travel to the extreme limit of the Great Western Railway, spend the Saturday and Sunday in the delightful Cornish Riviera, leave again on Monday morning and be back in time for business on the Tuesday morning, having covered 1,600 miles by train and spent two clear days in Cornwall.

Refreshment Rooms at Stations

At Stations where the Refreshment Rooms are held by tenants. The Station Masters to see that:—

The rooms are properly conducted, and to bring under notice any complaints made respecting them.

A printed copy of the authorised tariff of charges is suspended in a conspicuous position in each of the public rooms and is the only tariff exhibited.

Each room is kept neat and clean.

Supply of Luncheon and Tea Baskets and Cups of Tea to Passengers in the Trains

1. **Breakfast, Luncheon and Tea Baskets.**—Baskets containing Breakfast, Hot or Cold Luncheons or Dinner or Tea are obtainable at the Refreshment Rooms.

The charges for Breakfast, Luncheon and Tea Baskets are as shown below:—

	s.	d.
Breakfast Baskets.—Eggs and Bacon (or Cold Ham), Bread, Butter, Preserves, Tea, Coffee or Cocoa	3	6
Luncheon or Dinner Baskets.—Meat (Hot or Cold), (Roast or Pressed Beef, &c.), Bread, Butter, Cheese, Salad, &c.	3	0
Cold Chicken and Ham, Bread, Butter, Cheese, Salad, &c.	3	6
Chop or Steak, Bread, Butter, Cheese, &c.	3	6
Tea Baskets.—Pot of Tea, &c., Bread and Butter, Cake or Bun and Fruit. Per person	1	3

From the *Great Western Railway Appendix to the Service Time Tables.*

8
TRIALS ON OTHER LINES

GWR Locomotives Blazing the Trail

Locomotive interchange trials before the nationalisation of railways in Great Britain were generally thought to have originated from one party having uncertainty about its own equipment, and wishing to try someone else's. In 1910 it was imagined that the interchange of 4-6-0 locomotives between the London & North Western Railway and the Great Western was a continuation of the series of trials largely instigated by C. J. Bowen Cooke, Chief Mechanical Engineer of the LNWR in 1909, whereas the actual circumstances were far otherwise. On the GWR G. J. Churchward had been criticised, across the Board table, for the high cost of his express passenger 4-6-0s, in relation to those of the LNWR, and it was he who suggested the interchange to demonstrate the almost overwhelming superiority of his own design. In working between Euston and Crewe No 4005 *Polar Star* demonstrated this by quiet, easy running and low coal consumption rather than any very spectacular performance. Such records of his work as have been preserved indicate a lack of enterprise by its driver, and a disinclination to make up time lost by signal and other incidental delays. But the superiority of the GWR design was amply shown on its own line, where the lighter and less powerful LNW 4-6-0, handicapped also by the low water capacity of its tender, and the less lavish provision of water troughs, was no match for the duties required of it.

In the interchange trials of 1925, between new GWR Castle class 4-6-0s and the very much larger Pacific engines of the LNER, the competitors were more evenly matched so far as nominal tractive power was concerned. This trial was sometimes thought to have originated from the placing of examples of both designs on adjacent stands at the British Empire Exhibition at Wembley in 1924 with the Castle prominently advertising its higher tractive power. The interchange, at the end of April in 1925 was seen as a challenge from the LNER to prove that superiority. Actually this was far from the case, and one gathered afterwards that the locomotive department of the LNER entered into the trials with some reluctance. Although using coal of a nature somewhat different from that for which it was designed No 4079 *Pendennis Castle* did consistently good, and often really brilliant work with heavy trains between Kings Cross and Doncaster, creating an impression by the clean slip-free starts on the difficult, steeply graded ascent through the tunnels out of the London terminus. But it must also be conceded that the LNER Pacific No 4474 did some remarkably good work in hauling the maximum load of the down Cornish Riviera Express, punctually through the week of trials, not only in effecting an on-time arrival at each end, but in keeping accurate sectional point-to-point timings. Coal consumption was heavier than that of the Great Western Castle, but it is only fair to point out that the Pacific design was not fully developed, so far as valve gear and boiler pressure were concerned, at the time of the interchange trials. Nevertheless Gresley of the LNER clearly had the results in mind when he developed the original Class A1 design into the superior A3 class a year or so later.

In 1926 the LMS was in difficulties for motive power. All the principal English constituents of the group, LNWR, Midland, and Lancashire & Yorkshire, had different ideas on how the situation should be met, but there was no strong coordinating hand at the head of the engineering department, and a proposal to build a compound Pacific on French principles was vetoed. A suggestion from Sir Felix Pole that they might try a Castle was welcomed at Euston, and at the end of October engine No 5000 *Launceston Castle* went to Camden, on loan. There was no question of competitive running, but by way of recompense, the Midland shed at Kentish Town lent one of its three-cylinder compound 4-4-0s to the GWR for a short period. The Castle did some good work between Euston and Crewe, having no difficulty in maintaining current schedules with loads much greater than those taken unassisted by ex-LNWR locomotives at that time. The mastery was not so complete when the scene of the trials was extended to the Carlisle road, in bad winter weather. In a gale-force crosswind and heavy rain the dry sanding gear standard on the GWR did not prove very effective, and the engine fell a prey to slipping on some of the exposed and heavily graded sections of the North West. Apart from this the engine did well, and economically too, and gave the LMS locomotive department the basic proportions it needed for a new express passenger design, that eventually took shape as the Royal Scot class. Although so different in appearance and design features – three cylinders instead of four – and with the Southern Railway Lord Nelson class drawings alongside when the North British Locomotive draughtsmen were preparing the drawings of the Royal Scot, it is amusing to recall that when in the production stage these engines were referred to in official LMS correspondence as Improved Castles!

The 1948 exchanges
The top management of the Great Western Railway somewhat naturally took a poor view of railway nationalisation, and the attitude to it was epitomised by the refusal of the General Manager, Sir James Milne, to become the first Chairman of the new Railway Executive. In mechanical

Great Western on the Great Central. Resplendent in the last phase of the company's livery, number on the buffer beam and the style G crest W on the sides of its Hawksworth straight sided tender, No 6990 Witherslack Hall shows the flag during the 1948 locomotive exchanges. The train is the 8.25am from Manchester to Marylebone photographed on the Metropolitan & Great Central Joint line near Northwood.

GWR 2-8-0 on the NBR

After the first world war the North British Railway sought to satisfy its long-felt need for a powerful mineral engine. In Cowlairs drawing office there was a general arrangement drawing No 2662 dated 16 May 1908 showing Reid's design for a large 0-8-0 tender engine but Cowlairs showed no inclination to put the design into production. Instead, Maj Stemp, traffic superintendent, in 1920 looked round to see what other companies had to offer in the way of eight-coupled engines, and he was particularly attracted by the performance of the GWR 'E Group' 2-8-0s on the heavy gradients in the West of England. The NB's most powerful goods engine had to be double-headed when its load reached 28 wagons. From charts supplied by his GWR opposite number, Mr Nicholls, Stemp saw that the GWR 2-8-0 regularly took 28 loaded wagons over the 9 miles 22 chains between Lostwithiel and Doublebois, where the ruling gradient was 1 in 58, in 29 minutes. The same class hauled Welsh coal trains of 38 wagons over 1 in 90 gradients with regularity and apparent ease. Stemp was convinced that this was the engine for the NB and sought one for trial.

The company opened negotiations with the GWR on 14 December 1920. At first it seemed that there would be difficulty in obtaining a route between the engine's home territory and the Border because of loading gauge problems, but the difficulty was quickly overcome and on 19 December Charles Aldington, general manager of the GWR, informed Calder that he had given instructions for 2-8-0 No 2846 to be prepared for the journey to Scotland.

The test was fixed for 12 January, the location being the 6 miles 53 chains between Bridge of Earn and Glenfarg where an NE 0-8-0 had been tested in 1916. The GWR engine was handed over to the NB at Berwick on 10 January and at

engineering matters one can understand that a man of Hawksworth's stature, successor to the great office created by Churchward, and continued by Collett, and in its inclusion of all outdoor activities, locomotive manning and running, carrying considerably greater overall responsibilities than his fellow CMEs on the other British railways of the grouping era, did not look kindly towards intrusion from outside, and he took little interest in the locomotive interchange trials proposed immediately after nationalisation. It is important to bear in mind the management attitude in order to appreciate the rather colourless performance put up by some of the Great Western participants in the event, in such striking contrast to what had happened in 1925.

The programme of tests and the numerous conditions applying thereto were drawn up by the Locomotive Testing Committee of the new Railway Executive, under the chairmanship of the newly appointed Executive Officer (Design) E. S. Cox, a former LMS man; in the anxiety to achieve scrupulous fairness in operation for all the competing engines some of the conditions laid down savoured more of an academic approach, rather than a realistic examination of the practical job of running trains on the chosen routes. For example, insistence was placed upon use of a uniform grade of coal, regardless of route, instead of making each of the competing engines use the grade normally supplied. The fact that Great Western locomotives were required to use Yorkshire 'hards', instead of their accustomed soft Welsh coals was claimed to have intimidated their performance, but there were other factors that had a far more serious effect. From the outset, the fact that Great Western competitors were precluded by civil engineering conditions regarding clearances from working over *any* of the former LMS or Southern lines severely limited their participation in the trials anyway.

The manning of the locomotives was another important factor; no one was permitted to ride on the footplate other than the road pilotman, when the visiting crew accompanying the engine was working over a strange route, and a technical observer who would be one of the dynamometer car staff. It was a very different situation from the ordinary run of testing, when there would be a locomotive inspector at the driver's elbow to guide and advise. The drivers were very much on their own, and in many cases the actual working was far more a reflection of the driver's personality than the true capacity of the locomotive. Working the King class engines which represented the Western Region in the trials between Paddington and Plymouth, and between Kings Cross and Leeds the Old Oak driver chosen for both of these was a 'safe' man, rather than a fire-eater, and he gave an entirely adequate, but unspectacular display, showing a comfortable mastery of the use of a coal that was strange to him, and his fireman. The same driver, Russell by name, worked the Hall class 4-6-0 on the runs over the former Great Central line, between Marylebone and Manchester.

The mixed traffic group of locomotives was set a severe assignment in working the Penzance–Wolverhampton express in each direction between Bristol and Plymouth, and here an unexpected difficulty over the manning arose. It was intended that the duty should be worked as a double-home turn from Bristol, which was what the visiting enginemen from the other regions actually did; but the Bristol top link drivers had no lodging turns, and none of the regular men were prepared to work the train. It would, in any case have involved them in learning the road between Newton Abbot and Plymouth. As a result there was a call for a volunteer crew, and the only response came from a man of relatively short experience, and he too had to learn much of the route. The result, as might be imagined, was a totally unrepresentative performance from the Hall class engine involved. Allowing for signal and permanent way checks all the competing engines on the routes where the Great Western engines were involved kept their scheduled running times, and the basic coal consumption figures in pounds of coal per drawbar horsepower hour were as follows:

King class trials	Paddington & Plymouth	Kings Cross & Leeds
GWR King 4-6-0	3.74	3.39
LNER A4 4-6-2	3.19	2.92
LMS Duchess 4-6-2	3.24	3.04
LMS Converted Scot 4-6-0	3.64	3.26
SR Merchant Navy 4-6-2	3.61	3.73

Hall class trials	Marylebone & Manchester	Bristol & Plymouth
GWR Hall 4-6-0	3.84	4.11
LNER B1 4-6-0	3.32	3.96
LMS 5 4-6-0	3.29	3.39
SR West Country 4-6-2	3.90	4.28

When these results were published Great Western enthusiasts were surprised and disturbed to see that the King made the poorest showing of all on its own road, with a driver and fireman who, one would have thought, would have had an advantage over the visiting crews, who would have had to learn its many peculiarities. Could the use of hard Yorkshire coal make all that difference? When nearly new engine No 6005 had been put through a series of dynamometer car tests, and with Welsh coal returned a coal consumption of 3 lb per drawbar horsepower hour. The critics of Swindon practice regarded the King as an outdated design, and showing signs of its increasing age; but no such strictures could be applied to the Hall, which was one of the latest Hawksworth variety, with modified superheater.

In response to representations from Swindon the Railway Executive, later in 1948, agreed to a re-run of the trials on Western Region tracks with King and Hall class engines using Welsh coal. The former, working the same trains as in the main series of interchange trials, but in wintry weather, returned a coal consumption of 3.33 lb per dbhp hour, but allowing for the higher calorific value of the Welsh coal the equivalent value, related to the hard coal used earlier was 3.50 lb – not a great deal of difference. With the Hall class engine however the manning arrangements

6.15 that evening was lodged in Haymarket shed.

Conditions could not have been worse when the special train conveying NB and GW officers and observers from other companies reached Bridge of Earn. The test stretch was blanketed in snow and a near blizzard was blowing. The NB entrant was first at the post. With 23 loaded 16-tonners and two goods brake vans (437ton 8cwt exclusive of the brake vans) the 0-6-0 set off but stuck only a short distance up the bank. The train had to be hauled back to Bridge of Earn. The NB engine retired from the contest; it was quite unequal to the task allotted to it.

In the second test No 2846 in the charge of the GW crew and with a load of 29 wagons and two brake vans (552ton 4cwt exclusive of the vans) started away easily and, without faltering, reached Glenfarg in its scheduled time of 25min.

For the third test five wagons were added to the load bringing it up to 643ton 9cwt. Again the GW engine got away easily but about two miles from the start it encountered hard packed snow on the rails. It began to slip badly and was forced to a stand from which it failed to recover.

From *The North British Railway*, by John Thomas

V2 on test. Swindon Works was responsible for test trials of Sir Nigel Gresley's LNER V2 class 2-6-2 locomotive No 60845 during the winter of 1950. The engine had 21 coaches behind the tender including the GWR dynamometer car. There appears to be no trouble with this load on the 1 in 100 grade passing Hullavington as both recorder O. S. Nock and Swindon test engineer Sam Ell are looking out of the window.

of the earlier series of trials were not applied, and the engine was worked on a double-home basis by a first class crew from the Laira top-link, and the difference was astonishing. Instead of 4.11 lb per dbhp hour, this crew used no more than 3.22 lb, and even after this figure had been adjusted to take account of the difference in calorific value of the Welsh and Yorkshire coal the improvement was no less than 17.7 per cent, with an equivalent consumption of 3.38 lb.

The supplementary trials carried out in November and December 1948 had a further interest in that the first of the King class engines to be fitted by Hawksworth with a four-row high-degree superheater was also included, and gave excellent results. The actual coal consumption per drawbar horsepower hour was only 3.10 lb, which related to its Yorkshire equivalent was 3.25 lb.

The 1948 main trials also included 28XX class 2-8-0s, working on a Grade 2 hard South Midlands coal; but in slow, heavy mineral train operation the differences in the coal consumptions of the competing engines was not significantly more than might be recorded on different days with the same locomotive. Although the 28XX 2-8-0 had shown no disadvantage compared with its rivals, a re-run was also arranged in November 1948, between Acton Yard and Severn Tunnel Junction, and showed so substantial an improvement as to put the engine well ahead of the others, even taking account of the difference in calorific value of the coals used.

Freight Locomotive Trials

Engine Class	Coal lb per dbhp hour (Blidworth)
GWR 28XX class 2-8-0	3.54 (2.86 ★ with Welsh)
LNER Thompson O1 2-8-0	3.37
LMS Stanier 8F 2-8-0	3.81
WD (Riddles) 2-8-0	4.02
WD (Riddles) 2-10-0	3.59

★Actual 2.64 lb, Blidworth equivalent 2.86

The 1948 trials on the Great Northern route from Kings Cross to Leeds were run using No 6018 King Henry VI, the engine destined to be the last King to run in BR service. True to Great Western tradition and although in British Railways ownership the King appeared in its company livery complete with white spare headlamps on the running plate. The photograph shows a test train climbing from Beeston to Ardsley.

9

SUMMER SATURDAYS

The story was familiar: 'We raced down to just outside Taunton, and then crawled from signal to signal all the way to Newton Abbot and arrived two hours late.' Summer Saturdays in the West were enormous business, and at peak times it was just not possible to carry the crowds without delays. Yet Paddington was substantially remodelled with lengthened platforms, extra rolling stock built and maintained, and intermediate signalboxes and other facilities opened solely to cope with the extra business offering itself on at most a dozen Saturdays a year. What days they were!

Nowhere else in Britain, perhaps the world, was the traffic pattern so enormously different, either between seasons or on a single day of the week. It was yet another of those Great Western peculiarities. On Mondays to Fridays, even in summer, there was not even an average of a departure an hour from Paddington to the South West. On Saturdays up to eight trains an hour ran, all of them with restaurant cars, all of them travelling at least 200 miles.

Bristol Temple Meads with an engine change in progress. The King which has worked the 7.30am Paddington to Kingswear express thus far comes off with two coaches while No 7011 Banbury Castle waits to back on and take the train on to Kingswear. A Hall class 4-6-0 stands at platform 6 with the 6.55am Wolverhampton to Paignton.

Many stations in Devon and Cornwall despatched 90 per cent of their long-distance passengers, not only in a single day of the week, but within a few hours. But except for the war years and their immediate aftermath, it was rare for anyone to have to stand. In the 1930s in particular, it was assumed that the traffic was of prime importance and that passengers should be offered the best. Many restaurant cars were kept available solely for it, though they might also earn some keep on race and other specials. These resorts were of course highly dependent on the railway. No major holiday town ever developed without trains, and those served by the GWR remain more prosperous to this day than all but Exmouth on the LSWR.

An air of expectation hung over the system from early afternoon on Fridays as empty trains were marshalled and many services were strengthened. A whole train of restaurant cars victualled and staffed but without passengers made its way from Paddington to Newton Abbot, where the staff spent the night in the hostel over the booking office; some went on to Truro. They worked a dozen different services back to London on Saturday. Some trains ran with their normal destination boards reversed: the Bristolian set, for instance, for many years was used to make a Paddington–Paignton trip on Saturdays, showing blank boards. Other

112

Badminton 1958. The Pembroke
Coast Express *headed by Castle
class 4-6-0 No 5078* Beaufort
originally Lamphey Castle *but
renamed in January 1941 after an
RAF aircraft. Note the chocolate
and cream coaches re-introduced by
the W R for named trains in the late
1950s.*

Bristol Bath Road Shed 1961. A scene looking from the down platforms at Temple Meads Station showing King class 4-6-0 No 6002 King William IV and Castle class 4-6-0 No 5008 Raglan Castle waiting to take two up trains forward to London and Wolverhampton. The headboard on the Castle indicates that its train will be the up Cornishman. No 5008 had a short life with a double chimney; it was fitted in 1961 but the engine was withdrawn a year later.

Swindon Shed 1953. The last Castle to be built, No 7037, was aptly named after the works and town and carried the Swindon coat of arms on the splasher below the nameplate.

The classic view of Great Western holiday expresses – the sea wall between Dawlish and Teignmouth along the beautiful stretch of line running along the South Devon shore between the Exe and Teign estuaries. In BR days Castle class 4-6-0 No 7000 heads the down Torbay Express.

Dovey Junction in about 1958. The lonely station surrounded by marshes and distant mountains was an island platform complete with small refreshment room. It was the interchange point for the former Cambrian main line trains to Aberystwyth with the coast line to Portmadoc and Pwllheli.

Ashburton 1968. Although this is a
typical GWR branch line scene the
photograph was taken in the early
days of the privately-owned Dart
Valley Railway. Ashburton was
the terminus of the line from Totnes
but the section from Buckfastleigh to
the terminus was severed by the A38
road improvements. Ashburton
station is no longer a station but the
photograph shows the situation
virtually unaltered from GWR days
with 0-4-2 auto-fitted tank No 1420
standing just outside the Brunel
overall wooden roof so common on
country branches in South Devon.
This part survives in its new use as a
garage.

trains carried destination boards never used except on summer Saturdays: Paddington–Kingsbridge, Paddington–Perranporth, Wolverhampton–Minehead.

Many overnight trains from Paddington, the North and Midlands reached the resorts before breakfast, when platforms were covered with mounds of Passengers Luggage in Advance awaiting collection personally, or delivery to boarding houses and hotels. The passengers were in no hurry to collect their belongings since they would not be allowed into their accommodation until at least noon. Sometimes they hung around the station, perhaps holding an impromptu singsong, waiting to be served breakfast at the refreshment room; or they might take an early dip before going to a café for bacon and egg. Many cafés served as many eggs before nine on Saturday mornings as during the rest of the week. On the up platform after breakfast equally as many began to assemble for their homeward trains at the end of the holidays.

After the last of the overnight trains had passed there was a slight lull before the succession of morning trains from Paddington began, soon to be intermingled with services from South Wales, the Midland line, the GW's North Warwick route via Stratford-on-Avon, and the Hereford route from Crewe, Manchester, Liverpool and Glasgow. Though headways were close on all routes, it was Taunton where the Bristol and Westbury lines converged, that presented the first challenge. Beyond Norton Fitzwarren, everything for Exeter and beyond had to use the one pair of rails up Wellington Bank to Whiteball Tunnel. The headway was six minutes, so that at best ten trains an hour could be accommodated and then only if they had a clear run without slowing or stopping. Though splitting them into their separate sections at Taunton station might cause local congestion, the Minehead and Ilfracombe trains left the main line at Norton Fitzwarren.

Most trains were of at least a dozen coaches, many of the maximum 15. Not all were hauled by Kings and Castles in the prime of condition; 2-8-0s of the 47XX class were common, along with a mixed bag of Halls and later Counties and even 2-6-0s. If delayed at the foot of Wellington Bank they naturally took their time. Many stopped at Wellington for a banker. Once over the top, there might be a relatively smooth ride to the outskirts of Exeter, but on the busiest days most trains had to wait to get through St David's. A stopping train would have to wait its turn to occupy platform one, perhaps delaying a flier behind it. Numerous Southern services from Padstow, Bude, Plymouth and North Devon also had to be fitted in from Cowley Bridge Junction, and all requiring banking engines up to Exeter Queen Street, (later Central). The least miscalculation, such as the driver of the up Plymouth–Brighton service stopping slightly short on platform 3 and so not clearing the points at the up end, and everybody waited. Sometimes a train that should have stopped at Exeter was signalled for the through road and had to be set back into platform 1. Eventually all services ran with identification numbers on the front of locomotives, but for staff reading the already complicated timetable in conjunction with the daily supplement was by no means easy.

Slip Coach Working

Hitherto there has been accommodation in slip coaches for first, second and third class passengers, but owing to the comparatively small use made of the second class it has been decided to provide first and third class compartments only in slip coaches, except in those running between Paddington, Windsor, Taplow, and also from Birmingham to Warwick and Stratford-on-Avon, which convey a large number of residential second class season ticket holders. Passengers in slip coaches have hitherto had to depend upon footwarmers for warming purposes, but a system has now been devised, and will shortly be in general use on the Great Western Railway, whereby steam heating can be applied to the slip coach, and be cut off by the slip guard by means of a mechanical arrangement prior to the vehicle being disconnected from the main train.

From the *Great Western Railway Magazine* December 1907

Hire of Rugs & Pillows.

THE RUGS, PILLOWS AND PILLOW SLIPS ARE BRANDED "G.W.R." AND ARE COMMON USER TO THE STATIONS CONCERNED.

After rugs and pillows have been collected at the passengers' destination stations, they must be dealt with as follows:—

If destination station is a Rug Hiring Station—to be taken into stock.

If destination station is NOT a Rug Hiring Station—to be sent to the nearest Rug and Pillow Hiring Station by the next train, securely packed in paper and booked as a parcel.

From the *Great Western Railway Appendix to the Service Timetables.*

With their normal work on overnight fast freights Churchward's heavy 2-8-0s of the 47XX class were less often seen out on the line in daylight. The exception to the rule was summer Saturdays when they were pressed into service to head relief passenger trains. No 4707 leaves the up platform at Dawlish in 1936. It must have been a time of high seas as the repair gang is in evidence at the end of the down platform.

Between Exeter and Newton Abbot, unlucky trains would be delayed by the signals of the 13 intermediate boxes; yet it could be an exciting as well as slow journey as children caught their first ever glimpse of the sea. Part of the reason for the delay was that trains could not be handled quickly enough at Newton Abbot. Here nearly all locomotive crews changed, and as many as 50 pairs of men might be waiting around the hut at the down end of the down platform. Even nominally non-stops to Plymouth usually had to pick up a pilot engine. Paignton trains usually changed locomotives, the replacement going tender first in readiness for a return trip. Only just before dieselisation was a turntable added at Goodrington. Congestion at Paignton could also affect Newton Abbot, the queue of trains waiting to disgorge their passengers there indeed sometimes stretching back to Dawlish and affecting Cornwall services. Bank engine movements on the branch also caused delays, so much that in later days it was decided to keep all Torbay services to the load of a single locomotive. But by then the railway's share of the business was anyway in decline.

Beyond Newton Abbot, Plymouth and Cornwall trains took their time even if double headed throughout over the switchback road. Most services

A double headed St Ives to Paddington train passes Dainton box on 23 August 1958. The train engine is a King 4-6-0 but the pilot is Modified Hall No 7914 Lleweni Hall, then only eight years old. It is opportune to note that at this late hour the former Great Western branches in Devon and Cornwall, including the Kingsbridge branch, each had its own long Saturday trains through to Paddington.

Crowds on Torquay platform in 1958 before the car explosion in the 'never had it so good' years of the 1960s. Pannier tank No 5796 banks No 6957 Norcliffe Hall (a wartime engine built in 1943) out of the station towards Torre with the 8.40am Paignton to Nottingham train on 23 September. It will have been a heavy load to take up the 1 in 37.7 Lickey incline to Birmingham later on the journey, probably needing three engines.

were allowed extra time on Saturdays both for the slower pace when they had the road and for delays at signals. And so into Cornwall, the main line being extremely busy throughout to Penzance, though Newquay, Falmouth, Perranporth and St Ives, and once even Helston, all had their through services. Two locomotives, including the train engine, normally a Castle, in the front, and a third at the back, worked Newquay services up Luxulyan Bank. They terminated at a modern station with platforms able to take two locomotives plus 15 coaches. On Saturdays the major part of the Cornish Riviera Express went to St Ives, hauled by two 2-6-2 tanks, the first of which cut off before the train entered the long curved platform that epitomised Great Western on sea.

The return pattern differed sharply. While many people enjoyed an overnight trip at the beginning of their holiday, at the end they wished to leave before the official turning out time at boarding houses and camps, and be home in time to put the children to bed and collect the pet. The rush was much more concentrated. Though the reservation of seats was always encouraged, it was only with the introduction of compulsory Regulation tickets in the late 1950s that passengers could be forcibly directed to earlier or later trains when those at the most convenient times were full.

Up trains started at a large number of points, and generally also made fewer stops. The performance largely depended on what happened on the Torbay branch, the plan being to get as many visitors away from Paignton and Torquay ahead of those making longer journeys from Cornwall. But many of the morning departures from Paignton were made up of stock off overnight services, and if they ran late, chaos ensued as thousands of passengers waited to entrain.

There was absolutely no slack in the up service from breakfast to lunch time, any late running such as a Britannia Pacific of BR days slipping with a heavy Devonian on the steep gradient out of Torquay at the beginning of a non-stop run to Burton-on-Trent (though crews were changed on the Bristol relief line), or a vehicle with a hot box having to be detached at Starcross (involving a shunt via the down main line), resulting in the whole kaleidoscope being delayed. At one point on the sea wall near Dawlish you could sometimes see the train before and after you halted at signals. But on a good day, when it all worked smoothly, the Torbay Express and Cornish Riviera Limited would shriek their way through Exeter St David's and Taunton overtaking other trains.

As the day wore on, every available siding in the West Country became chock-a-block full of stock, much of it several decades old and not to be used until the following Saturday. When Long Rock, Truro, Newquay, St Blazey, Laira, Tavistock Junction, Goodrington, Newton Abbot and Exminster could take no more, the surplus had to be run out of the West Country. Between six and eight every Saturday evening a succession of empty stock trains could be seen running along the sea wall to places as far away as Didcot, Tyseley and Severn Tunnel Junction.

By then, the tension was easing. Many drivers and firemen had completed their long turns of duties. Supernumerary porters had gone off duty for another week. At the locomotive depots most engines had been watered and coaled and the 2-8-0s made ready again for freight duty. Ticket collectors had time to start sorting and counting the tickets ready to inform district office who would pass the figures on to the Press, who would comment on the day's performance as though it had been some mighty sporting event.

The impression is inevitably one of the average over the years, but each season brought its individualities. The quality never quite regained its 1930s excellence, when even on services provided exclusively for the use of third class passengers, you still expected the best service in the restaurant car. Incidentally, no extra long-distance services were normally run on Saturdays before 1914, and even by the mid-1920s there were only a handful, though by then the trains would normally have been fuller on Saturdays than on other days, and relief services were becoming more common, starting early in the season when a series of specials took

The Great Western's last class of 4-6-0, No 1016 County of Hants, *with a Plymouth to Liverpool express via Hereford and Shrewsbury near Dawlish on 15 April 1957. These engines were originally painted by British Railways in lined black but the new 'Hanks' regime was in full swing and No 1016 is GWR green, spotlessly clean and with all brasswork sparkling. It was an Indian summer.*

North Wales in 1938. Churchward 2-6-0 No 6303 leaves Barmouth with a train for Ruabon, Shrewsbury, Birmingham and London with nine heavily loaded coaches to take over the hills through Dolgelly, Bala Junction and Llangollen. This was a normal route for the 43XX class until the coming of the Manor class 4-6-0s. The third coach is one of the then new wide window end door vehicles which were extremely comfortable in the third class compartments.

Swindon's own workforce to Devon and Cornwall. Not until well into the 1930s and the expansion of paid holidays had the business so blossomed that the Saturday timetable had to be printed quite separately.

Not merely was the carriage of these extra long-distance passengers seen as highly desirable in itself (how else could you increase business in a depression?), but of course those visitors taken to the resort by train would buy runabout and excursion tickets as they explored the locality. Some occupied the Camping Coaches, another Great Western speciality.

In the war it was different. The state of the trains automatically raised the question 'Is your journey really necessary?'. Thereafter the holiday explosion continued to overwhelm the railways. Despite the enormous increase in motor road traffic, the peak railway carriage of summer Saturday passengers did not occur until 1958. For the 13 years since the end of the war, more and more resources continued to be poured into the business, the management never challenging the economics or wondering whether a rationing system might not have forced the staggering of holidays – staggering the holiday week as well as lengthening the total season. Some resorts received nearly a third of their total season's influx of visitors on just two Saturdays, on each of which over 30,000 people making journeys of well over 100 miles went down the Torbay branch and 6,000 to Newquay.

Sadly, the railwaymen who performed miracles in keeping the wheels turning were at least partly misguided. So long as the railways could add extra trains and coaches, people still opted to travel at the season's peak. Once a substantial proportion of tourists had transferred to road, however, they were not prepared to suffer the intolerable delays on the Exeter bypass and elsewhere. It was traffic congestion, in searing heat or heavy rain, that ultimately resulted in the season being staggered, which in turn led to more healthy tourism.

Instructions to be observed in dealing with the receipt, storage, and delivery of articles deposited in cloak rooms.

1. The charges to be made for Cloak Room deposits are as follows:—

(a)

Bags.
Baskets.
Boxes.
Bundles.
Cases.
Coats.
Hat-boxes.
Hucksters' Luggage.
Mail Carts, Folding (folded).
Packmen's Luggage.
Parcels.
Portmanteaux.
Rugs.
Sewing Machines, hand.
Typewriting Machines.
Umbrellas.
Walking Sticks.

If removed on day of deposit or next day. Each article. 3d.

For each day than the days of deposit and removal. Each article. 1½d. (min.) 2d.

(b)

Bass Viols.
Bath Chairs.
Bicycles (ordinary).
Cash Registers.
Hand Carts.
Harps.
Ice Cream Carts.
Ice Cream Freezers.
Invalid Chairs.
Mail Carts (children's).
Organs (street).
Perambulators.
Pianos (street).
Scissor Grinders' Machines.
Sewing Machines, treadle.
Side Cars.
Violincellos.

If removed on day of deposit or next day. Each article. 6d.

For each other day than the days of deposit and removal. Each article. 3d.

From the *Great Western Railway Appendix to the Service Time Tables.*

As well as being the peak year for rail business, 1958 was the last in which over half the West Country's visitors came by train. Almost every season since has witnessed some reduction in the number of trains run, but in 1983 the Saturday timetable was still printed differently and many familiar features, such as trains to the Midlands and North making unexpectedly long non-stop runs, were retained.

At the end of the 1930s, the summer Saturday timetables for most main lines were printed separately, and an amazing range of cross-country and industrial, as well as coastal branch lines, enjoyed at least one extra service, probably the only one not calling at all stations and halts. The West Wales junction of Whitland would have been an interesting place to spend a summer Saturday, while a variety of curiously-routed services connected South with Mid and North Wales. Along the Cambrian Coast, Aberystwyth, Barmouth and Pwllheli were among the places worked to capacity and beyond. The North Wales system was different in being virtually all single track as well as steeply graded, but armies of holidaymakers were conveyed each Saturday from Birmingham and Wolverhampton alone. Many travelled in trains used on the West Midlands suburban services during the week, hauled perhaps by Tyseley's 43XX class 2-6-0s skilfully pushed to their limit on the hard Ruabon–Barmouth line.

Punctuality was never brilliant along the Cambrian Coast. Any late running of through trains from Paddington, Birmingham, Manchester, Liverpool and Birkenhead, or from Euston via Afon Wen, immediately upset crossing arrangements, as did heavy traffic including calls at more than the usual proportion of request stops and bad weather. But most of the long-distance services were genuine expresses with long non-stop runs, and one still hears Midland people talk nostalgically of the days before they became car owners and the journey to Aberdovey or Criccieth was a highlight of the holiday. This staff-intensive system was highly dependent upon tourism, and while many facilities were only justified on a dozen Saturdays a year, the visitors that came then accounted for much of the local traffic during the following week.

Cardiff, Bristol, Oxford, Birmingham and many other large provincial stations handled enormously-increased traffic, their platforms ever crowded with families eager to get to the sea. You could immediately sense the difference on a summer Saturday at Birmingham Snow Hill, always a civilised station, which at the season's peak despatched up to 25,000 long-distance passengers in a few hours. In addition to the trains for North and South Wales, Weston-super-Mare (a Birmingham favourite), Weymouth and numerous destinations in Devon and Cornwall, there was a variety of through services to the Southern serving nearly all the large resorts from Margate to Bournemouth. And whether you went to Margate, Eastbourne or Portsmouth, you had a choice of several trains, again most of them with restaurant cars. But then when the blanket factory went on holiday, you could even get an advertised through train from Witney to Portsmouth, while other trains for Portsmouth via Oxford came off the LNER from places like Sheffield. The range was truly prodigious.

10

HOW THE PASSENGERS TRAVELLED

Despite a unique continuity of administration over a century and a half, Great Western carriage design, both in detail and standards of accommodation, showed remarkable contrasts. At different periods in its history it produced some of the finest examples of the coach builders' art and some of the worst in terms of passenger accommodation. In some aspects the company was a pioneer with innovations well in advance of their time, yet there were periods of mundane conservatism when from the passenger's point of view progress over periods of a quarter of a century and more seemed to stand still. Right at the start the Great Western Railway's policy towards passengers was one of strict adherence to the class apartheid which characterised early Victorian Britain and which lasted in its fairly precise divisions for much of the Company's first 80 years, and to a lesser extent until the second of the two world wars and subsequent changes in attitudes brought a more equal society, though still with some more equal than others. Yet the Great Western in its pioneering days in hardly considering it necessary to carry third class passengers, that is the poorest and the lowest in the land, was probably no worse than the other railways of the period which if they did carry them treated them with indifference and the bare minimum of accommodation. Indeed, third class carriages did not appear as such in the early Great Western stocklists, even when the company decided to carry third class passengers, for they were no more than open goods wagons with benches, and holes in the floor to let out the rainwater. While the railways were built for the masses, the masses, it was thought, could not afford to, or even have a need to travel.

For the first few years third class carriages only ran in goods trains taking up to 9hr between London and Bristol. The first major Great Western accident occurred to one of these trains on Christmas Eve 1841 when it ran into an earthslip in Sonning cutting, as a result of which the two open carriages were crushed with eight passengers killed and 17 injured. The low sides of the wagons in any case probably contributed to passengers being thrown out, and the height of the sides was increased soon after. In contrast, the early Great Western first class coaches were

The early Great Western broad gauge first class coaches were six-wheelers and fairly sumptuous inside with well padded and upholstered seats of generous proportions allowed by the width of the broad gauge, by comparison with the contemporary standard gauge stock of other lines. The 4ft diameter wheels protruded through the floor and were enclosed within wheel splashers which in the end compartments just encroached into the doorway to trap unwary passengers. The original vehicles for carrying third class passengers were no more than open wagons with wooden benches, with holes in the floor to let out rainwater. They were described in the stock lists merely as 'trucks'.

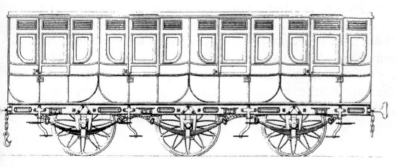

FIRST CLASS CARRIAGE

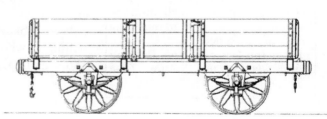

TRUCK

Coaches Requiring to be Disinfected.

When application is made to convey the body of a person who has died from an infectious disease the authority of the Superintendent of the Line must be obtained. No such application must, however, be entertained until the Medical Officer of Health certifies that the body may be removed, and if necessary the vehicle used must be subsequently sent to Swindon to be disinfected.

Bodies of persons who have died from Spotted Fever must not be accepted unless coffins are hermetically sealed and a certificate is received from the Local Medical Officer of Health certifying that there is no danger in handling and conveyance by rail. The vans used must, in all cases, be disinfected.

The following are the charges agreed generally by Railway Companies for the disinfection of coaching vehicles:—

Saloon or corridor carriage or compartments in corridor carriage or complete non-corridor carriage 30 0

Compartment in non-corridor carriage 10 0

Guard's van conveying corpse 20 0

The charge to be credited to the Company performing the disinfection.

It is imperative that all carriages used for the conveyance of FOREIGN Emigrants should be thoroughly disinfected immediately after the journey is completed, and before the vehicles are utilised for other traffic.

This applies not only to Foreign Emigrants travelling in large numbers, but also to small parties for whom one or more compartments are reserved. In the latter case it is essential that any small number should not be allowed to mix with ordinary passengers.

From the *Great Western Railway Appendix to the Service Time Tables.*

sumptuous indeed, and spacious by comparison with standard gauge vehicles of other lines. After an early essay into four-wheel coaches most of the early broad gauge vehicles were on six-wheel underframes, and in a coach 24ft long with four compartments the 6ft by 9ft compartments could seat eight in considerable comfort. Some of the compartments were sub-divided with a longitudinal partition and door into four-seat compartments, ideal for small families.

From the beginning and for the first decade and a half the body style of GWR first class coaches followed very much the designs of road coaches, with curved body panels and windows on each side of the door in the shape of a quarter circle. Inside everything was plush with well padded seats and backs buttoned in, and with arm rests. Second class coaches were at least covered, but with open sides and no windows were open to wind and weather. They seated 72 passengers on wooden bench seats, extremely cramped in a coach no more than 27ft long and 9ft wide.

The poor conditions which had to be endured by third class passengers were brought to the attention of Parliament, which in 1844 approved a bill which stipulated that all railways must provide enclosed third class accommodation and run at least one train a day conveying third class carriages at an average speed of not less than 12 miles an hour with fares at no more than 1d per mile. The provision of covered accommodation was taken literally and the new third class coaches were little more than almost totally enclosed goods vans containing bench seats.

For the opening of the Birmingham line service in 1852 the Great Western built what were to be the largest broad gauge coaches of that period, 38ft long, 9ft 9in wide, with three centrally placed first class compartments flanked by two second class compartments at each end. They retained the road coach style of three cornered windows on each side of the doors; more importantly they were carried on eight wheels in two groups of four, placed towards the ends, and were the first eight wheelers in regular passenger service in the country. Because of their size these Great Western vehicles were known as 'Long Charleys'.

By this time the Great Western was also involved in standard gauge operation but the coaches provided were no better or worse than those on other standard gauge lines, and were inevitably much smaller than their broad gauge contemporaries. The type of accommodation was much the same. With the provision of mixed gauge between Oxford and Birmingham and the mixing of the former purely broad gauge line between Oxford, Reading and Basingstoke in 1852/6 already the future of the broad gauge seemed in doubt, even though it was to last for another 40 years until 1892 before it finally disappeared. Nevertheless, however fine the broad gauge first class vehicles of the 1840s and 1850s might have been when built there was little incentive during the 1860s for the GWR to spend large sums replacing them if the broad gauge was not to have a long term future, and at a time, moreover, when financially the company was at a very low ebb with bankruptcy staring it in the face. Indeed, it still did not seem willing to woo the mass market of third class passengers, for in the early 1860s its total of third class carriages of just over 200 compared with 380 second class and 270 first class, and even allowing the higher seating capacity of the thirds, showed that the middle and upper classes were its main source of passenger traffic. With further gauge conversions more broad gauge coaches were replaced by standard gauge vehicles and the expanding third class traffic of the 1870s was catered for on broad gauge lines by demoting old second class coaches. Even on the standard gauge, new types of coaches were still mostly of the small four-wheel pattern, including those for service on fast expresses.

In 1873 came a development in railway carriage design which was to produce a revolution; at one and the same time it gave a far better riding coach and permitted the introduction of longer coaches. This was the pivoted truck or bogie which allowed coaches to take curves more easily and smoothly. Originating in North America it was seen first in Britain on the narrow gauge Festiniog Railway and its importation on Pullman cars for the Midland Railway in the following year brought its first use on a British standard gauge line. It was immediately taken up by the Midland for some of its ordinary stock and by a number of other railways but not the Great Western. Instead, when the new Swindon Carriage & Wagon Works, which had been opened in 1869, resumed the production of coaches for the broad gauge in 1876 although they were eight-wheelers like the 'Long Charleys' of 24 years earlier, the axles were grouped in two pairs towards the coach ends suspended from the underframe. The coaches were purely of the compartment type but were very spacious, for with bodies 10ft 0in wide inside and 7ft between partitions of the first class compartments they were much larger than anything on the standard gauge. Moreover, they were equipped with the clerestory roof, that is with a raised centre section, and were thus much higher than coaches until that time. The clerestory was a feature of Great Western coaches for the next 30 years for new construction.

Three classes continued to be catered for, the first class with well padded seats, backs, and armrests, the second class with smaller dimensions between partitions and nominal padding in seat cushions and backs, and third class still largely with wooden seats. Nevertheless with the improvement to third class facilities initiated by the Midland Railway in 1875 when that line abolished second class, neighbouring companies had perforce to improve the standard of third class accommodation in succession as one line strove to keep up with another on competing routes. Thus even third class seats in GW coaches were eventually given a semblance of upholstery, and from then on the difference between third

In the later years of the broad gauge thoughts were turned to the production of coaches which could be converted for use on the standard gauge after the abolition of the broad gauge. By this time broad gauge coaches were around 40 to 50ft in length, on eight wheels, some of which were grouped in pivotting bogies. None had corridors, few had between compartment toilets and there were no refreshments, even on long distance services to the South West. This tri-composite carriage behind Churchward Atlantic No 189 Talisman was built for the broad gauge and seen here in the early 1900s after being narrowed.

Damage to Carriage Windows, Etc.

The following amounts must be collected from persons responsible for the breakage of windows:—

Top side light	..	.. 3s. 6d.
Ordinary door light		.. 10s. 0d.
Corridor door light		.. 7s. 6d.
Ordinary quarter light		.. 13s. 6d.
Corridor quarter light		.. 11s. 6d.
Lavatory drop light ⎫		
Lavatory fixed light ⎬		.. 4s. 6d.
Quarter light "Smoking"		17s. 6d.
Door light frame	..	..20s. 6d.
Large light in corridor or saloon coaches, under 34 inches wide	..	..30s. 6d.
Large light in corridor or saloon coaches, 34 inches and not exceeding 50 inches wide		..35s. 6d.
Large light in corridor or saloon coaches, over 50 inches wide	..	..47s. 0d.
Ventilators, large, in Rail Motors	..	....74s. 6d.
Ventilators, small, in Rail Motors	..	..25s. 0d.

The same amounts shewn above should also be charged in the event of breakage of windows in other Companies' stock.

Where difficulty is experienced in identifying soldiers and sailors who have broken windows, or otherwise damaged the vehicles in which they were travelling, owing to the men giving their wrong names and numbers, the proper regimental or official numbers can be obtained from the men's clothing, a soldier's regimental number being inside his tunic or cap, and in the case of a sailor inside his cap or underneath his collar.

From the *Great Western Railway Appendix to the Service Time Tables.*

and second grew rapidly less distinctive, often being little more than a few inches in compartment sizes and thus passenger leg room, and the provision of a carpet in the seconds.

But six-wheel coaches continued to be built for both broad and standard gauge, including two six-wheel sleeping cars for the Paddington–Plymouth night service in 1877. Each car had two dormitories, one for ladies, the other for gentlemen, where passengers slept in rows side by side. There was no attempt at privacy. But only four years later the two six-wheelers were replaced by a pair of new eight-wheeled sleeping cars, with bodies 46ft 6in long but only 9ft wide and thus suitable for the standard gauge, but carried on broad gauge bogies. Thus these coaches were not only the forerunners of the convertible stock built to be easily adapted from broad to standard gauge, anticipating the end of the broad gauge which did not come for another decade, but also anticipated the design of the typical side corridor coach of later years, with its layout of individual compartments and toilets linked by an internal side corridor.

On matters of detail this was also a period when gas lighting began to replace oil lamps and the first experiments were being conducted with vacuum brakes, which in its turn allowed the development of improved passenger communication facilities so that in an emergency passengers could pull the communication cord and apply the brakes on the train.

With William Dean in command of locomotive and carriage design from the late 1870s and the inevitable end of the broad gauge approaching, the need was for large numbers of coaches of standard gauge dimensions but temporarily fitted out to run on broad gauge bogies to replace the older life-expired purely broad gauge stock, not only of the Great Western but also for the South Devon and Cornwall railways which had come into the Great Western fold in 1876. Indeed the later convertibles were standard gauge vehicles in all except the bogies themselves and the wider footboards needed to bring them close to the broad gauge platforms. Conversion in Swindon Works to the standard gauge took no more than ½hr with the coach bodies and underframes supported by blocks as the bogies were dropped out from underneath and replaced by new ones while the wide footboards were unbolted. Some of the older wide-body coaches had a slice taken off each side to make them narrower.

A year before the end of the broad gauge the Great Western took another stride forward with the introduction of the first British side corridor train equipped with flexible gangways between the coaches, and placed in service on the standard gauge Paddington–Birmingham–Birkenhead route. It had toilet facilities for all three classes and gas lighting and set a new standard for long distance travel. It was not the first train to have flexible gangways between the coaches since that had first been seen on coaches for public use on a set of Brighton line Pullmans in 1888, and on some special LNWR saloons of the same year, with its origin in the pair of LNWR Royal coaches two decades before. In the Great Western train the gangways were at the side, as they were in succeeding trains built for the South Wales and West of England services, but this soon proved to be a disadvantage and the central gangway became standard.

126

During the decade from the mid 1890s to about 1905 the Great Western built some handsome corridor coaches of William Dean's design with clerestory roofs, as part of the dramatic improvement in passenger facilities on long distance services. A feature of many of these coaches was a small open saloon at one end for smokers, since smoking at that time was not permitted in compartments of these vehicles.

With the end of the broad gauge it seemed that one common type of stock could be used on all routes, yet in the new century with Churchward now at the helm of mechanical engineering, new designs took advantage of the fact that former broad gauge routes even with 4ft 8½in gauge track and corresponding clearances for platform faces and other lineside equipment could still pass vehicles with wider bodies than on original standard gauge routes where clearances were tighter. Churchward was bold in his approach and the new standards of 1904 eliminated most of the features of the preceding century with some of the biggest coaches that have ever run in Britain before or since. The new vehicles were no less than around 70ft long with bodies 9ft 6in wide, carried on two four wheel bogies; the most dramatic advance was in the internal layout since although they had side corridors, which changed sides halfway along the coach, entry from the platforms was by end and centre doors, and access to the compartments was from the corridor alone. The coaches were so large that they soon gained the nickname 'Dreadnoughts' after the then new British battle-ships. Moreover, the clerestory roof which had characterised Great Western coaches for more than three decades gave way to a high elliptical section, giving a much more spacious interior. Much the same profile was adopted for restaurant cars built at the same time which with their open saloon interiors seemed much more generously proportioned than the narrower diners on other lines.

The Great Western was relatively late in introducing dining facilities on its long distance trains, the first appearing in 1896, but one reason was the existence of the clause in the concession for the operation of Swindon refreshment room requiring all trains to stop for a brief refreshment halt. The clause was not removed until the GWR bought out the lease.

The Dreadnought corridor coaches alas were not a success, for the British travelling public did not take to the end door entrances and the approach to the compartments by the corridors. The compartments

---

Steam Heating of Passenger Trains.

1. (a) All steam heating pipes and valves to be fitted and pipes coupled up for use by September 1st.
   (b) Heat to be applied:—
   Sleeping car trains/Boat trains . . . First Monday in September.
   All express trains running during the late evening, night and early morning, also morning business trains . . . Third Monday in September.
   All other passenger trains . . . October 1st
   (c) Heat to be discontinued on all trains May 31st.
   (d) The removal of the pipes and valves to be commenced on June 14th.

From the *Great Western Railway Appendix to the Service Time Tables.*

themselves still had three windows, the two quarter lights flanking a drop window exactly as though there had been a door there. Seemingly the designers had not considered fitting the single wide windows used on the corridor side because of ventilation problems. Equally the travelling public was not over-enamoured by open saloon coaches with seats flanking a centre passageway. Two such trains had been built for the Paddington–Milford Irish boat trains in 1900/1 but they were also in advance of their time. The Great Western never built any more except for excursion use 30 or so years later and the open saloon-style coach never found favour on the GWR as it did on the other three Group companies between the wars. Curiously though, many of the single class corridor clerestory coaches of the 1891–1905 period included a two- or three-bay open saloon for smokers, seemingly without complaint. It was not until the 1970s that the open style became more general on former GWR lines as British Rail abandoned the side corridor compartment coach.

Thus from the Edwardian years until the end of the Great Western's independent existence in 1948 the side corridor coach was the standard for all its long distance expresses, and until the mid 1930s external doors were provided to each compartment. The details of the various batches over that 30 year period naturally varied. One feature, the provision of small toplight windows above the main windows, although only standard for about 15 years for new construction, virtually became a trade mark of the Great Western, for large numbers of these coaches were built and lasted until the late 1950s in general service. As for technical developments electric lighting had become standard during the early 1900s and steam heating from around the same time allowed the replacement of the foot warmer, that very Victorian aid to travel, at least for the upper classes. This was virtually a tin hot water bottle which included sodium acetate to assist in keeping the water hot. In coach construction steel underframes had replaced timber and by the 1920s coach bodies were steel panelled instead of wooden panelled with mouldings, altough painting styles continued to have panels picked out in contrasting lining as though the mouldings were there.

Coaches built in the 1920s varied from batch to batch, both in length between 57ft and 70ft, and width between 9ft and 9ft 7in, the latter primarily for former broad gauge routes, particularly to the West of England for the Cornish Riviera service which was undoubtedly the prestige train of the Great Western.

Included among the coaches built at this time, and, indeed before and later, were slip coaches equipped with a guard's compartment containing special uncoupling apparatus which allowed a slip coach at the back of a train to be uncoupled from the main portion while travelling at speed, and with the guard controlling the brake brought to a stand at the station while the main portion continued ahead without stopping. Slip coaches detached from non-stopping trains were inaugurated on the Great Western in November 1858 at Slough and Banbury and although other companies used the system it was practised to a far greater extent by the Great Western where it lasted longest, the last slip service not being

The Great Western operated numerous slip coach services; to ensure that signalmen could see whether trains were correctly carrying the right number of coaches and that a slip coach had not been accidentally detached, a special code of tail lamps was applied to slip coaches. The red and white display here was placed on the back of a single slip coach, or the last to be slipped where there was more than one.

Ladies' Compartments
One or more compartments of each class, as required, must be provided for "ladies only" on semi-fast trains, other than business services, which are formed with non-corridor stock; also on the express night trains.

The compartments must be labelled before the commencement of the journey, and Guards and Ticket Collectors should be instructed that they must inform lady passengers who are unaccompanied that there are Ladies' compartments in the train.
From the *Great Western Railway Appendix to the Service Time Tables.*

128

withdrawn until September 1960. Some trains carried more than one slip portion – the Cornish Riviera at times up to three – with a complex system of 'tail lamps on each slip portion and the main train to confirm to signalmen on the way that the right number of slip portions was still attached to the train and that they had not become uncoupled accidentally. On the Great Western there was no corridor communication between the slip portions and the main train so that passengers were denied access to any restaurant car facilities although at one period a four-coach portion including restaurant car was slipped at Taunton for Ilfracombe.

As for local trains non-corridor compartment type stock had become standard by the turn of the century, mostly still four- and six-wheelers and until then with little difference between coaches for main line and local use. Following the abolition of the broad gauge and the introduction of corridor trains, longer bogie non-corridor coaches became the norm on local and main line stopping services. On the longer cross-country journeys a few coaches equipped with between compartment toilets passed down from long distance services of the pre-corridor train era were used on a number of routes.

To counter road competition soon after the turn of the century the company sought ways of reducing costs of suburban operation by the introduction of steam railmotors in which single cars had their own steam engine unit which cost less to operate than a conventional locomotive and separate coaches. In the 1930s the idea was developed into a diesel powered railcar, described in Chapter 14.

The final development of any note in Great Western main line coach design came in the 1930s, first with the building of some superb saloons very much on the lines of Pullman cars, which had been tried on the Great Western on a Torbay Pullman service in 1929 without much success. The

The GWR pioneered moves to reduce train operating costs by using railcars on lightly used and branch services. In the first decade of the present century came steam railcars, then came motor trains with small tank engines working with saloon trailer coaches push-pull fashion, and in the 1930s came diesel railcars described and illustrated in a later chapter, which laid much of the foundation work for today's diesel multiple-units on BR.

Great Western carriage design at its best is epitomised in the train sets for the Cornish Riviera service, built in 1935. They took full advantage of the generous clearances bequeathed by the broad gauge after its abolition having a width of 9ft 7in, that seven inches providing more room in seat width than could be found on other companies' stock. They were distinguished by angled recessed end doors and were similar in outline to coaches built for Plymouth–London boat trains in the late 1920s, known as the Super Saloons, which had Pullman style interiors.

GWR saloons were intended primarily for the boat train traffic between Plymouth and London. They took full advantage of broad gauge clearances with bodies 9ft 7in wide and 61ft 4½in long. Internally they had single armchairs arranged at tables for four or two, wall to wall carpet, curtains and a very Pullmanesque feature – a table lamp. Some of the ocean saloons were equipped with kitchens to provide meal service to all passengers at their seats. Because of the width of the bodies the end doors were recessed into the sides to keep the coaches within the loading gauge.

Very similar in profile were the sets of coaches built to mark the centenary of the Great Western Railway in 1935 and placed in service on the Cornish Riviera. They had side corridor compartments but with end door access only; this time the arrangement was accepted by the travelling public unlike 30 years earlier. The centenary stock and ocean saloons had wide picture windows and, later, to improve ventilation, had sliding window ventilators fitted in the top quarter, a feature which was used in other Great Western coaches for ordinary services and excursion work built from then on.

From the early 1950s production of Great Western designed coaches ceased and new designs of the BR all-steel Mark I type soon appeared on former Great Western services. Even then there was deference to Great Western operating practice since BR coaches for the Western Region had eight seats without armrests in each third (later second) class side corridor compartment while similar coaches for the LM and Eastern Regions were fitted with armrests to give six seats per compartment. Was there some broad gauge thinking here even though the BR coaches were no more than 9ft wide?

Although future BR coach construction seemed to owe nothing to Great Western practice, in 1964 the wheel appeared to have come almost full circle, for a new prototype BR train, XP64 produced by industrial designers, included side corridor coaches with end and centre doors with the side corridor changing sides halfway. Could the ghosts of Churchward and the Dreadnoughts of 60 years earlier have been at work? And then in 1976 when the Inter-City 125 high speed trains entered service between London and Bristol back came the 70-footers, for the new BR Mark III coaches, built to metric dimensions, are roundly 75ft long.

Family, Saloon and Invalid Carriages.

1. Applications for Family, Saloon and Invalid Carriages are to be made to the Divisional Superintendents or District Traffic Manager, and it must be stated for whose use a coach is required, the number of passengers, by what train, on what day it is wanted, and where it is to work from and to. Family carriages must not be supplied for composite parties of First and Third Class passengers attending Race meetings, Horse Shows and similar events.
From the *Great Western Railway Appendix to the Service Time Tables.*

11

THE FREIGHT SCENE

At the end of the second world war the heavy freight and modern mixed traffic engines of the 2-6-0 and 4-6-0 types outnumbered the purely express passenger 4-6-0s by more than three to one. It is true that a number of the Hall class 4-6-0s were used in regular passenger service, quite apart from summer holiday 'extras' at weekends, but the mere statistics of the motive power involved do no more than begin to lift the curtain upon the volume and importance of the freight traffic conveyed by the Great Western Railway.

In 1912 the total traffic receipts from freight of all kinds no more than slightly overtopped those from passenger business – in round figures £7½ million, against £6.95 million; but in 1936 freight accounted for 58 per cent of the total traffic receipts. This was despite an increasing loss of business to road transport through the unfavourable conditions in which railway freight traffic was governed by law, and from which relief was later sought in the 'Square Deal' campaign of 1938–9.

The great bulk of it went by night. The Great Western was one of the foremost users of vacuum-fitted freight stock, and beginning at 8.5pm no fewer than 12 express freight trains left Paddington Goods Station in the ensuing 4½ hours. Their destinations were Bristol, Birkenhead, Carmarthen Junction, Laira (Plymouth), Cardiff, Weymouth, Wolverhampton, Bristol, Newton Abbot, Worcester, Fishguard, and Bristol. At around the same time similar processions would be setting out from Birkenhead, Bristol, Cardiff, Westbury and Wolverhampton. Great Western men had always been adept at giving nicknames to their freight trains. In broad gauge days there had been 'The Tip', and the 10.45pm Exeter goods was known as 'The Flying Pig', while the 'Didcot Fly', far from doing anything approaching 'flying', was reputed to take about 12 hours to cover the 24 miles to Swindon!

In the 1930s when strenuous efforts were being made to arrest the declining trend in freight traffic the GWR produced a *Guide to Economical Transport* for traders, giving particulars of the fast services available, but revealing also the nicknames used in railway circles of no fewer than 73 express vacuum and accelerated Class E trains. It was evident from this booklet that the company set considerable store on the use of the nicknames, seeing them as terms of affection that would instil in all concerned throughout the run a sense of personal responsibility, for ensuring prompt despatch and avoidance of delay. It is amusing to see that the old broad gauge name of 'The Flying Pig' was revived for the more modern 4pm Exeter to Old Oak Common, while traders would be

---

Milk Traffic

Having regard to the highly perishable nature of this commodity and the severe road competition now obtaining, it is most important that Milk Traffic shall be afforded the best possible service and special attention paid to the working of returned empty churns. If any difficulties are experienced in this connection, the Divisional Superintendent or District Traffic Manager must be advised.

When churns are received at a station, they should be either loaded direct into a Milk Truck (when one is provided), or placed, as far as possible, upon trolleys, which should be wheeled to a position on the platform, as nearly as can be judged, opposite the spot where the van into which the Churns are to be loaded will come to a stand. In the event of there not being sufficient trollies, the Churns must be placed on the platform, in such a position as will cause the least possible delay on loading into the Milk Van. In either case the milk should be placed as far as possible in the shade.

Care must be taken to stand the trollies so that they will be well clear of the open doors of incoming and outgoing Trains.

From the *Great Western Railway Appendix to the Service Time Tables.*

Special traffic. A special train load of the famous excellent quality Witney blankets for Maple's store in London. Note the protective straw packing on the horse drawn carts.

encouraged to consign by 'The Spud', 9.45pm Cardiff to Saltney (Chester), by 'The Carpet', 8.20pm Kidderminster to Paddington, or 'The Moonraker', 4.20am Westbury to Wolverhampton.

There were long non-stop runs. The 9.10pm Paddington to Birkenhead used to run through from Greenford to Shrewsbury, 145.1 miles, at an average speed of 38mph. This was one of the duties on which the special 5ft 8in 2-8-0s of the 47XX class were used, and in maximum loading conditions it could be a very heavy task, with a gross load of about 800 tons. It was a lodging turn for the men, but when it was revived in 1946 the working arrangements were changed, and a stop was made at Banbury South to re-man.

The 4700 class 2-8-0s were also used on the long night runs to Newton Abbot and Plymouth. The speed of all these fast freight trains was limited to 60mph and the stock used was always maintained in first class condition. The special vans built by the Great Western for various purposes were a fascinating study in themselves, no less than their attractive telegraphic code names, such as Mogo (12 ton motorcar van); Vent-Insulmeat; Bloater, for the big, long wheelbase fishvans; or Asmo, another long covered van with opening doors at each end.

A 1920s photograph of Moor Street goods shed Birmingham; it had been open about 10–15 years as part of the area's modernisation plan, including the construction of Moor Street station to take the extra traffic from the new North Warwick line from Stratford-on-Avon. Note the greengrocery; the Vale of Evesham was an important source of vegetables and fruit.

Vacuum goods. One of Churchward's 47XX 2-8-0 locomotives built for fast freight services between London, Bristol and the South West, as well as London and Wolverhampton. In these early days these engines were not normally seen by day as their employment was principally on night express freights. This is an early 1920s photograph; the distant signal arm is still painted red.

Although suffering a grievous setback during the long strike of 1926, coal traffic was always heavy, and on the long haul to London the 2-8-0 locomotives of the 28XX class were almost exclusively used. But for the special measures adopted, the severe gradients and operating conditions at the Severn Tunnel would have presented a serious obstacle with loose-coupled trains of such weight. A large stud of tender and tank engines was based at Severn Tunnel Junction, and the coal trains stopped there to take an assisting engine, usually a 3100 class 2-6-2 tank. Because of the difficulty in controlling such trains through the deep V of the tunnel itself – 1 in 90 descending from the Welsh side, and climbing out of it on 1 in 100 – the assisting engines were always coupled ahead of the train engine through the tunnel rather than banking in rear. But on the English side the hard work was not finished when level ground was reached at Pilning. A second ascent at 1 in 100 lay ahead, but this time through the single-line bore of Cattybrook new tunnel. Because of the severe exhaust conditions in so confined a space from two engines at the head of the train, a stop was usually made at Pilning and the assisting engine transferred from front to rear for the passage through the second tunnel.

In 1921 when Sir Felix Pole became General Manager the coal was conveyed in open four-wheeled wagons of 10-12 tons capacity and almost entirely owned by the colliery companies or by the larger coal merchants in London and elsewhere. Wagons used for coal were naturally not suitable for any reciprocal traffic, and long trains of returning empties were

Severn Tunnel Junction layout in the 1930s, one of the most important freight marshalling yards on the GWR.

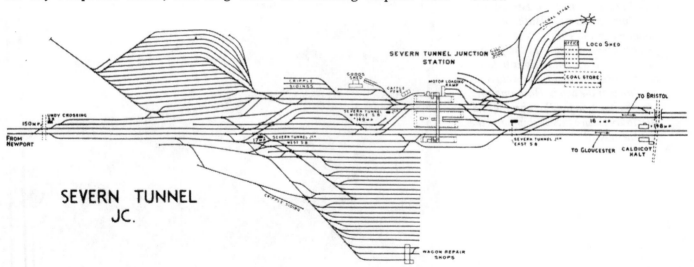

SEVERN TUNNEL
JC.

Cross country freight. Dean Goods 0-6-0 No 2456 heads a Bristol to Salisbury goods near Bathampton sometime in the 1920s. Note the private owner wagons at the front of the train, an everyday sight before nationalisation, and the first class condition of the track. Bathampton was the junction for Trowbridge and Westbury thence to Salisbury and the Southern Railway.

involved. Sir Felix Pole became a fervent advocate of larger coal wagons, which by taking up less space on the line per ton conveyed would be more efficient to handle. It was not proposed to go to the huge 30-ton and 40-ton bogie wagons used by some of the northern lines for locomotive coal, but to a 20-ton all-steel four-wheeler of special design, by which a 35 per cent reduction in siding space would be made possible. Sir Felix went so far as to offer a five per cent reduction in carrying charges for coal conveyed in 20-ton wagons. He received no more than a qualified approval in South Wales, because the new wagons, being longer than the old, could not be accommodated at many of the collieries. Nevertheless orders for 1,000 of them had been placed by the GWR by August 1924. The advantages that Sir Felix foresaw however were not to be realised, because the disastrously prolonged strike of 1926 brought the South Wales coal industry almost to the brink of ruin.

While the Great Western did not use large bogie wagons for moving coal (except loco coal) it had a variety of long vehicles for special tasks, one of which was the 73ft Macaw C for carrying rails, lengthy lattice girders, and the like. Another was a 45ft long covered van for motorcar body traffic. Nine bodies could be accommodated, loaded from the side, and having the roof and sides covered by tarpaulin sheeting. The Crocodile trucks were built in considerable variety for carrying heavy bulky loads. The C type was a low-loader mounted on two four-wheel bogies, with the carrying portion between set as low as possible – just to clear the rails; but the 120-ton Crocodile L was a tremendous affair mounted on no fewer than 24 wheels – two six-axle bogies at each end and used for such things as giant transformers for sub-stations and the like. The actual carrier could be either of well or straight section; but while the mounting ensured the necessary flexibility on curves and in sidings, the lateral overhang with some loads could be such as to require special track occupation, which could be provided only on Sundays.

The Great Western was always proud of its association with the life of the country, and often it was not merely a case of transporting a few animals or implements but of moving an entire farm – all the animals, machinery and personnel – by special train, sometimes up to 100 miles or more; but that was nothing to the job of moving an entire circus! It is on

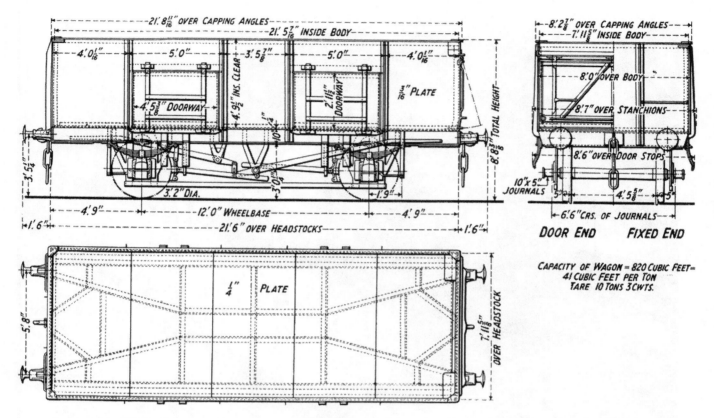

record that the GWR did one such job in a special train of 20 vehicles. Cages containing lions, tigers, bears, leopards and monkeys were loaded on to 16 Crocodile wagons with the well type of transporter. The elephants were conveyed in two Pythons (covered bogie vans) with end doors, from which the animals could walk out in appropriate dignity on arrival, while all the circus paraphernalia was loaded on to Scorpions, the code name for an open carriage truck. For less specialised forms of removal, of course, the familiar type of container was used, loaded as required on to a flat railway truck, or a road motor vehicle.

A much cherished seasonal traffic was the conveyance of Cornish broccoli from the Penzance area to markets in various large cities. The broccoli specials were given preferential treatment on the line; the rolling stock used was specially selected, and usually express passenger engines were used for the haulage. As with all the vacuum-fitted freight trains, the Control Office kept a special watch on their running, and an equally close check had to be maintained on the flow of empty wagons to Cornwall. Ample reserves had to be kept available for this highly-prized perishable traffic, and those responsible had to be aware of the farming conditions that could affect the crops. The weather could seriously interfere with the railway rolling stock position. A spell of March frost, for example, could retard the crops, and careful regulation of wagon movement was essential to avoid a glut of vehicles accumulating at Marazion and Penzance, and congesting the sidings against other more regular business.

Then there was milk, of which the Great Western at one time brought

Diagram of the 20 ton coal wagons advocated by Sir Felix Pole in an endeavour to cut costs.

135

Cattle special. An Armstrong goods 0-6-0 with a cattle train near Warwick in 1928, when most of the survivors were working in the Wolverhampton Division. The train is almost certainly en route to Bordesley Junction where there was a large cattle wharf handy for Birmingham market. With this type of traffic, unknown today, it is not always easy to imagine the vast number of such trains that worked into the big cities.

more into London than any other single transporter, rail or otherwise. Its daily total was around 240,000gal. Before the turn of the century special attention was being given to this traffic, and the Great Western milk van of the early 1900s, likened once to 'a prison-on-wheels' was a long semi-open-sided six-wheeler which held a vast number of the old traditional milk-churns. By the 1930s however milk was being conveyed in 3,000-gallon glass-lined tanks, mounted on six-wheeled railway undercarriages, and designed for running at passenger train speeds. Though not measuring more than about 25ft overall, when fully loaded they weighed about 28 tons, much the same as a 57ft toplight corridor passenger carriage. The county of Carmarthen was a big supplier of milk, and the one-time 3.50pm milk special from Whitland to Paddington very often conveyed as many as 18 tanks. It was worked regularly by a Castle class 4-6-0 locomotive. An occasion is recalled of the 5pm up express passenger train from Chester, when four of these milk vans from Dorrington were attached to the rear of the train at Shrewsbury. The engine had to be worked hard to keep time onwards to Wolverhampton.

There was another form of milk transport in which road milk tanks were loaded on to rail trucks. These tanks carried 2,000 gal – not so much as the special rail tanks – but they were convenient where the milk had to be conveyed some distance by road, and were really the fore-runners of container style tanks of more recent times although this type of conveyance was not developed for milk traffic.

12

SIGNALLING, AUTOMATIC TRAIN CONTROL AND SAFETY

Outwardly, the mechanical signalling practice of the Great Western was entirely conventional, albeit distinguished everywhere by large smartly kept semaphore blades and exceptionally clear geographical display on bracket post structures and the occasional gantry. In the Grouping era, when the other main line companies changed to the upper quadrant arm, where semaphores were retained the Great Western stood firmly by the lower quadrant type, even after nationalisation. Indeed, after some changes in the Regional boundaries which brought certain parts of the former LMS and SR into the Western Region, ex-LMS and SR upper quadrant arms were replaced by ex-GW type lower quadrant arms at certain places when renewals became necessary. Apart from outward display, however, Great Western practice included certain adjuncts and refinements to the basic block system of working that considerably enhanced the safety of operation.

One of the most important of these was the track circuit control on the block telegraph instruments. A track circuit was installed between the distant and the home signal, and the block section in rear could not be cleared until the train passing through the section had passed the distant signal, actuated the track circuit, and then passed clear of the home signal. There was thus an assurance that the block section was clear up to the home signal. Another very important feature was the 'Line Clear' control on the starting signal. Electrical interlocking prevented the signalman from lowering his starting signal, and so allowing a train to proceed to the next signalbox down the line, until the signalman in that box had accepted the train and pegged his instrument to Line Clear. There was thus a double check, because he could not do this until the arrival of the preceeding train had been proved by the track circuit control between the distant and the home signal.

There was however one classic case when even these two-fold precautions failed to prevent a serious accident. At its best the safeguard was no more than intermittent, and the section of line between the starting signal at one block post, and the distant signal at the next one ahead was unprotected by track circuit. It was this 'dark area' that in a combination of unfortunate circumstances led to disaster near Shrivenham, in the early hours of 15 January 1936. To facilitate the working of the numerous and heavy coal trains, for which paths had to be found amid the busy passenger service from Bristol and South Wales, the line had been plentifully equipped with running loops, into which slow and heavy trains, not equipped with continuous brakes, could be run direct, without the laborious and time consuming business of drawing ahead and then setting back into refuge sidings. East of Highworth Junction, Swindon, the line was double-tracked as far as Shrivenham, beyond which there was a long loop extending for 2½ miles to Knighton Crossing. But there was also an entry into this running loop at Ashbury Crossing, about 0.7 miles east of Shrivenham.

At 5am on this fatal morning a heavy loaded coal train of 53 wagons, Aberdare to London, was signalled away from Highworth Junction; it was passed on by the intermediate block post, at Marston Crossing, from which the signalman at Shrivenham received the 'train entering section' signal. It had been agreed between the signalmen concerned that the coal train should continue on the main line through Shrivenham, and be turned into the loop at Ashbury. This was necessary to clear the main line for the up Penzance sleeping car express, which ran via Bristol. In fact the signalman at Shrivenham had only just given train out of section for the coal train when he was offered, and accepted the express. It so happened that the signalbox at Shrivenham, like that at Ashbury crossing, was on the down side of the line, and just as the coal train was passing, in the darkness of an early January morning, a down train of milk empties was also passing, and the signalman was not as perspicacious as he should have been in observing the coal train, before he gave train out of section back to Marston Crossing, because the train was *not* out of section. There had been a breakaway, and the brake van and five loaded wagons were lying completely unprotected in open country. The signalman at Ashbury Crossing also failed to observe that the coal train had no tail lamp, and the elements of disaster were consummated by the marooned guard, who

The west end of Box tunnel with a characteristic Great Western disc and crossbar signal of the 1840s on the left. With the disc showing face on and the fishtail caution arm displayed, the signal was set for a train to proceed into the tunnel cautiously. After the electric telegraph had been installed in 1847 for signalling trains through the tunnel this indication would have meant that the preceding train had left the far end of the tunnel, but the caution board was displayed for a further period of time. The policeman is handsignalling 'all clear – proceed' to the train emerging from the tunnel.

The same location in 1962 with a Warship-hauled down train leaving the tunnel. Box down distant signal has replaced the policeman's hand signal, but the signal controlling entry to the tunnel is further back from the tunnel mouth and controlled by Box. The milepost had become 101 instead of ¾ in the Bourne view which would have been 100¾ miles from the original Paddington station.

apparently took some little time to wake up to the fact that the train had not stopped normally, and that he was out on his own. By the time he realised this, and the acute danger of the situation it was too late. The Penzance express running under clear signals and hauled by a King class locomotive came up at full speed and hit the obstruction at 55mph.

The Great Western always prided itself on the sense of responsibility shown by even the humblest of its employees in the discharge of their duties, and that three of them were lacking in this respect on that January morning could, perhaps, be quoted as the exception that proved the rule. Certainly the company had a very notable record of freedom from accident, and the disastrous affair at Norton Fitzwarren in 1940, in circumstances so exceptional because of war conditions, and the inexperience of the man primarily concerned, cannot really be held to dim that record. The men involved with train running, and particularly the locomotive enginemen, felt that the Company was doing all it could to help them in their job by the general application of automatic train control on all the main lines, and on some secondary routes too, and that was greatly appreciated. It is interesting to recall however that the first steps were not aimed previously at an automatic form of train control at all, but at assisting drivers in foggy weather.

In these days of smokeless zones, and other measures to ensure clean air in cities, it is difficult to appreciate just what the fogs of 60 years ago, and earlier, were like. For those who had to run trains the conditions were often very trying. The traditional method was to call out fogmen, who stood beside each distant signal and fixed two detonators on the line when the signal was at danger. Not only was the procedure labour intensive, and placed an unpleasant responsibility on permanent way men, but it did not give a truly satisfactory signal to the driver. When the signal was in the clear position the detonators would be removed, and no audible signal at

---

Signalbox Titles
There is a fascination in the odd titling of some signalboxes. The Southern had a Bo-Peep Junction on the outskirts of Hastings; the North Eastern named one after a Roman Emperor, Severus, while in Ireland there was a Two Pot House. But the Great Western was always precise and comprehensive, but sometimes with lengthy inscriptions like Dr Day's Bridge Junction Signal Box. One of the most compact and euphonious however was that to be seen at the main line country station five miles east of Bath – Box Signal Box.

By the 1860s semaphore signals were used on many GWR standard gauge routes with disc and crossbar signals on broad gauge lines. Gradually semaphores took over and by the turn of the century the two-position semaphore was used all over the system. Except for details – pressed steel arms instead of wood, tubular steel instead of wooden posts, and the painting of distant signal arms yellow instead of red, for example – Great Western signals have changed little in style or meaning since then. GW drivers were well directed by the clear indications with possibly more signals than would be provided on other lines, and supplemented by what was called until recent years automatic train control, an audible cab indication of distant signal positions transmitted to the engine by the ramp seen between the rails in this photograph.

The interior of a GWR signalbox was always neat and tidy, for in most cases the signalmen took a pride in the 'housekeeping', with windows sparkling, floor polished and the lever handles burnished bright and kept so with a cloth in the hand when operated. Woe betide a man who handled a lever with sweaty palm, which would soon turn the handle rusty. A particular feature of GWR lever frames was that facing point lock levers normally stood reversed (that is towards the signalman) when the points were locked. This is the interior of Newton Abbot East signalbox, one of the last of the large GWR mechanical boxes, originally with provision for 206 levers although in its closing years only about 90 were in use.

all given. This was fundamentally wrong because, in effect, it meant that no signal at all was all clear; but the fact that no detonators were on the line could also mean that the fogman had not yet arrived at his post, or if he had been on duty for a long time he might have succumbed to fatigue, or some other form of physical exhaustion. Yet up to the turn of the century this principle of fog signalling was the generally accepted method of operation on the British railways. Indeed, when Vincent Raven was responsible for locomotive running on the North Eastern Railway in the 1890s he designed and installed, at every signal along the line, a stop arm mounted in the middle of the track, which co-acted with the signal arm. If the signal was at danger it would be in the raised position and struck by a pendulum lever mounted below the engine cab. The movement of this lever blew a warning whistle in the cab, though when the signal was in the clear position, as with conventional fog signalling no audible indication was given to the driver.

On the Great Western it came to be felt that this was not good enough. In conditions of bad visibility it was just as important to give the driver a positive assurance that the distant signal was in the clear position, as to warn him when it was not. About the year 1905 an entirely new system of audible cab signalling was devised jointly by the Signal and the Locomotive Departments, in which certain fundamental principles were laid down. Audible signals should be given when the distant signal was in the clear and in the warning position, but they should be totally different; the actuating device in the track should have no moving parts, and should not be physically connected in any way to the mechanism controlling the signal arm, and any failure of the equipment should lead to a warning signal being given in the engine cab. The device that triggered off the action was a ramp varying in length from 40ft to 60ft according to the ruling speeds of the trains. The top, or contact-making portion of this was a 4in by 2in inverted T-bar, which was electrically energised if the distant signal was clear, but dead when the signal was at caution.

The fundamental safety feature of the system, however, lay in the plunger of the locomotive equipment, which made contact with the ramp in the track. The ramp was sloped down at each end, but in its central portion was 4in above rail level. The plunger normally stood 2½in above rail level, but it was spring-loaded downwards, and when passing over a ramp it was raised 1½in. The important feature was that the plunger was raised every time the locomotive passed over a ramp, irrespective of whether the ramp was energised or not.

An apparatus box containing the audible signalling equipment was fixed in the driver's cab. The lifting of the plunger when passing over a ramp caused a small air valve to be opened, and on a dead ramp this would sound the warning siren; but if the ramp was energised and electric current was picked up by the plunger, electromagnets in the engine-cab apparatus box would be energised, closing the air valve and blocking the admission of air to the siren, and instead ringing a bell while the plunger remained in contact with the ramp. There were thus not only two highly distinctive audible signals – a bell for all clear and a siren for warning; but there was

Train staff ticket from the Ashburton branch on which the staff and ticket system was used between Buckfastleigh and Ashburton.

141

A Track Circuiting Innovation

Railway signalling history was made at Royal Oak, just outside Paddington, in 1925, with the installation of the first ever direct current track circuit to be fed from an alternating current supply through a metal rectifier of the copper oxide type. At that time the Union Switch and Signal Company, of Swissvale, USA had a substantial financial interest in the Westinghouse Brake and Saxby Signal Company. Interchange of information was frequent, with many goings and comings of senior personnel. On one such occasion an English engineer learned of the discovery, by an American research chemist, of the rectifying effect of the junction between a copper oxide film on a copper base. Current would flow one way through such a junction but not the other. Although no steps had been taken in the USA to exploit this discovery the Englishman, Major L. H. Peter, realised its immense potential value; he quickly arranged for world-wide patent rights to be assigned to Westinghouse, and its very first application, anywhere in the world, was on the GWR, at Royal Oak, in July 1925. For nine months it remained the only track circuit thus fed; but thirteen more were installed at Plymouth in the following March, and it thereafter became the standard system of track fed on the GWR.

the overriding safety feature that if through a faulty contact current was not picked up, the warning signal would be given in the cab. The apparatus was very soundly designed in the Locomotive Works at Swindon, and in the Signal Works at Reading, and gave very reliable service.

While originally designed purely as an audible cab signal, to assist the working of trains in foggy weather, it was soon realised that the principle could readily be extended to a form of automatic train control, by arranging that the air valve, when opened, not only admitted air to the siren but also to the brakepipe, so that if no action was taken the train would be stopped. But here a psychological as well as a practical point emerged. The distant is a warning signal, and the GWR audible apparatus was intended to ensure that the driver observed it whether in bad visibility or not. When the brake control was added the original requirement that every audible signal must be acknowledged became even more important. Originally the driver simply silenced the siren; but with the brake control added, if the siren were not acknowledged the train brakes would be applied, and this should occur only in an emergency.

The first full description of the Great Western system, with working drawings, was published in a paper read before the Institution of Mechanical Engineers by W. A. Stanier in December 1914 when he was Assistant Manager of the Locomotive Works at Swindon. At the time 180 miles of track and 90 locomotives had been equipped. Extension of the system continued after the first world war, and by September 1931 no fewer than 2,130 route-miles were equipped. When Government funds were made available for schemes to relieve unemployment during the early 1930s the Great Western allocated part of its allotment to completing the ATC system over its entire main line network. Manufacture of the locomotive equipment to cover the entire stock, up to 3,000 units, had to be placed with signalling contractors to ensure delivery in the time required.

Engineering and operational development on the British railways was sometimes bedevilled by a parochial outlook, with the result that the GWR system of audible cab signalling and its associated automatic train control were not regarded with much favour by certain other administrations. And some manufacturing companies with strong Transatlantic business associations continued to advocate systems that involved continuous rather than the intermittent control the Great Western had standardised. The unfortunate accident at Shrivenham, referred to earlier, was quoted as an example of a situation in which intermittent ATC was no good.

Then towards the end of December 1937 there came a terrible accident on the LNER at Castlecary in Scotland, in blizzard conditions of almost nil visibility. During the subsequent enquiries a number of references were made to the GWR system of automatic train control, which it was considered would have prevented the accident. On Sunday 22 March 1938, with a number of LNER officers as guests, a special run was made from Paddington to Reading to demonstrate the working of the system,

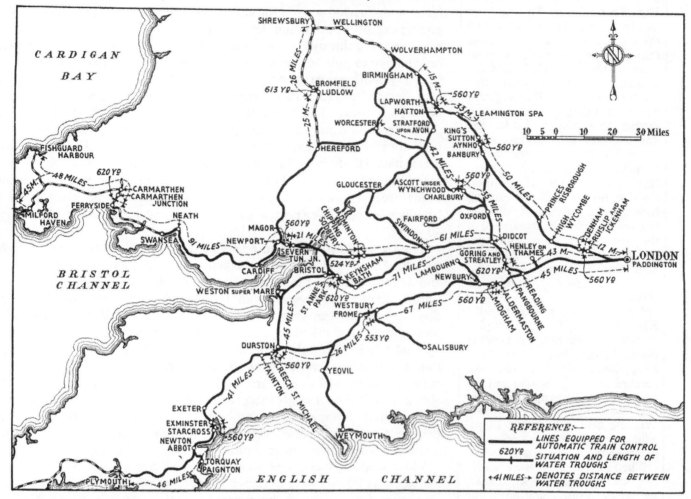

Map of GWR lines equipped with automatic train control, and the position of water troughs in the 1930s.

and to allow the visitors, taking it in turns, to observe the functioning of the equipment from the footplate of the locomotive. For test purposes a 10-coach train of 300 tons was made up, and hauled by one of the then latest Castle class engines No 5055 *Earl of Eldon*. From the operating viewpoint the most significant of the tests was one made on the down journey approaching Maidenhead, where the distant signal was kept at caution and the driver was instructed to ignore it and continue at full speed. An extraordinary mistake was made in the very full report published in *The Railway Gazette*, in which the speed on passing the distant signal was given as 59mph. It was actually 69mph and made the subsequent deceleration all the more impressive. On passing the signal the siren began to sound, but no acknowledgement was made, and with full steam still on the train was brought to a dead stand in 900yd, all on dead level track. The ramp was 318yd ahead of the distant signal, and as that signal was 1,032yd ahead of the home signal the train was stopped 450yd short of the danger point – a very impressive demonstration, and significant of the safety with which operation on the Great Western Railway was conducted.

But the GWR pioneered other signalling developments too. There was a

High Speed Bridge Testing

One of the schemes undertaken by the GWR under the Government scheme for the relief of unemployment in the early 1930s was the quadrupling of the main line southwards from Birmingham, which until then had extended no further than Olton. Under the improvement scheme two additional running lines were to be provided for a further 7¾ miles, as far as Lapworth. On the new lines, built to the west of the existing lines, there were six double-tracked underline bridges, each of the plate girder 'through' type, and arrangements were made for all of them to be given a live-load test in a single day, Sunday 25 March 1934.

6001 *King Edward VII* and 6014 *King Henry VII* were coupled together and running light, while No 6017 *King Edward IV* and 6005 *King George II* had the two coaches. At first, the two pairs of locomotives, keeping exactly in line, were steamed very slowly over the bridge, at about 2mph, while engineers took measurements of the resulting deflections.

The few spectators were hardly prepared for what happened next, for on the word being given the four locomotives were immediately opened out to nearly full power, and started away in a tremendous acceleration. As the speed rose they were little eased, and to the accompaniment of a terrific and increasing roar from the four exhausts they bore down upon the bridge. It was noted that when starting away the pair running light drew slightly ahead of the other two at first, but the driving was superbly managed for the crews had been instructed to keep together and when approaching the bridge and reaching the stipulated test speed of 60mph the two leading locomotives were exactly in line (*right*). It was the railway spectacle of a lifetime.

trend in the period around the end of the first world war to reduce to a far greater extent the amount of lever pulling a signalman had to do by use of route working throughout; in other words the ideal was aimed at of a man only having to pull one lever to set up an entire route. Practical details of such a system were worked out between L.M.G. Ferreira of the signalling firm Siemens and R. J. Insell, then Assistant Signal Engineer of the Great Western Railway. The system was first installed at Winchester Chesil, on the Didcot, Newbury & Southampton line; and having been thoroughly tried out at this small and not very busy station, the Insell-Ferreira system was installed in the late 1920s at Newport (Monmouth) on the South Wales main line of the Great Western. This form of route working, using miniature levers, was destined to be the only one of its kind; although very heavily worked at Newport, it gave excellent service and lasted for nearly 40 years.

The Great Western put into service large installations of colour-light signalling in connection with the station reconstructions at Paddington and as far down the main line as Southall, Bristol Temple Meads, and Cardiff. In all cases the searchlight type of signal was used, but while these three large areas were completely track-circuited and fully equipped with power-worked points, the system of signalling remained essentially that of manual block, while the aspects displayed were the same as the *night* indications of semaphore signals. So far as drivers were concerned no new code of aspects had to be learned. Two searchlight units, one vertically above the other on a single mast, were simply a stop and distant signal in combination. None of the searchlight mechanisms included more than two positions, and in the instance just mentioned the upper unit would display either green or red as required, and the lower one green, or yellow.

Block working was in operation between all signalboxes, and the power interlocking frames were designed to incorporate on their facia boards, a miniature form of block instrument. At that stage in Great Western history it was clear that there was no trend towards multi-aspect colour-light signalling as used on the other three group companies and particularly on the Southern from the mid 1920s. That was a development not seen on GWR routes until British Railways days from the late 1950s onwards as part of major signalling modernisation schemes.

13

PUBLICITY

Few British organisations have conducted their publicity so successfully, and made so much money even out of the direct sales of publicity material to the public, as the Great Western Railway. Not one produced so much material that was to become collectors' pieces in later generations. The story is astonishing, especially when placed against the background of the slow development of commercial publicity generally before the 1930s.

The GWR had been publicity conscious from the start. Timetables were well publicised in the Press and at stations, and the publication of guides to the railway and its scenery by commercial publishers was firmly encouraged. Several guides appeared even in the early years, the most famous being *Bourne's*. An advertising agency was used fairly early in history, mainly for announcements of 'Tourist Arrangements', but dropped to save money around 1870. Thereafter the creation of such material was pretty haphazard until 1886 when a small advertising

An evocative 1930s poster showing a late but unnamed King with the Riviera stock. It could be seen on advertising boards all over the company's system.

SPEED TO THE WEST
CORNWALL DEVON SOMERSET WALES

department was formed in the General Manager's office, soon to be transferred to the traffic side under the Superintendent of the Line. Its work was more notable for quantity than quality.

Enthusiasm for publicity grew in the 1890s when the fortunes of the railway itself were in the ascendancy. But it was the decade before the outbreak of war in 1914 that produced truly remarkable activity. In 1904, for example, the railway took the then most unusual step of addressing its customers through a whole page illustrated advertisement in the *Daily Mail*. 'Old shareholders must have rubbed their eyes with astonishment at the sight of such a show of enterprise', said a financial journal, but more such surprises were in store. 1904 was also the year that the first Great Western book reached the bookstalls: *The Cornish Riviera Express*, its white card cover also bearing the GWR coat of arms in gold. It deserved its instant success. Though costing only threepence, (the old 3d – little more than today's 1p), it was well-written, by A. M. Broadley, a prolific topographical author (who was not acknowledged on the title page). It was even better designed, setting standards that were immediately recognised as revolutionary in commercial publicity. A quarter of a million copies were sold of the first edition and four more followed.

Two years later came the first issue of the most important single publicity item, *Holiday Haunts*, containing hundreds of advertisements of accommodation plus illustrations and editorial. One of the railway's own advertisements announced the opening of the shorter Castle Cary route to the South West. This first issue also made first use of the slogan 'The Holiday Line' invented by a South Wales artist.

Other events before the first world war include the appearance of the first of the 'Engine' books, but all this was a dress rehearsal of what was to follow in the 1920s. While Britain's other railways were developing new identities under their larger Grouping, the Great Western restored its chocolate-and-cream livery and combined the appeals of permanency and nostalgia with fast innovation. 'Go Great Western' was everywhere, newspaper advertisements and quasi editorial features, the 'GWR series of travel books', *Holiday Haunts*, posters and soon even jig-saw puzzles, children's painting books, postcards and much more boosting that irresistible combination of a solid 4-6-0 green locomotive with tapering boiler hauling a spotless chocolate-and-cream train through beautiful countryside or beside the sea. Glorious Devon and the Cornish Riviera were both GWR inventions, maps showing a similarity in the shape of Italy and Cornwall being used to boost the Royal Duchy's attractions as a mild winter resort.

In the West Country and in Wales, the railway keenly co-operated with resorts wishing to tell the world of their attractions. Substantial contributions were made to Press advertisements if they mentioned the GWR's services, and liaison at local level was surprisingly strong and effective. When Newquay became Cornwall's premier resort and perhaps the fastest-expanding holiday town in the whole country, the publicity committee acknowledged that it would not have been possible without the GWR. And Paddington realised that it would not have been able to keep

An 1898 handout describing cheap weekend bookings and half day excursions.

its head as high as it did during the difficult inter-war years without the massive sales generated by publicity.

Publicity was taken seriously in every way. Even inkwells told you to 'Go Great Western'. The Great Western Whisky, a special blend bottled at the Great Western Royal Hotel, and the use of popular authors for GW touring books had a common purpose. Lantern lectures, films available for free hire, competitions in newspapers and magazines, special restaurant car menus, luggage labels for the Shakespeare Express and – after years of conflicting styles – a steady introduction of higher typographical standards from around 1922 (Winchester Bold became the standard for posters and the similar Cheltenham type for general purposes) . . . it all counted. The scale of operations was enormous, the stationery department stocks of books and other publicity material often being greater than those of famous book publishers of the day, while at least half a dozen printers claimed that they specialised in railway work with the GWR as their main customer. In the 1930s there were something like 25,000 cheap trips and excursions each year, announced by notices in around 250 newspapers, 250,000 full-size posters and many million handbills. Every compartment of every carriage had its complement of photographs of beauty spots on the system, generations of travellers immediately checking on entering a train how many of those in their compartment they had yet visited; and thousands of the photographs were sold at a shilling a time for framing.

In 1924 the advertising department, still in the Superintendent of the Line's office, became a fully-fledged publicity department still under him. Felix Pole was then in command; his earlier editorship of the *Great Western Magazine* had, as we will note anon, helped bring him to power, and he was ever ready to acknowledge the importance of publicity. He made a number of inspired appointments, notably that of William Henry Fraser, who became the first publicity head. Fraser was a GWR man through and through, having been with the railway since 1892 and as well as having charm, drive and integrity was bubbling with new ideas. He was also

Penny a Mile. The front page of a leaflet extolling the virtues of monthly return tickets in the 1930s. This was one of the many give-away leaflets always available in station booking offices.

The front cover and an inside page from a fascinating 1920s leaflet in connection with the new GWR paperback book The 10.30 Limited. *Like most of the Great Western literature aimed at youth it was an educational as well as a promotional exercise. One would like to have seen the winning 500 word essay.*

River-Keeping for the Great Western Railway

Of the multifarious jobs connected with the running of a railway none seems more remote and completely incongruous than that of river keeper; yet the Great Western Railway has need of such an employee. Strange and unusual occupations of certain members of the staff excite comment from time to time, but comparatively few people are aware of the Company's interest in a Welsh river and the consequent need for a water bailiff, or river keeper, as he is officially termed.

In catering for the needs of a public with a wide diversity of interests and tastes, the Great Western Railway has acquired the exclusive fishing rights over eight miles of the Western Cleddau River in North Pembrokeshire, and to this fast-running mountain stream come enthusiastic anglers from all parts of Britain.

The Cleddau passes through some of the most picturesque and unspoilt scenery in the country, flowing swiftly through belts of pine and oak trees, open meadowlands, and reedy curlew-haunted moors. The Company's rights begin at Pont-y-Duan near Mathry Road station and extend as far as Wolf's Castle Halt. The river is stocked with speckled brown trout, and the stream is fortunately free from pike and roach.

A river, contrary to popular belief, needs a good deal of attention and the river keeper is a busy man. Although his duties might appear to be merely the apprehension of poachers and the prevention of infringement of the Company's rights, there is actually much more to do than that. River-keeping is a job which demands very early training and acclimatization. Usually such a calling runs in families, handed down from father to son.

From the *Great Western Railway Magazine*, September 1937

fortunate in his boss, for no top manager could have been more open to suggestions than Pole. Later Pole also appointed a former news editor of *The Times*, George E. Beer, as publicity consultant. The spirit of pragmatic enterprise is perhaps illustrated by the fact that when Beer moved on to the *Daily Mail*, he offered the GWR a book on cathedrals, which was not merely accepted but produced to a remarkably high standard.

Though the whole publicity machine got results, it was undoubtedly the books and other printed material that was so specially Great Western. In his *Go Great Western: A History of GWR Publicity*, Roger Burnett Wilson lists 132 'sale publications' including new editions. Not only is the list formidable but varied. A. M. Broadley's pioneer *The Cornish Riviera Express* was followed by a sheaf of other topographical works on all parts of the system, including Southern Ireland and Brittany served by GWR ships. *North Wales: The British Tyrol, The Cathedral Line of England: Its Sacred Sites and Shrines* and *Rural London: The Chalfont Country and the Thames Valley* all enjoyed several large editions.

The first Engine book of 1911, *Names of Engines*, was followed by 16 variations down to the fourth edition of *GWR Engines: Names, Numbers, Types & Classes* under the authorship of W. G. C. Chapman just before nationalisation in 1946. It was one of the most popular railway publications of all times, an omnibus collection still being offered by the publisher of this work. Chapman was also author of the famous 'For Boys of All Ages' series. Here was another example of the railway able to capitalise on the enthusiasm of native talent. Joining the service in 1896, Chapman was a keen youngster in the general manager's office when he took a course in the railway department of the London School of Economics and was awarded one of the first three I. K. Brunel Medals for performance. The first of the 'Boys of All Ages' titles, *The 10.30 Limited*, an outstanding bargain at a shilling (5p), sold 71,000 copies in six months. *Cheltenham Flyer, Track Topics*, and *Locos of the Royal Road* were not only outstandingly successful in their day but continue to be collected and referred to; their tone may be a touch patronising, but they are a store house of information and illustration.

Greater variety was yet to come. Top-ranking topographical writers of their day did some of their best work for the Great Western, S. P. B. Mais on *The Cornish Riviera* and *Glorious Devon*, A. G. Bradley on *Pembrokeshire and South West Wales*, Maxwell Fraser on *Southern Ireland*, and W. Heath Robinson on a lighthearted centenary *Railway Ribaldry* in 1935. Curiously the only other centenary publication (though there was a film and much else) was a reprint in book form of a supplement of *The Times* for which a wide range of authors and journalists wrote signed articles. One was E. T. MacDermot, whose two-volume *History of the Great Western Railway* had been published by the GWR in 1927 and 1931. Just as no other railway had issued details of its locomotives in book form before the first Engine book of 1911, this broke entirely new ground and commanded a respectful audience among Great Western men themselves, railway enthusiasts and even professional historians. No other company

Tyseley shed 1967. This painting by Terence Cuneo shows the interior of a typical GWR roundhouse – sadly at the end of its days. Inside are the two preserved Castles Nos 4079 Pendennis Castle and 7029 Clun Castle together with 0-6-0 pannier tank No 1638. The painting was executed to recapture the atmosphere of a Great Western shed before it was too late and while it was also possible to get the two Castles together. No 7029 is still in Birmingham, No 1638 is on the Dart Valley Railway and No 4079 has been sold out of the country to Australia.

Overleaf:
Swindon 1974. Out of step as usual, the Western's internal combustion express locomotives were diesel hydraulics in the form of Hymeks, Warships and Westerns. Here, in A shop, they have come to their last rest and are being stripped of useful parts before scrapping.

Bath 1966. A down Paddington to Weston-Super-Mare express leaves behind a Western class diesel hydraulic in its then new blue livery.

Sonning Cutting 1981. An Inter-City 125 HST unit heads towards London. These units have transformed the South Wales and West of England routes with fast frequent services.

A luggage label issued to passengers on The Cheltenham Flyer; the Paddington Publicity Department did not miss a trick.

Jigsaw Puzzles. Made by the well-known toy firm of Chad Valley these coloured wooden jigsaws of 150 pieces retailed all over the Great Western system at 2s 6d (12½p). In the early days some (such as Oxford illustrated in the centre) were black and white. The other three here are The Cheltenham Flyer, Warwick Castle and The Night Mail

Britain's Riviera for Health and Sunshine. The Great Western always pressed the case for British holidays and its posters often compared the Cornish Riviera with the Italian Riviera as here.

history perhaps anywhere in the world has been so read and commented upon – and its original research so used by later writers.

Books for walkers and anglers, for those who enjoyed exploring North Wales by mountain railways, and innumerable souvenir booklets, some commemorating exhibitions, also poured forth from the presses. From the 1930s, many contained the famous folding map printed in red of the company's system and its ramifications, which is reproduced also as part of the present work. One wonders what new titles would have come had it not been for nationalisation, since innovation was active until the end, postwar publications including *Dunkirk and the Great Western* and Christian Barman's *Next Station*, surveying the railway's hopes and aspirations, and, for instance, containing fascinating details of hotel purchases and holiday camp plans.

But though all these publications kept the estimators, progress chasers, packers and invoicers at the stationery department busy, the real pressure came when the annual edition of *Holiday Haunts* arrived each Easter. As already stated, this was launched in 1904, and though it contained descriptions and illustrations of the holiday areas and a map of the system, its main value lay in the advertisements and lists of accommodation. Said the introduction to the 1906 issue: 'The object of this little volume is to impart to holiday-makers of all classes, noble and simple, rich and poor, strong and weak – such information as will enable them to secure a maximum of change, rest, pleasure or sport at a minimum of expenditure and fatigue'. The volume did not remain so small. The 1934 edition, for instance, totalled 1054 pages; by 1928 sales were 200,000 copies. It was big business in itself, though its object was really to attract passengers to the holiday lines. Stationmasters were expected to canvass for advertisements, and such was its pulling power that some small hotels and boarding houses found that they did not need to advertise elsewhere. Photographs came from the engineering department whose cameramen were expected to capture the scenic beauties of Great Western land as well as bridges and engine sheds. The covers were colourful, sometimes *avant-garde*. The title page however remained unchanged for two decades down to 1931. The sale publications, 'The Holiday Books of The Holiday Line', were of course extensively advertised, along with the jig-saw puzzles and restaurant car meals.

Finally, but by no means least, there was *The Great Western Magazine*, a cut above anything published by other railways. Ignoring an earlier unsuccessful venture of a more literary type, the magazine began in 1888 as the tool of the GWR Temperance Union, and though it included details of the company's traffic receipts and occasional articles on aspects of the GWR, most space was devoted to staff appointments and news of the Temperance Union and the growing number of welfare organisations attached to the company. After taking over two of the GWR Coffee Tavern Company's branches that were losing money, the Temperance Union itself got into difficulties, and to help pay off its debt, the company bought the magazine for £750. Felix Pole, still a junior in the chief engineer's office, saw the editorship as a chance to make his way and in August 1903

Hunting Country
Every care must be taken to avoid running over Packs of Hounds which, during the Hunting Season, may cross the line. All Railway Servants are hereby enjoined to use every care consistent with a due regard being paid to the proper working of the Line and Trains. From the *Great Western Railway Service Time Tables*.

153

got himself moved to the general manager's office at a salary of £50. The editorship was, however, only part of his workload in an era demanding high output.

Next year he published the first of a series of lists of locomotive names and numbers, and up went the circulation, quickly reaching 20,000. Then followed a long and distinguished editorship under Edward S. Hadley, who not merely enhanced the editorial content but used the magazine to promote an effective 'Is It Safe?' campaign later adopted by the other railways. Felix Pole edited the magazine for 15 years, and its success helped get Pole the post of assistant general manager at the then early age of 42.

For most of its history the price of the ordinary edition remained at a penny, which meant that for a shilling a year the readers were receiving between 400 and 600 pages including much inside information on the operation of the railway. By 1937 the circulation topped 44,000, but with a much greater readership since one copy might be read by many staff, and even a copy ordered by a member of the public would be read in the booking office first, though if you wanted the cover afforded by the insurance edition at an extra penny an issue, you of course had to have your own copy.

The last issue, in December 1947, carried an advertisement for back issues to 1888 and a poem 'Goodbye, Great Western' which ended:

Alas! the curtain falls, the lights are low:
Pride of Brunel, now it is time to go;
But when the old days are dim, when we have gone,
May all thy grand traditions still live on.

In lighter vein. The foreword and a cartoon from Railway Ribaldry, *a unique railway publication by the GWR and one which actually laughs at itself.*

INGENIOUS PLAN FOR FIXING THE APPROXIMATE TIMES FOR TRAINS TO COVER THE REQUIRED DISTANCES, USED SUCCESSFULLY IN THE COMPILATION OF THE FIRST TIME-TABLE

FOREWORD
—

THE GREAT WESTERN RAILWAY celebrates its one hundredth birthday this year, but unlike other centenarians such as trees and turtles, grows more youthful after a century of existence.

The Company, serious in its determination to maintain the enviable reputation that it has acquired in the past, is, as will be seen in the pages that follow, not without a sense of humour in giving Mr. W. Heath Robinson a free hand to apply his skill to the portrayal of certain events in its history.

Occasional excursions in a lighter vein help us to take life a little less seriously than we are generally called upon to do. It is hoped therefore that this contribution to the library of humour will be appreciated by our patrons, present and to be.

G.W.R.
May, 1935

The Great Western Railway on Film

It has always been a source of some surprise that the Great Western Railway never had a film unit. Considering the high quality of GWR publicity during the 1930s and the extent to which it was concerned with its public image, it would have seemed a most logical step in an age when the Gas Council, the Post Office, Shell, ICI, the Grand Union Canal and many smaller organisations were deeply committed to the making of in-house films for public exhibition, clubs, societies and what in those days was called the 'non-theatrical market'. The LMS made over 150 films between 1933 and 1939. The Southern was slow off the mark but started its film unit in 1938. The LNER and the GWR stood aloof. In the case of the LNER, we know that Sir Nigel Gresley was not keen on the 'cinematograph' ever since a feature film in 1929 showed that the Flying Scotsman train was apparently not fitted with the continuous vacuum brake and broke into two parts both of which gaily rolled on down the track! In the case of the GWR, it seems that Sir Felix Pole and his contemporaries came to the conclusion that it was better (and cheaper) to get other people to make the films or offer their services to film companies in exchange for publicity.

Indeed, this had been the approach in pre-grouping days when films made 'through the courtesy of the Midland/London and North Western/South Eastern and Chatham Railway Company' abounded. It was under just such circumstances that the first film record of the Great Western came to light a few years ago. A film appeared in the National Film Archive catalogue entitled 'Building a Locomotive at Crewe'. It was described as being 'courtesy of the London and North Western Railway' but in a footnote, none less than Sir Arthur Elton commented:

'Under Film No 461, recording the building of a locomotive at Crewe, there is a scene of the initials 'G.W.' being transferred to the tender. How could any cataloguer, save a loco-spotter, know that the initials 'G.W.' belong to Swindon, and that this shot must have been interpolated in error?'

Unfortunately, Sir Arthur, usually meticulous in these matters, had not actually looked at the film itself or he would have discovered that it was not only the cataloguers who were wrong but himself. The film was a print of *Building the Locomotive* PRINCE OF WALES *No 4041 of the Star Class at Swindon*, produced by the Kineto Film Company 'by courtesy of the Great Western Railway Company'. Made in 1913, it is an excellent record of the great plant as it was in Churchward's day.

Meanwhile, the GWR began to specialise in letting out its services to feature film companies in exchange for publicity. A famous lost film was the original sound version of *The Ghost Train* of 1936, with Jack Hulbert and Cicely Courtneidge; the negative disintegrated in a vault at Pinewood Studios and was discovered too late to salvage a single foot. It used the Limpley Stoke-Camerton line, with one of William Dean's standard 0-6-0 goods engines, No 2381, painted white for ghostly effects! The crash on the swing bridge was done partly at Barmouth and partly with a Gauge O 0-6-0 at Shepherds Bush Studios. The station of Fal Vale in the story was provided by Camerton. Interestingly, the same line was used again with Jack Hulbert for making *Kate Plus Ten* in 1937 with GWR mixed traffic Churchward 2-6-0 No 4364 doing most of the work. In this case scenes were also shot at Brentford Docks (with Churchward's own saloon) and on the line from Westbury to Bath. The Limpley Stoke-Camerton branch had a final fling with the making of *The Titfield Thunderbolt* in 1952, now into British Rail days, but using GWR 1400 class locomotives as well as the famous Liverpool & Manchester *Lion*.

On all these films, the GWR got special credit for its help; a typical title was that on the front of *The Last Journey* in 1936:

'Twickenham Film Studios desire to express their grateful thanks to the Great Western Railway Company for the facilities which they have courteously extended to them in connection with the filming of "The Last Journey".' It included photographic runs from Paddington to Plymouth (Millbay Docks) behind Castles and complete occupation of the Reading–Basingstoke line for two Sundays from 9.30am to 8pm; a spectacular near-collision was staged in the vicinity of Bramley signal box.

Despite the free publicity from films produced by other people there was an exception for the celebration of its Centenary in 1935 when the GWR decided to commission a film and pay for it itself. A complete Maidenhead Station was built on a bit of waste ground at Swindon and *North Star*, with replica coaches, was propelled forward by an unseen early diesel shunter; this was to show the opening of the Paddington–Maidenhead line in 1838. The breakthrough on the Severn Tunnel was filmed in a tin shed at Blackheath (which is exactly what it looks like!); the main parts were played by professionals but the crowd and small parts were taken by members of the Great Western Railway Amateur Operatic and Dramatic Society (which is also exactly what it looks like!). The film was never released. It was given a certificate and registered with the Board of Trade for circulation but then a private viewing was requested by the GWR directors at Paddington. No one knows what happened. There was supposed to be a disagreement about what the Chairman had said at the end on the future of the GWR. Whatever the cause, the film was quietly dropped. It was never seen in cinemas as had been intended and the negative was finally discovered some years ago in the wine vaults of the Marylebone Hotel when British Transport took over.   John Huntley

155

14
PIONEERS OF
TRANSPORT

When the first commercially viable maglev vehicle speeds along its track it will be time to think more kindly of J. D'A Samuda and his atmospheric system of propulsion without adhesion between wheel and rail. Brunel was sufficiently impressed to install the system on the South Devon Railway, where the experiment proved costly and unrewarding. The idea was in advance of the technology and materials available at the time.

The Great Western Railway was more successful in enlisting the road motor vehicle as an ally. It was not the first railway to do so, having been preceded in 1903 by the Lynton & Barnstaple, but when the L&B wished to dispose of its two Milnes-Daimler 'motor wagonettes', which were frightening the local horses and agitating the police by exceeding 8mph, the Great Western bought them. Apparently the horses in Cornwall were made of sterner stuff, for the Great Western road service between Helston and The Lizard inaugurated on 17 August 1903 was the forerunner of many others and established the Great Western as the first of the major railways in this field.

The Helston-Lizard route was in lieu of a light railway which the GWR was being urged to build, but which it was unwilling to undertake without testing the traffic potential. Other services were introduced similarly as test cases and were usually found to meet local needs without the heavy expense of railway building.

After Helston-Lizard came Penzance–Newlyn–Marazion on 31 October 1903, and in the following year the railway prepared for road operations on a larger scale by ordering 30 Milnes-Daimler vehicles. The GWR was active in opening routes throughout its territory which served both as feeders to the trains and for general local transport. Shortly before the first world war some 31 GWR services were working, employing about 112 vehicles. After some contraction in the war years the road service network was expanded rapidly again. The company had no special powers for these operations but having been so early in the field was never challenged. By the time railway road activities were put on a more formal footing in 1928 the GWR was working 168 bus services and had 300 buses on the roads.

From 1928 direct railway operation of buses declined, for the new road transport legislation allowed the railways to have large (but not controlling) shareholdings in the major provincial bus companies and to make co-ordinating arrangements with them. In the case of the Great Western there were financial links with Western National, Thames Valley, Western Welsh and Midland Red bus companies, among others.

156

An interest in bus operations did not offset the effect of loss of traffic to the roads on some railway services. When the Associated Equipment Company (AEC) proposed a diesel railcar for secondary and branch lines, the GWR, long a firm believer in steam auto-trains, took up the suggestion. On 4 December 1933 the first of the railway's streamlined diesel cars began operating a range of local services from its base at Southall depot. Its duties in the area between Slough, Reading and Didcot included trips on the Windsor and Henley branches. The 69-seater car had

Road vehicles like this were, however, used exclusively to take goods to and from the nearest station. Judging by the expression on the driver's face, the responsibility must have borne heavily and journey's end with a full load been reached with relief.

The Great Western streamlined railcars were introduced in December 1933. They were diesel mechanical vehicles, designed for cross-country express services up to 80mph. No 15, had twin engines each of 121 brake horse power; it is seen here passsing Stapleton Road, Bristol on a Bristol–Cardiff working.

The last four diesel railcars built for the Great Western were designed as two pairs of twin units with a driving compartment at one end of each vehicle; they were built with a view to replacing earlier single railcars on the Birmingham to Cardiff service. A buffet counter and lavatory accommodation were included and the set could take a trailer coach in between the driving units. In later days one set worked between Bristol and Weymouth (seen here at Fairwood Junction approaching Westbury) and the other between Reading and Newbury.

a 121hp London bus engine and other mechanical and internal features common to the London buses of the day. The external streamlining was a concession to fashion, top speed being 60mph, although it was claimed to be based on wind tunnel tests.

Satisfied with the performance of the first car, the railway soon ordered three 260hp twin-engined cars with more spacious accommodation (but fewer seats) for cross-country services. The main saloon had 44 one class

seats in facing pairs with tables between them, and there was a small buffet with four seats. These vehicles were put on the Birmingham–Cardiff through service, with a fastest schedule of 142min for the 116¾ miles, which was 34min less than the best previous time. The average speed was a modest 49.3mph but the improvement was considered to justify a supplement of half-a-crown (12.5p) on top of the third class fare, though it was later withdrawn. More cars were built for shorter-distance services, and in 1937 a parcels car geared for hauling a trailing load of up to 60 tons was introduced. All these vehicles were double-ended but shortly before the second world war four single-ended cars went into service, designed for running in pairs back to back or with an ordinary passenger coach between them. The time of these longer formations on the Birmingham–Cardiff run was short, for after the war the traffic on the route called for locomotive-hauled trains and they were transferred to Bristol–Weymouth and Reading–Newbury services. On the eve of nationalisation the Great Western's diesel fleet consisted of 37 units, the later ones having more angled ends instead of the curving streamlining of the original units.

In the same year that the first of the railcars was sent to Southall to help keep the railway flag flying in the face of competition from the road, the Great Western reacted to a new challenge. By the 1920s the Southern Railway was already losing some of its first class Continental traffic to the airlines, and soon the four Groups decided to arm themselves with powers to operate air services. Their Bill received the Royal Assent on 10 May 1929. The first railway to use the new powers was the Great Western. By 1932 several internal air services were being run by independent operators, mainly where a sea or estuary crossing was involved. The Great Western stepped in with a route which by-passed the rail detour from South Wales to the West of England via the Severn Tunnel by hopping straight across the Bristol Channel from Cardiff to Torbay (Haldon, near Teignmouth) and on to Plymouth. Flights began on 12 April 1933 with a Westland Wessex three-engined high-wing monoplane on hire from Imperial Airways, wearing GWR livery. From 22 May they were extended from Cardiff to Birmingham. The service was withdrawn at the end of September. In 1934 railway air operations were resumed by the newly-formed Railway Air Services Ltd which operated routes at the request of the individual companies. The first RAS service was a revival and extension of the pioneer Great Western venture, restored on 7 May 1934 and extended to Liverpool.

From 30 July 1934 RAS worked a joint GWR/SR service between Birmingham, Bristol, Southampton and Cowes. Financial results from air operations were disappointing, and the Southern decided it would do better to 'go it alone' with the Great Western as partner. Great Western & Southern Airlines Ltd was formed on 3 December 1938. The war brought numerous reshuffles, with the Great Western still active in arrangements which by 1943 had given the railways full control of all domestic civil aviation in Great Britain. After the second world war a nationalised British European Airways operated internal air services and railway participation in air services ceased.

Airborne Great Western

The GWR thrived on ritual and its airborne forces had got it off as pat as the railborne. The door would open as the aircraft taxied to a halt and the Haldon mechanic would run in and place a small set of steps at the passenger door. Then the incumbents of the cabin would emerge – the ladies often rather gingerly backwards. Three minutes elapsed; then back they trooped again, the doors were closed and at 4.25 precisely the aircraft would move bumpily across the heather, to reappear in a few moments roaring steadily if slowly upwards, turning to gleam in the sun and head north-eastwards, rapidly assuming the shape of a bumble-bee seen stern-on in the general direction of Wild Wales. Once again the best, and only the best, would do for the Great Western; whereas there were still passenger aircraft flying on foreign and internal routes where the pilot sat alone outside, muffled up in the best Blériot tradition, in the Westland Wessex *he* had an enclosed cabin or "flight deck".

From *More Great Westernry* by T. W. E. Roche

ORGANISATION AND MANAGEMENT

Opposite: Genealogical table showing railways absorbed by the Great Western

From early days the Great Western senior management rested almost exclusively upon four men, Charles Russell, the Chairman, Charles Saunders, Brunel and Gooch. Between them they ran the railway. Saunders in particular had a remarkable assignment, for he combined in his own person the offices later designated as Secretary, Superintendent of the Line, and General Manager. One might have thought he was Accountant as well, but for the fact that the Engineer and the Locomotive Superintendent managed their own accounts – a situation that was to become a major bone of contention in the early years of the 20th century. In 1863 when Saunders retired the immense responsibilities that he had carried, single handed, for nearly 30 years, were split three ways, with each independent of the others and each reporting direct to the Board. Frederick Saunders succeeded his uncle as Secretary; G. N. Tyrrell was made responsible for traffic, with the new title of Superintendent of the Line, while James Grierson was appointed General Manager. This latter, far from signifying the commander-in-chief as it came to do later on most other railways, involved the Parliamentary work, and looking after what could well be described as the remaining odds and ends.

At that time it must be remembered that these newly appointed officers acted only for the original Great Western Railway, and the lines it had absorbed in the West Midlands, the North, and in South Wales. The Bristol & Exeter, and lines west, though closely associated for traffic purposes, were still independent, and at times dangerously so. There was a strong anti-Great Western faction on the Bristol & Exeter Board, with talk in Bristol about the grievous error of adopting the broad gauge in the first place; and with the Midland on the doorstep there were vivid memories of January 1845 and the way Charles Saunders had been out-manoeuvred in the battle for control of the Bristol & Gloucester, and the Gloucester & Birmingham.

In the 1870s the Midland was certainly in a highly expansionist mood, and in other circumstances, sensing the attitude of a strong section of Bristol & Exeter shareholders, it might have swooped, as John Ellis had done in 1845, and with advantageous terms scooped the B&E into the Derby empire. Fortunately for the Great Western, however, the Midland was very committed financially at that time with construction of the Settle & Carlisle line, though the situation around the B&E board table remained extremely volatile. While a preponderance of sympathy still lay on the Great Western side, the General Traffic Manager, J. C. Wall, felt that the nettle should be firmly grasped to eliminate once and for all the undoubted

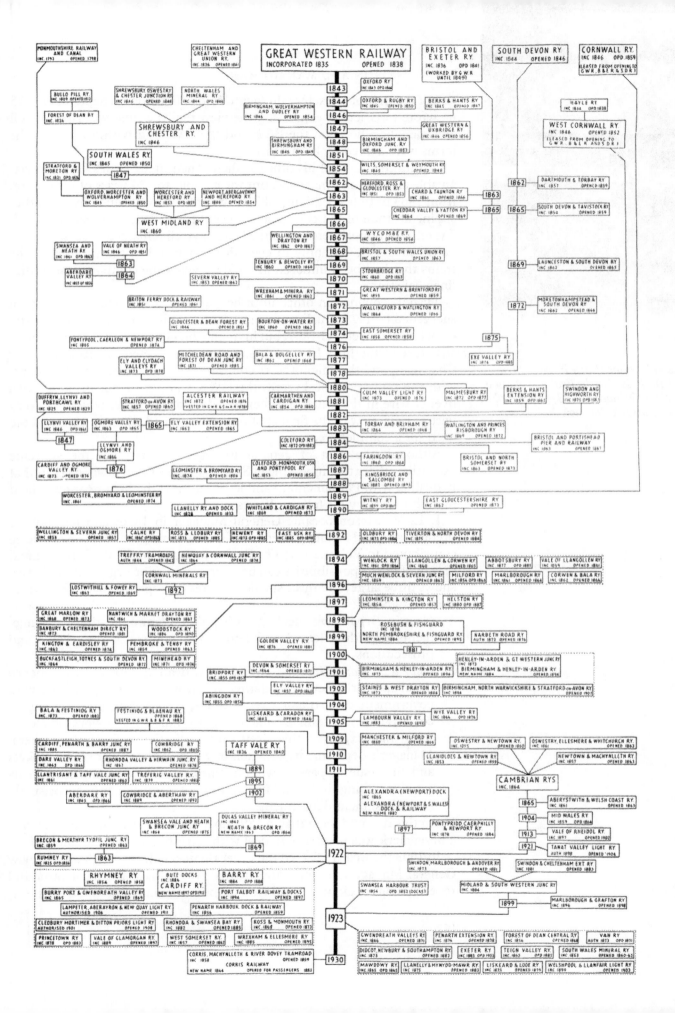

*Let Us Now Praise Famous Men
(a) The End of the Era: nameplate of
No 5069 built in 1938, photographed
at Old Oak Common shed.*

risk of the Bristol & Exeter falling into Midland hands. In September 1875 he wrote to Grierson expressing the view that the time was ripe for full amalgamation between the B&E and the GW, and within a month the terms were agreed by both boards.

Within the limits of his office as then constituted, James Grierson was an able and popular manager, but throughout the 24 years of his tenure, from 1863 until his death in 1887, he was much constrained by the rather supine attitude of the colleague who could have helped so much, G. N. Tyrrell, the Superintendent of the Line. Tyrrell remained obsessed by the policy of drastic economy in everything involved in the running of the trains that had been imposed in the days when the company was in dire financial straits.

Tyrrell remained in office until he was 73 years of age, and was then succeeded by N. J. Burlinson, who had been his assistant for nine years. Gooch died in October 1889, but his going did not change the management structure of the line. Frederick Saunders was elected to succeed him as Chairman, and the chief officers continued to report direct to the Board; with the retirement of Tyrrell, the GWR had got in Burlinson a much livelier wire in the office of Superintendent of the Line, which was very necessary in view of the final abolition of the broad gauge in 1892 and the need for a complete recast of the train services.

Although the post of general manager was not yet the supreme executive officer that it became in Sir Felix Pole's time, it was evident that in dealing with Parliamentary and legal business the incumbent was held in high regard by his fellow officers.

J. L. Wilkinson became General Manager in 1896, and he, like his predecessor, had formerly been Chief Goods Manager. From an article he contributed to Volume 1 of *The Railway Magazine*, in 1897, the limited nature of his responsibilities can be appreciated. The organisational 'tree' shows three large, and three smaller spheres of responsibility. The former were designated:

1 *General Department*, dealing with public communications, arrangements regarding leased and joint lines, compensation, claims and prosecutions.
2 *New Works and Government Enquiries*, dealing with correspondence (legal and parliamentary) relating to new works; correspondence with government departments; registration, distribution and copying of correspondence; train arrangements, irregularities in working etc.
3 *Staff and Expenses*: this dealt only with the staff of the General Manager's department, a section of which looked after season tickets and the issue of passes, while a third main section included in its activities 'filing, indexing, distribution of minutes', and, surprisingly the refreshment department.

From this it would seem that in 1897 no more exalted a staff member than a filing clerk was necessary to deal with refreshments on the railway!

In 1903 the Board selected the Chief Engineer, James Inglis, as the new General Manager, an appointment that was to have the most profound repercussions. Taking a broad view of the situation on the Great Western,

162

while he could have appreciated the autonomy he had enjoyed as Chief Engineer, its disadvantages became apparent when viewed from the chair of the General Manager, particularly in that there was no financial control. This was the more important, seeing that his previous department and that of the Locomotive, Carriage & Wagon Superintendent were easily the biggest spenders on the railway – and necessarily so. Moreover, the level of expenditure was constantly rising. Inglis was becoming painfully aware of all this, but could not penetrate the iron curtain that surrounded the finances of the engineering departments, and he became convinced that the only way to break through was to change the top-level organisation to something like that of the London & North Western, or the Midland, having the general manager as the executive 'commander in chief!' At one stage, by some back-stage manoeuvres, Inglis secured some comparative costs of building 4-6-0 passenger locomotives at Crewe and Swindon, and asked Churchward across the Board table why his engines cost so much more. The reply, so one gathered, was in language more suited to the workshop floor than to the board room! The situation had not been resolved when Viscount Churchill succeeded Alfred Baldwin as Chairman, but eventually a majority of the Board passed the scheme, and Lord Churchill signed copies of the new organisational tree, to be issued to all the chief officers concerned. But Inglis never sent them out. The strain of the contest had told heavily upon his health, and in 1911 he died.

The management structure of the Great Western Railway remained unchanged for another 11 years. Then came Felix J. C. Pole. That forthright, very determined, and still relatively young man had been in the general manager's office all through the troubles of 15 years previously, and was fully aware of all that had transpired.

As a great admirer of Inglis, Pole was convinced that the organisation he had· proposed was the right one for the future. From 1921, with a management team led and virtually dominated by Sir Felix Pole, as he had become in 1924, the GWR entered upon one of the most dynamic periods in its entire history, with an organisational structure exactly as planned by Inglis in the early 1900s. It was able to weather smoothly and effectively what could have been a very difficult time with the amalgamations with the local Welsh railways, and to achieve a notable degree of coordination among what had previously been warring interests. The Great Western was fortunate in not having to endure the strains of major amalgamation occasioned elsewhere by the Grouping scheme, and was favoured – remarkably for any British railway – in receiving the commendation of a friendly, and at times even enthusiastic Press! For this, much was due to the energy and enterprise of Sir Felix Pole, who, as he once said, was the first *real* General Manager of the Great Western Railway.

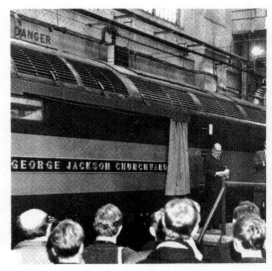

(b) New Day Dawns: Brush 2750hp diesel George Jackson Churchward *is named at Swindon works.*

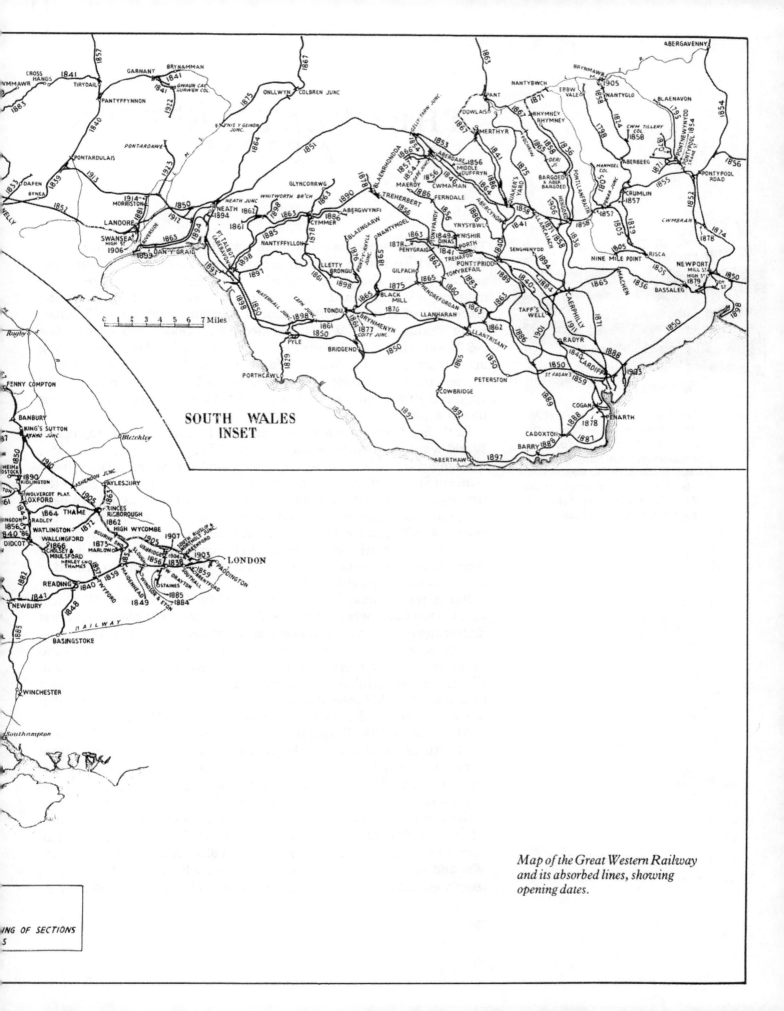

Map of the Great Western Railway
and its absorbed lines, showing
opening dates.

SOUTH WALES
INSET

0 1 2 3 4 5 6 7 Miles

16
THE GREAT WESTERN AT WAR

Dean Goods No 167 (ex GWR No 2463) at Algiers in 1943 during the second world war. Behind are briquettes specially shipped out from South Wales as fuel at the conclusion of the North African campaign. No 167 with her sisters was later sent to Italy; they never came home.

Together with other main line companies the GWR was hard pressed during both world wars, not only in the movement of evacuees, munitions and troops but also in the provision of locomotives and ships to the military: in World War II Great Western seamen played their part in the evacuation of Dunkirk with honour. Locomotives sent to the Western Front during World War I included Dean Goods and 43XX class 2-6-0s with a few of the former finding their way to Salonika (some ending up in Turkey); in the Second World War the Dean Goods went even further, to such far flung areas of combat as France, North Africa and Italy. A few even ended up in China as part of United Nations Relief, their ultimate fate.

Little has been written of the exploits of Great Western engines in World War I, but two stories are worth the telling. On one frightful night, 25 March 1918, when the Germans were bombing the important railway centre of St Pol, a train of troops was setting out with leave at the end of the journey. With the situation becoming serious the train was ordered back as all leave was cancelled, and on its return to the depot at Tachincourt the engine (43XX class No 5325) was hit and the tender badly holed, but the crew were fortunately scrounging tea in the cookhouse so all was well for them. They plugged the holes with wood and the locomotive remained in service in that way until the war ended.

But it was a Great Western engine, Dean Goods No 2531 which, coupled to a Caledonian 0-6-0, took the Staff train into Cologne – the first British engines to cross the Rhine. Imagine the feelings of the enginemen, used to the relatively primitive conditions of pre-war locomotive sheds and the exigencies of war service to discover the German depot complete with slipper baths and a full sized swimming bath as well as electrically operated turntables. No 2531 made one more run, to Audruicq and home. But that was not the end of the story, for it went *back* into WD service in 1940.

At the end of 1942 British railway troops on the railways of Algeria in North Africa heard rumours that locomotives were on the way to them from Great Britain. There was a rumour as well of a powerful new locomotive type for the War Department – the well-known Austerity 2-8-0 – and something tough like that was needed for African gradients.

Great was the disappointment when six locomotives were landed at Algiers in February 1943 for once again, the GWR 0-6-0 Dean Goods had been sent to war, although by now 25 years older than in the First World War and very much under-powered for the loads they had to handle on steeply graded lines. Most military railwaymen had worked with the type before and (although it did not occur to anyone at the time) the six locomotives were to follow the railway troops about like a bad dream for the next three years – out of Algeria to Tunisia and northwards up Italy getting more decrepit all the way.

At Algiers the locomotives went on shunting duty in the Maison Carrée yards, some miles outside the city, with British drivers, as well as working trips to the port. French drivers were thus released for the main line, although not, God forbid, the ex-PLM 0-6-0 locomotives of the 1860s formerly used for shunting. The GWR locomotives as shunters lost their air brake pumps and apparatus and thence-forward relied on the steam brake alone.

After a couple of months 172 and 174 were sent east from Algiers to Bône, being used by the Americans for a short time at Ouled Rhamoun on the way. One would have liked to have seen and heard the reactions of an American railroad engineer of, say, the Santa Fe when told to work on this particular design of Swindon footplate.

In mid-1943 the other four were transferred to the Tunisian Railways and as a variation from shunting were put on banking duty at Medjez el Bab and on the Mastouta-Mateur line. No 171 was the only one of the class to reach Tunis, running up from Mastouta for wheel turning in the running shed there. While making these various transfers the Dean Goods piloted Algerian and Tunisian locomotives, or USA 2-8-0s.

Along the way No 171 was given some attention in the Sidi Mabrouk works of Algerian Railways. The actual work was carried out by backshop members of American units, who failed to grasp that Swindon not only lubricated tender axle-boxes by a trimming from above but also by a pad from below. Finding holes in the tops of the tender axlebox brasses the Americans thoughtfully filled them up, thus effectively stopping any lubrication from the top oil box. Out on the road 171 was later stationed at Mastouta (a junction in the middle of Tunisia) and banked trains for 20 miles or more towards Mateur. At Mastouta the staff were quite unable to fathom why all 171's tender axleboxes ran warm at once.

Normally the Dean Goods at Mastouta banked USA 2-8-0s and sometimes Tunisian 2-10-0s up to the top of the gable between there and Mateur; the ruling gradient was 1 in 50. One night in order to clear an accumulation of wagons forward a Dean Goods was put on a lessened load as the train engine and banked by another. For about an hour after starting the glow from the fireholes of the locomotives could be seen reflected in the low cloud as they struggled slowly towards the hills.

The locomotive crews had a dreadful time that night and the stories that they brought back of what went on grew taller and taller in the telling. According to the drivers one of their difficulties in the later stages of the journey was that if they tried to run at more than 10mph downhill or on the level, the brakesmen screwed the brakes on hard. Afterwards, if one saw a crowd of shadowy figures crouched round a dung fire in their djibbahs with a voice holding forth in monotonous Arabic until cut off by hoots of laughter, one could be pretty sure that what went on at Ksar Mezour as two Dean Goods tried to get a tenderful of water was being told yet again.

Crossing the Bosphorus. It is difficult to imagine anything less warlike than the Dean Goods 0-6-0, with its associations of peaceful rural branch lines. Yet the class became one of the most successful military locomotives of all, serving in both world wars. This photograph dates from the 1914–18 war when a number of Dean Goods locomotives were transported to Macedonia for use by the British Salonika Force. They were then moved over the Jonction–Salonique–Constantinople Railway to Constantinople for use by the British Army on the Chemin de Fer Ottoman d'Anatolie. One is seen here being moved across the Bosphorus on barges from Sirkedji, the terminus on the European side, to Haider Pacha on the Asiatic side.

Engine-naming in Algiers
A kindly and tolerably skilled hand added names on the centre splasher of the Dean Goods in Algiers – 100 *Virginia*, 167 *Margaret*, 168 *Rosemary*, 171 *Voiara*, 172 *Wavell* and 174 *Jean Ann*. The name *Wavell* had been given to 172 in Kent, but if authority happened to ask about the rest the story was that the names were those of base hospital nurses. Much more likely the inmates of a far less respectable female establishment were involved, an establishment at Algiers in which English names were popular at the time as a come-on for the passing military trade. By the time the locomotives reached Italy the names had been obscured by fresh coats of dark green paint.

17

GREAT WESTERN INTO WESTERN

GWR in Perpetuity
Disposal of Old Books and Papers.
TO BE RETAINED PERMANENTLY.
Comparative Returns.
D.G.M.'s Weekly or Periodical printed Circular.
Dock Rate Book.
Fare Books.
General Instructions relating to Merchandise Traffic.
General Railway Classification and Supplements.
Guard Books containing circulars, balance sheets, etc.
Handbook of Stations and Appendix
Important correspondence where questions of Agreements, history, principle and other similar questions have been reported upon and settled. To be specially indexed and kept apart.
Instructions to Country Stations re London Traffic.
Irish Traffic—General Instructions.
Merchandise Route Books.
Pier Head Arrivals & Sailings Book.
R.C.H. Coaching Arrangements Books.
R.C.H. Instructions to Railway Companies' Staffs relating to Passenger Train Traffic and Merchandise Traffic.
Rate Books.
Regulations, General Instructions, and Scales of Charges for Warehouse Rent, Wharfage, Demurrage, Labourage, etc.
Season Ticket Rate Books.
From the *Great Western Railway Appendix to the Service Time Tables.*

Nationalisation

On 1 January 1948 the four group railway companies were vested in the British Transport Commission. The BTC, under the Transport Act of 1947, had the duty to provide an integrated system of transport in Britain which was to have due regard to safety and efficiency and had to comply with a complicated instruction drafted by a Parliamentary lawyer which has been commonly interpreted as requiring it to 'break even financially taking one year with another'. The British Transport Commission organised its activities under separate functions: a Railway Executive, a Road Haulage Executive, a Road Passenger Executive, and a Docks and Inland Waterways Executive and the London Transport Executive – thereby ensuring the failure of its principal duty of integration.

The four companies, banded together as the Railway Companies Association, had opposed the Transport Bill. They urged that 'the Bill provides no practical or constructive plans for the improvement and co-ordination of transport but on the other hand proposes an unwieldy and bureaucratic control with no proper safeguards for transport users'. No company was more resistant to the principle of nationalisation than the Great Western. In common with other companies no director took service with the BTC. Unlike other companies only one senior officer joined the Commission – David Blee, who became the Commercial Member of the Railway Executive. This was not because the GWR had no able officers; Sir James Milne was an outstanding General Manager and Cyril Dashwood had a towering reputation as Chief Accountant and as general adviser to the Board. Many officers later took promotion to top jobs at headquarters or in other Regions, among them Keith Grand, as General Manager, M. H. B. Gilmour, Solicitor, A. N. Butland, Maintenance Engineer, F. F. C. Curtis, Architect, A. W. Woodbridge, Signal Engineer, and K. J. Cook, Assistant Chief Mechanical Engineer. Milne and soon Dashwood retired. The rest of the Region rolled itself into a hedgehog.

Sir Cyril Hurcomb, Chairman of the BTC, had made the mistake of organising rail, road and water in five separate Executives, and had selected incompatible people for the Railway Executive, which left him no hope of integrating road with rail, and no chance of integrating the four railways. Who snuggles up to a hedgehog?

According to Roger Wilson, author of *Go Great Western*, some of the outward and visible signs which distinguished the Great Western were chocolate and cream livery, taper boilers, shining brass, slip coaches, lower quadrant signals, pannier tanks, Paddington spotlessly clean, idyllic stations far from the villages they served, and four-a-side seating in third class. Ten years after nationalisation one could detect no change. No, that is wrong: there was one upper quadrant signal at the approaches to Birmingham. Otherwise traditions continued unbroken.

The Western Region was 'the territory of the former Great Western'. It went on with its former officers, its former equipment and its former practices. It admitted no light from outside. Far worse, it shed on others no light of its own. Almost to a man the managers had been servants of the Great Western. They had grown up in the tradition. They had, moreover, come through eight years of managerial nationalisation under the wartime Railway Executive from 1939 to 1947. They expected – and resolved – to continue what the Rev W. Awdry has more recently and most aptly expressed in the phrase: 'There are two ways of running a railway; the Great Western Way and the Wrong Way.' For the managers then, no change. For the railwaymen at large on the Western, nationalisation meant a remote British Transport Commission, headed by people of whom they had never heard, a Railway Executive manned by people only one of whom they knew, and a Western management who obviously would go on playing the traditional tunes. By no stretch of their imagination could they see the appointments of NUR's John Benstead and of ASLEF's W. P. Allen to the corridors of power as fulfilling a hope for a 'due measure of control and responsibility'.

Eventually, years later, the staff settled to obstruct the road to efficiency, economy and scientific administration. British Railways suffers from that obstruction today. The general immediate attitude of the staff on the Western, as elsewhere, was 'Oh, well we didn't expect any different'. A peculiarly Western reaction was '. . . and not a bad thing, either, if they leave us alone'. So for the staff too, no change.

The Great Western's Indian Summer. For a short while in the late 1950s the various BR Regions enjoyed a certain measure of autonomy; the Western Region immediately set about painting its stock used on named trains in chocolate and cream, and many locomotives in Great Western green. As the summer of 1958 moves into early autumn the familiar sound of a hard working Castle echoes across the Golden Valley with a Cheltenham to Paddington express climbing the final 1 in 60 gradient to Sapperton tunnel; the livery is as near Great Western as could be allowed.

Punctuality was also a story of success up to a point. No figure looks good when one quotes a full year. For one thing the timetables do not time trains with full recovery allowances in the winter for the extra rolling resistances, long hours of darkness, slower moving passengers and slower moving staff. So let it not come as a shock that the percentage of express trains to time on the Western Region in 1948 was 22; by 1955 it was no better than 25 per cent but in 1962 there came a lift from 36 to 48 per cent and in 1964 52 per cent. No wonder no one was keen to accelerate services between 1948 and 1961, that is, before the diesels arrived in numbers. In 1963 and 1964 we had a lot of fun. By then we had some 750 main-line diesels and I didn't see why we should be bumping around near the bottom of the punctuality league.

We set out to teach *homo sapiens erectus railwayanus regionalis occidentalis* to abandon his casual habits and to run trains to time. The first task was with ourselves. 'Will officers kindly instruct their stations that trains will no longer wait for passengers strolling down the hill or from one platform to another? Will officers kindly instruct their controls not to stop trains where they are not booked to stop for anyone except the Sovereign? Will officers no longer stop trains for themselves? Will the engineers kindly keep off the fast lines during "expfess" hours? Will officers get out and about and encourage louder whistles, more noisy slamming of doors, more dramatic waving of flags?' And they did.

G. F. Fiennes

The 'Break-Up' of Paddington

The performance of the Western Region between 1948 and 1958 posed a serious problem to the British Transport Commission. When Sir Brian Robertson succeeded Sir Cyril Hurcomb he changed his predecessor's policy of centralisation, setting up Regional Boards of Directors and delegating very large powers to the Regional General Managers. He converted the BTC into a body which held a watching brief, staffed increasingly by officers who were most excellent chairmen of committees but were not dynamic executives. Under his benevolent eye three Regions were performing well, the Eastern, the North Eastern and the Southern; two were struggling, the London Midland and the Scottish; one, the Western, was slipping down the hill.

Sir Brian had other preoccupations, notably the ominous noises coming from the Government as it became clear by 1958 that the aim of the Modernisation Plan of 1954 to take BR into the black by 1961 or 1962 was not going to be realised. Spurred by the setting up of an Advisory Group outside the railways, Sir Brian summoned Keith Grand from Paddington to the BTC to head the Railways Sub-Commission. Supported by those excellent chairmen of committees, Grand had as much hope of turning the tide of BR's deficit as King Canute.

At Paddington J. R. Hammond took over as General Manager. He faced a dismal prospect of ageing steam traction, industrial recession, and stiff competition. The financial results were worsening fast. The outcome of the continuing slide was on the one hand the arrival of Dr Beeching at the British Railways Board and on the other the appointment of S. E. Raymond as Chairman and General Manager of the Western Region in 1961. Some hallowed Paddington traditions and practices suffered from the customary attentions of a new broom, and then a new management team got down to serious business. Only the Civil Engineers and the Staff Department remained under old Paddington hands. The new team set about the Western Region manfully. They initiated a thorough review of both passenger and freight timetables. They unrolled the hedgehog and co-operated – no less – with the BRB and their neighbouring Regions in a review of geography. They spearheaded an inquiry, mostly carried out by divisional managers, into the benevolent levels of manning, especially in the Motive Power Department. They asked, disagreeably, why Swindon so often happened to have a spare boiler, spare wheels, spare everything, and they carried the process into all the holes and corners of the Region. The Western Region became very quickly and very violently aware that stray wagons, idle road trailers, cans of surplus paint or a rusty siding could attract displeasure as heavy as the wrath of God.

The effects of the new policies began to be seen between October 1963 and December 1965. The Western Region deficit had grown from nil in 1953 to £20m in 1958; to £30m in 1961; and then in two years had been cut to £16m in 1963. By 1965 it was down to £6m. The old Paddington hands naturally took the wrath of God hardly. The import of managers would have been seen to be reasonable if it had not been regarded at first as breaking up a family group. In time, as the results began to appear in monthly statements, the stunned expressions wore off and their cheerful natures recognised that to be again on the up grade was fun. The case for the 'Break-up of Paddington', as these events have been called, rests first on the deterioration in results during the first 13 years of nationalisation, and secondly on the dramatic improvement in the four years which followed.

Geography

The Western Region did well geographically under the Act of nationalisation. The Great Western's great slice of cake with its centre in Paddington and its outer icing stretching smoothly from Pwllheli to Weymouth was not easy to divide in the same way as the LNER and the LMS. Great Western loyalties thickly embedded in the cake made it difficult to carve. In any case, the Great Western seldom penetrated the territory of other companies in the same way as the constituents of the other Groups. The two penetrations of importance were the joint line from Chester to Birkenhead, and the line from Yeovil to Weymouth.

On the other hand the LMS cut across Central Wales for about 150 miles from Shrewsbury nearly to Carmarthen. That Group had outliers from Pontardulais and Brynamman into Swansea, and from Abergavenny across the heads of the valleys to Merthyr, with tentacles half way to Newport and Cardiff. More important, it owned the main route from the industrial North East and Midlands to Bristol and Bath. At the bottom of the slice the Southern ran wholesale west of Exeter into North Devon and Cornwall.

The British Transport Commission approached its duty of integration timidly and naïvely. Perhaps it remembered the Western's stationmaster at Yeovil replying to the general managers of the Great Western and Southern when asked whether he clearly understood his new function as joint stationmaster. He briskly repeated the lessons which they had read to him and added: '. . . and to give they Southern b.....s 'ell'. In 1948 the Western took over the LM lines in Central and South Wales. In 1950 it took over the LM territory south-west of Birmingham, and the Southern's west of Exeter. But it did not take over the operation of the lines. The intransigent operators, spearheaded by Sir Michael Barrington-Ward at the Railway Executive, stuck to the doctrine that as far as possible the two terminals of each service be under the same manager. The effect of the changes was to raise the Western Region from second to first place in size, from around 4,000 route-miles in 1948 to 4,350 and from around 1,600 stations to over 1,900. Quite a large chunk of railway. It was unfortunate that the organisation chosen by the BTC hindered the railway's efforts at integration.

Within the railways integration meant two things: rationalised operation between competing lines, and closure of unwanted branch lines. For the first of these the BTC had organised badly. The Western's competitive routes were firstly to Chester via Birmingham and

......and Staff

The other principal task was with the most important man on the railway, the driver. A diesel was like a first watch to a boy. He treated it like an egg in case it came apart in his hands. And of course the diesels often did come apart in their hands. The locomotive inspectors were straitly charged to tell drivers to run to time – or to make up time, if late – and if the nuts and bolts fell off, it would not be the drivers' fault but ours. Finally, we charged the mechanical engineers to see that the nuts and bolts did *not* fall off. And in the winter of 1963–64 away we went.

By January 1964 we had the best result ever achieved by the Western Region, 55.7 per cent of trains to time and we were second in the league. In February we were top with 68.2 per cent, the second best figure ever recorded in February by any Region. In June we had 73.7 per cent, the best ever for the Region in any month. We maintained our position for three more months. But by October we were back to fifth in the league. However, the worst figure for any month was 54.7 per cent and in December, with 56.4, we were back to second. I am not sure what the moral of this is. Three things are for sure: that *homo sapiens* is a casual, unpunctual character; that you have to keep after him all the time; and that it is no way to make him deny that character by doing as British Railways now do in giving him an alibi by quoting their figures of punctuality as 'trains up to five minutes late'.

G. F. Fiennes

The Importance of the General Manager's Saloon

The number of times is legion when I took out a special saloon. This was quite deliberate. It was a unique way in which I could entertain. It was memorable to the guests. The saloon was a place where the Paddington team could get a captive audience for their spiel. So, I did this not only quite deliberately but also very often; Ministers, MP's, County Councillors, Mayors, Trades Union leaders, customers – not in that order of importance – came with us. One lady MP told us that we were proposing to close all railways west of Plymouth by the simple expedient of declaring the Saltash bridge unfit for traffic. To that I replied: 'Well, the simplest way to deny that rumour is to declare it fit for traffic. Will you go up in the overhead tube while a couple of trains go by and tell us that it won't fall down?' All she said was 'May I wear trousers?' and in due course the District Engineer took her up the ladder. The rumour died.

Another success on a special was to persuade the Cornish MP not to oppose our plans for capturing from Coastal shipping much of the traffic in china clay from Cornwall to the Potteries in Staffordshire and to Kent. This exercise in persuasion was not all that easy because the law was against us. Coastal shipping had protection from competition by the railways. Indeed the then Under-Secretary for Transport, Vice-Admiral Hughes-Hallett, fired broadsides at us on the subject, so there had to be a conspiracy of silence. Our argument was that 'there is neither the population nor the industry in Cornwall to support the traditional forms of transport, coastal shipping and railways and the newcomer, road. If much of what goes coastwise now does not transfer to rail we may lose the railway. You choose.' They chose to support us.
G. F. Fiennes

Wolverhampton, competing with the London Midland out of Euston; secondly to Devon and Cornwall competing with the Southern; and thirdly the lines from Birmingham to the South-West and Wales, competing with the former Midland line to Bristol, and the former LNW line across Central Wales to Llanelli. Eventually – nearly 20 years and many millions of pounds later – the Western's route to Wolverhampton and the Southern's route to Exeter were relegated to the status of secondary lines. The massive benefits might have been reaped earlier if the BTC had appointed an integration 'Supremo' at the Railway Executive, or had at once handed the Western's route to Wolverhampton to the LM and the Southern's to Exeter to the Western. As it was, after 15 years of Western Region ownership when the writer came to Paddington as General Manager in 1963 the Central Wales line was still carrying heavy freight traffic with huge engines hauling tiny loads over the mountains, traffic which could have been, should have been, and soon was, integrated with the flow over the flat, well-equipped economic route via Newport and Cardiff.

On the other hand the Western was quite active in closing branch lines. Adding up the final score, the situation in the area south and west of Bristol was:

Branches closed or in process of closure before 1963 (ie Beeching report)	by WR	14
	by SR	nil
Recommended for closure by Beeching	by WR	9
	by SR	14
Closed after Beeching	by WR	7
	by SR	13
Closed by BR but open in private hands		3

So it was not Dr Beeching who swung the first axe at the Western's branches. The Beeching plan made virtually a clean sweep of the former Southern Railway's branches west of Salisbury. Another of its effects was to stimulate opposition to closures in general. Nevertheless, the peculiarly Great Western reactions to an uncertain future were pre-Beeching. The formation of the Great Western Society in 1961 was aimed at preserving locomotives and rolling stock threatened by the coming of diesel traction. The Group which eventually formed the Dart Valley Railway was negotiating long before the Beeching Plan.

In 1960, as soon as Dr Beeching had endorsed the plan for electrification from Euston to Birmingham and Wolverhampton, the writing was on the wall that the route out of Paddington would be secondary. Beeching also transferred the Western Region's territory north of Banbury and Craven Arms to the London Midland. The two General Managers, Raymond and Johnson, were in full support. The outcome was spectacular. The primary service from Euston was the most frequent Inter-City service in the country, half-hourly for much of the day. The secondary service diverted from the route via High Wycombe to that via Oxford, gave Oxford a vastly better service and improved out of all recognition travel from the south via

End of an era. Local trains only into Snow Hill. Commuters from a Leamington train leave platform 5 on 7 March 1967.

Reading to the Midlands. For cross-country travel between north-east and south-west the majority of transfers between formerly competitive routes were concentrated at one station, New Street in Birmingham. The cross-country route via Birmingham and Derby had lagged behind the radial routes from London both in capital investment and in timetable planning. Services remained frequent and reasonably fast, however, and the introduction of HSTs in 1982 gave full effect to an integration most intelligently master-minded and planned.

Along the southern fringe of the Western Region's territory ran the line from Salisbury to Exeter. In the same territorial shuffle Dr Beeching transferred it to the Western Region. A working party looked into the facts about the routes to Exeter via Westbury and via Salisbury. They were given some complicated options to consider but basically the situation was simple. The Western route had always been the primary route to Exeter

Castle Leaseback

September 1965 was given as the deadline for the cessation of steam on the Western Region main line including the Paddington to Worcester expresses which were Castle hauled. The last job should have been in mid September but there were not enough diesels to go round and this caused some head scratching, for Worcester's Castles (and maybe some from Old Oak), had already been sold for scrap as from that date at figures of around £10 per ton for a 140 ton locomotive and tender. To get over the situation some engines were actually hired back at £100 per week so Nos 4079 and 7029 were not in truth the first privately-owned Castles to run over British Railways tracks.   D. Green

173

Some thirty branch lines were closed during the early days of nationalisation and, strange to relate, only nine of these came under the Beeching recommendations. One was the section of the Moretonhampstead line from Heathfield to the terminus (all traffic), and Newton Abbot to Heathfield (passengers). Moretonhampstead station stands quite derelict in 1967.

and beyond. The Western route was the public's choice. With the prospective closure of the former Southern branches to North Devon, their trains for London would come to Exeter from the west. They would not only have to reverse at St Davids but have to be assisted by a banker between St Davids and Exeter Central at a great cost. And in the future Waterloo would be under far greater pressure than Paddington.

It was change for sixpence between the routes both for length and for ruling gradients. The Western had 1 in 81 at Bruton and 1 in 80 at Whiteball; the Southern 1 in 80 at Templecombe and again at Honiton but plus the 1 in 37 up to Exeter Central. The timings from London would have been as good by either route. But the services between Salisbury and Exeter were earning little more than a third of those between Westbury and Exeter. The Western's freight trains loaded 67 per cent better than the Southern's. The cost of the bankers at Exeter Central would be over £30,000 a year. And at Waterloo the effects of the electrification to Bournemouth were still to come. A new 'foreign' administration at Paddington insisted on terms which could not have been surpassed by Sir Felix Pole, Sir James Milne or Keith Grand. 'Go Great Western. The Going's Good'. They prevailed. As with the services to Birmingham, results counted and now the HSTs have done for the Western what the electrics did for the LM.

For a short time in 1965 there was a risk that the improvements would not happen because there *could* have been no railway on which they *could* happen. In February 1965 the great and good Doctor published, in the teeth of all advice from the Regions, the 'Red Peril' – The Report on the Development of the Major Trunk Routes. He did this secretly at headquarters. In spite of assurances being given that the West Country would have a first class service via Westbury and that the line between Exeter and Salisbury would be preserved for a semi-fast service, the 'developers' were planning that all the traffic should be diverted via Bristol. Not only that but development would end at Plymouth; no development in Dorset or Wiltshire; nothing beyond Swansea; no Oxford/Worcester; no Chester/Shrewsbury/Newport. Paddington said 'No, it can't happen here'. And it hasn't happened yet.

Motive power
Generally in the age of steam it was easy to lay track, to instal signalling and to build carriages, all of which were in advance of the locomotive capacity. It was therefore the locomotive on which a railway depended for success or failure. In this sense the Great Western was supreme. From the time in 1904 when George Jackson Churchward produced the first four-cylinder Star until the 1930s the other railways at first ignored, then envied and finally copied what came out of Swindon. Doubt did not arise until 40 years later, after the second world war.

The Western Region's fleet in 1948, then, was largely the one which had earned the Great Western's laurels pre-war. We are accustomed to think of the Western striding along ruling gradients of 1 in 1320, but it was not like that at all in Wiltshire, Dorset, Devon, Cornwall and what are euphemistically called 'The Valleys' in Wales. There the railway plugged and pounded round tight curves up and down the high hills with no chance of speed. Good acceleration, high tractive effort and powerful brakes were needed, and the Western had them in no fewer than a couple of thousand 0-6-0 and 2-6-2 tank engines. So in 1948 out of a fleet of nearly 4,000 locomotives the Great Western as its crack express passenger fleet owned only 30 Kings and 171 Castles.

In 1948 the Railway Executive held a series of trials between a Great Western King, an LNER A4, an LMS Duchess and a rebuilt Royal Scot, and a Southern Merchant Navy as described in Chapter 9. Similar trials were held between mixed traffic engines and with heavy freight. The object was to establish a basis for the design of a range of standard steam types for British Railways. The outcome proved how well Gresley and Stanier had done their homework. The King at over 40,000 lb tractive effort was the most powerful locomotive but showed no more than marginal advantage in running. And, what was worse, it proved to be more costly in coal than any of the others except the Merchant Navy. The Western Region, reasonably enough, argued that the Great Western had designed for the use of soft Welsh coal and that the trials had been with Yorkshire South Kirby Hards. So the King went out again with Welsh coal and proved again to be more costly than any except the Merchant Navy. Nothing daunted, the Western sent out a King which had been modified from Collett's design to have high superheat. This time at 3.10 lb per dbhp hour the Western led the field and even succeeded in approaching the original figure of 2.83 lb achieved by the Castles in 1924, on test soon after their introduction.

The outcome of the trials gave the impetus to S. O. Ell and the new Chief Mechanical Engineer at Swindon, R. W. Smeddle from Doncaster, to undertake a comprehensive programme for modifying the Kings and Castles. Ever since the test plant at Swindon had been modernised in 1935

In March 1950 the Western Region took delivery of a gas turbine locomotive ordered by the Great Western in 1946. This was the Swiss-built No 18000 by Brown-Boveri. Taken into stock in May 1950 it was placed in service between Paddington and Plymouth and was generally restricted to routes authorised to the Kings. A second gas turbine locomotive, British built by Metropolitan Vickers Electrical Company Ltd, No 18100, was delivered the following year. Both had short working lives as they were found to be very wasteful, consuming almost as much fuel when idling or running under low power as they did under full load conditions. The normal regular working for No 18000 was the 9.15am Paddington to Bristol returning with the 4.15pm and this lasted intermittently until 1960 when the locomotive was withdrawn. Old and new pass each other in Sonning Cutting on 19 April 1954. No 5092 Tresco Abbey (a rebuilt Star) is heading a Worcester to Paddington train while No 18000 heads west on a down afternoon working. The steam engine was the last Star built in 1923; conversion to a Castle was in 1938 and it was withdrawn in 1963 – a total life of 40 years.

research had been going on. The principal aims were to improve the rate of steaming and to reduce the back pressure in the cylinders. Therefore the design of firebox, of tubes, of smokebox, of blastpipe, of chimney and of the steam passages were all in question. Swindon could do nothing about the narrow fireboxes without a wholesale re-design but the other items were altered. The outcome was an improvement in the Kings' rate of steaming from 25,000 to 30,000 lb/hr; of the Castles from 20,000 to 26,000; of the County class from 18,000 to 24,000; and so on. Swindon was reaching the stage at which the limit on performance would be the fireman's capacity or willingness to shovel coal.

Simultaneously with this programme the Railway Executive was designing a new range of steam locomotives of which two, the Class 7 mixed traffic Britannia Pacifics and the Class 9 freight 2-10-0 were among the most successful ever built in this country. The designs were centrally controlled under E.S. Cox but farmed out in parts to the principal works. Crewe had the lion's share; Swindon a humble role. Only 15 Britannias went to the Western, which received them without enthusiasm. Later, the drivers at Canton, Cardiff, gradually took to them and began to put up performances of which a Castle would not be ashamed.

Let us not be deceived into thinking that Paddington was only a hedgehog, secure, defiant, immobile. The Western was not immobile. Before the war it had commissioned a report from Merz and McLellan on electrification. Maybe the remit was not intelligent. The rural areas west of Bristol and the Welsh valleys are not among the best candidates for electrification. But the intention was sincere and was not a repetition of the Great Eastern's Decapod 0-10-0 tank engine designed to defeat a political move and never intended for service or reproduction as a class. When after the war electrification again became a live issue, the Western was low in the queue. The Eastern got in first with Liverpool Street–Shenfield and Manchester–Sheffield–Wath; the Southern second; the London Midland third. The electrical industry told the BTC that it could not undertake more than one major scheme at one time and the modernisation plan proposal for the East Coast main line was shelved. The Western spoke of electrification no more.

Paddington's next move before nationalisation was to toy with gas-turbines. In September 1946 the Great Western Board authorised £99,000 for a prototype from Brown Boveri in Switzerland and soon afterwards a rival from Metropolitan Vickers both delivered after nationalisation. Neither was a success. They spent much time under repair. They were noisy and unpopular with the drivers and when Paddington went for conversion to diesel traction there was no moaning at the bars. However, the point to remember is that these two units were of 2,500hp and 3,000hp. Nevertheless, when Paddington stated its diesel requirements in a memorandum, it showed that the stimulus for the change was the shortage of good coal, and that which was sought was a straight diesel replacement for the Castles and Kings, for which 2,000hp was the largest unit needed.

Paddington was represented on the Railway Executive's Traction

---

Fiennes on Tour

I remember walking on an inspection from Reading to Southcote Junction, a matter of not more than two miles. I went up the steps of the signal box, opened the door and said in due form: 'Fiennes, General Manager, Paddington.' Usually the reaction was a wipe of the right hand on the seat of the trousers and a handshake. This time it was:

'You can't be.'
'Why not?'
'General Managers don't *walk*!'
G. F. Fiennes

Committee by the Region's Assistant General Manager, Herbert H. Phillips. He argued that at 70/80 tons a diesel-hydraulic locomotive of 2,000hp would weigh about 30 tons less than a diesel-electric with its generator and traction motors. The BTC thought the extra weight would be useful for adhesion, but Phillips countered by pointing out that in the Kings and Castles there was about 70 tons on the driving wheels. And he reminded the BTC, which was dubious about 2,000hp with hydraulic transmission, that the Germans were using it successfully. It meant high-speed engines to keep within the weight, but Paddington was not worried on that score. The upshot was approval, a visit to Germany to see diesel-hydraulics in action, and then an order to Swindon to build three Bo-Bos with Maybach engines and Mekydro transmission. An order was also placed after some delay with the North British Locomotive Company to build further 2,000hp diesel-hydraulics under licence. The original five came out at 117 tons, which was almost as heavy as a corresponding diesel-electric largely because of BTC insistence on the use of conventional 'heavy' engineering with orthodox underframe, but North British later

The crack Bristolian was one of the first expresses to be dieselised as can be seen by this photograph of the eastbound train as it accelerates past Stapleton Road Junction, north of Temple Meads, and begins the long ascent of Ashley Hill bank to Filton Junction. But it is still very much a Western scene. The locomotive is a diesel hydraulic, the signals lower quadrant and that signification of safety, the ATC ramp prominent on the right hand track.

177

Fewer BR standard steam locomotives came to the Western Region than most but Newton Abbot's ageing Bulldog 4-4-0s soon fell prey to the new motive power. In the summer of 1959 Standard Class 4 4-6-0 No 75028 was performing pilot service over the South Devon banks and is seen here heading a Castle class 4-6-0 up Dainton just past Stonycombe.

It was Swindon's lot to construct the very last steam locomotive to go into service for British Railways, a Standard Class 9F class 2-10-0. A competition was held to find a suitable name for it and scarcely to anyone's surprise a Great Western series was perpetuated in the highly appropriate Evening Star. The ceremony was held at Swindon Works on 18 March 1960 by the Chairman Reggie Hanks. In Swindon's view it was equally appropriate that the engine be painted standard GWR passenger green and bear a copper capped chimney. The engine ran in this form throughout its short working life and is now in the National Collection.

built a batch of the Swindon pattern locomotives based on the German lightweight style body weighing about 78 tons. The Western followed the 2,000hp Warships with the 2,700hp Western class. Yet the whole diesel-hydraulic fleet was plagued with problems. As late as June 1965 Sidney Ridgway, the CME at Paddington, listed a whole mass of general defects: 'bearings in Voith transmissions, bearings in final drives, big end bearings in Maybach engines, camshaft wear, torsional vibration in engines, modifications in Mekydro transmissions'. The same report noted that steam locomotives had been reduced from 1,181 to 448. There were then 349 diesel-hydraulics and 206 diesel-electrics on the WR. Raymond, the General Manager, had chivvied the BRB into giving the Western a diesel-electric allocation out of its proper turn.

Logic was on the side of Paddington. The power/weight ratio of the lightweight diesel-hydraulics was equivalent to hauling an extra coach for nothing, as Churchward had said about the Stars' advantage over the Saints. But Paddington went wrong in again behaving like a hedgehog and not admitting the engineers at BRB fully into their counsels, in not refusing the design when the original North British design came out as heavy as a diesel-electric, and in not insisting that the experience of the German Federal Railway (Bundesbahn) should be incorporated in the designs for Britain.

Raymond's action in insisting on diesel-electrics for the Western gave the Region the distinction of being the first to abolish steam traction. On 3 January 1966 the last regular train worked by steam travelled over the Region's metals – another Western 'first'.

The Western Today

By 1983 an era had ended. Some had wondered whether the Western Region could survive as a unit of effective management. The latest reorganisation by the British Railways Board had appointed national 'Sector' managers to control the Inter-City services, the commuter services, local and cross country services and the freight and parcels services. What was left for the General Manager of Paddington to manage?

> **Managerial Lessons at Golf**
> Stanley Raymond in a memorable speech to the annual dinner of the Great Western (London) Golfing Society, urged that golf courses should be given over for municipal housing. I, on the other hand, regard golf as the finest training I know for managers. Everything you do at golf is your own fault. The little white ball is stationary; your opponent is still and silent. Unless you are disturbed, as you should not be, by the uproar of the larks ascending, you should strike the ball truly, as you well know how to do. At golf you have no alibi for poor performance. Nor had the old Paddington hands an alibi for the events which led to the break-up in the early 1960s.
> G. F. Fiennes

The Western goes it alone, diesel-hydraulics not diesel-electrics: Class 52 No D1013 Western Ranger *passes Fairwood Junction box with a Witham to Westbury block stone train on 1 June 1976.*

New prestige Pullman diesel trains appeared in 1960 running west to Bristol and north to Birmingham. Painted Nanking blue with a white centre band running through the window sections and with the Pullman coat of arms on the ends of the units, the train was smart and popular. Seat service was available in both classes for meals and refreshments. When the Birmingham train was out of service for repairs a relief set of orthodox Pullmans (diesel hauled) was used known affectionately as the Wells Fargo set; they were not so popular on cold winter mornings. The photograph shows an up Birmingham Pullman passing West Ruislip in July 1962.

So the plan for 1984 was for him to move to Swindon. The new headquarters at Swindon – 77 miles from London on the Inter-City 125 routes serving Bristol and South Wales – came 142 years after the Great Western Railway established its headquarters at Paddington. Swindon was chosen because the new-style HQ organisation needed greater accessibility to major centres of revenue and traffic. Indeed many of Gooch's arguments made to Brunel in 1840 in favour of convenience for the siting of the locomotive works there apply just as much today, given the geography of the Western Region.

The four-storey building, a minute's walk from Swindon station, accommodates about 500 rail staff who transferred from London, Reading, Bristol and Cardiff. The move coincided with the introduction of a new streamlined organisation based on a merger of existing headquarters and divisional offices. Elimination of one management tier will improve productivity and save £3m a year. Time will be the arbiter of whether the move was justified. In any event, what happened during the 17 years before 1983 had been the responsibility and often the doing of the General Manager at Paddington and it says a great deal for the massive continuity of the Western that however quickly general managers came and went progress was spectacular by any standards.

Let us now consider the Western under the three heads – geography,

Cross country service. The 14.10 Weymouth to Bristol dmu passes the 15.43 Bristol to Salisbury dmu at Limpley Stoke (close to the now abandoned branch where the film The Titfield Thunderbolt was made) near Bradford on Avon on 14 June 1969. These units, which have main line type low density seating, are used on many BR medium distance services.

Running over continuous welded flat bottom track, Class 50 No 50050 passes Flax Bourton near Bristol with the 10.45 Paddington to Weston-super-Mare train on 21 June 1974.

timetables and staff. Since the mid 1960s the Western had lost, partly by transfer and partly by the Beeching axe, about a thousand miles of route. In 1984 it stood at 1,855 miles or nearly the average for a Region forming one-fifth of British Railways. The Region is good geography, linking large centres of population in the West Country, South Wales and the Midlands with each other and with London. The centres are 'good railway distances' from London: over a hundred miles for competition with coach and car; less than 300 miles for competition with aircraft. The centres moreover are not in a straight line, for the main lines are like a four pronged fork allowing at least that number of Inter-City trains an hour to leave Paddington with prospects of a good load for the West Country, Bristol, South Wales and the Midlands. If any Region is geographically ideal for Inter-City services it is the Western.

One last word on geography. The Western in the mid-1960s successfully resisted a 'discussion paper', Dr Beeching's 'Main Line Red Peril'. People fly kites but one and all they come down to earth: the railway continued to exist west of Plymouth, west of Swansea, from Salisbury to Exeter, even the Berks & Hants.

The fact that the Western is a sensible geographical entity implies that it can have a sensible timetable. Through the timetables of the Great Western and the Western Region there has always run a strong principle, that of pattern. In 1839 the service between Paddington and Maidenhead left on each hour (except two) between 8am and 8pm. Incidentally the early timetable did not tell passengers how long the journey took. In later years the pattern remained; arrival times were published, high speeds were vaunted, but the high speeds were for one train on each route, the Limited, the Bristolian, the Cheltenham Flyer. The rest of the service was slow, not only by comparison with the one Steam Spectacular but with other companies. Sir Felix Pole is the suspect for this act of charlatanry. In

Sadly the east front of Bristol Temple Meads is now marred by the ugly GPO transporter bridge but, in spite of that, modernisation has served the passenger well. The picture shows a west to north express in 1976 behind a Class 45 locomotive and on the right, a London bound HST. Today several West of England to Birmingham and the North services are also worked by Inter-City 125s.

Bulk transport. A southbound tank train near Pontrilas behind a Class 47 diesel in April 1980. The only sign of times past is the Great Western lower quadrant signal.

the 1960s the pattern was still there but the drive was to accelerate the whole service to what French Railways call a *vitesse commerciale*. In terms of competition with the car this had been shown to be an average end-to-end speed of 75mph. It had also been shown that such speeds required 4,000 horsepower under the bonnet. This horsepower and therefore these speeds were beyond the 'rude mechanicals' of the 1960s. The London Midland Region with electric traction could average some 72mph; the Eastern with the 3,300hp Deltics around 70; the Western with 2,700hp Westerns in the high 60s.

However the new timetables of the 1960s brought the railway a great deal of traffic. But it was not enough. Luckily help was seemingly just around the corner. In 1962 Dr Sydney Jones, head of BR Research, had come to the Chief Operating Officer BR and asked: 'How would you like a train with a top speed of 150 miles an hour which does not have to slow down on curves?' The answer was: 'Very much – when?' He replied: 'In about seven years.' That made it 1969, and it was the answer to a prayer because Chief Mechanical Engineer Harrison had just dismissed with scorn a request for 4,000 horsepower in a locomotive. Now, in the Marylebone Road 'Kremlin' at that time were certain agnostics who disbelieved in Dr Jones' project for the Advanced Passenger Train by 1969. They went away and designed the High Speed Diesel Train which, with its average end-to-end speeds between 85 and 90mph put the railway beyond the reach of road competition in speed. The Western laid claim to the first fleet of HSTs. In the timetable of 1977 the Region went to the top, – not only of Britain and Europe but almost of the world, being second only to the Japanese Shinkansen. What happened – or didn't happen – with the Advanced Passenger Train is another story outside the scope of this book, save to say that the experimental unit did capture the title of Britain's fastest train in August 1975 with 151mph on – where else – Brunel's main line between Reading and Didcot.

The writer was brought up in an environment in which men talked

---

First Steps Towards the next 150 Years?

Proposed Organisation Changes Western Region

It is clear that the targets set for this Region in 1983 to curtail expenditure upon administration cannot be achieved by the methods we have successfully employed in the past 5 or 6 years. It has been possible hitherto to obtain economies by 'slimming in situ' and by 'good housekeeping' schemes, but the scope this now provides is insufficient and a more fundamental approach is necessary.

It has therefore been decided that the Organisational structure should be simplified and plans are being developed to put the Region's Traffic Management on a two tier basis. Work has now started with the utmost urgency. The objective is to introduce the necessary changes as quickly and as smoothly as possible consistent with the desire to minimise the period of uncertainty and to cushion the effects of disturbance to those concerned. Office accommodation at various locations, including Regional Headquarters, will be subject to examination for its suitability and adequacy.

Meanwhile it is of the greatest importance that all Managers and Staff are not deflected from the main task of effectively running the day to day railway while the changes briefly described above are being progressed.
(Western Region Management Briefing, 1982)

Bulk transport. A British Steel Corporation Llanwern to BSC Ebbw Vale freight carrying steel coil headed by Class 37 No 37972 passing Llanhilleth on 24 May, 1979.

Where the railway can show its advantage. Two Class 56 diesels haul a Port Talbot–Llanwern merry-go-round train with iron ore in bulk. There are 27 bogie wagons making these the heaviest trains on BR in the early 1980s.

about 'the Bloody Company'. On the Western, 15 years after nationalisation, men still talked about 'the Company' but never does one recall hearing the words used derogatorily or resentfully. Individuals might have uncomplimentary adjectives attached to their names but the 'Company' itself was an object of respect and affection. Rightly so: the Great Western Company had cherished its staff; the loyalty was reciprocal. And after nationalisation Keith Grand as General Manager had resisted for 12 years the attempts to bring alien practices and alien managers on to the Western. Not only that, he had resisted attempts to reduce the numbers of the staff. And Western Man had responded by continuing the Great Western's tradition of cheerful service to the customer and to the timetable beyond what on other Regions was regarded as the call of duty.

Even now, almost two decades after the first swings of the Raymond axe at the staff establishment there are no great changes in the attitudes of the real railway – the drivers, guards, signalmen, staff on the permanent way and in the locomotive depots although inevitably there are worries about the future with cuts real or imagined in service and staff, and a seeming reluctance by government to invest more than the minimum in new equipment. Certainly in 1982 the Western, like the other Regions, came out on the strikes called by ASLEF and the NUR but so they did in the 1920s against the Great Western Railway Company. And they went back to work, maybe a little shame-faced, and apologised by producing outstanding results for punctuality. The grades mentioned, thanks to the lack of recruitment over the previous ten years, were old hands. In 1983 over 50 per cent of the drivers were due for retirement in the next five years so the attitudes dated back to the Great Western. But have no misgivings about the younger entry. Just as with the rest of us, in our time, old hands look at the newcomer and say 'He'll never make a railwayman'. But again like the rest of us, by trial and error and a bit of luck in covering up his early mistakes, he will.

18

BRANCH LINES

The Great Western branch line will for ever be remembered for its rhythmic orderliness. It was like a stage – a very clean stage with a colourful set – upon which was enacted a variety of familiar pieces. Seldom did anything outright new happen, but the daily and seasonal variations gripped the attention as though one were looking at another production of *Macbeth* or *Othello*. Yes, one had basically seen it all before, but how could one be bored?

The ingredients that went into the unique mix that made up the Great Western branch were of course of two kinds: the track, stations and other pieces constituting the physical railway, and the traffic along it and all that working it entailed. The Great Western was distinguished on both counts.

The physical branch was usually well built and splendidly (often almost wastefully) maintained. Weeds seldom encroached upon the permanent way, and though the components of the track often reached a substantial age, the rails having first done main-line service, the alignment and general attention to detail were outstanding. If not actually commissioned in the Brunel era, the branches were mainly built by men who had been brought up in the Brunel school. They might not be quite to the standard of the Paddington–Bristol main line, but that had set an example it was hard to forget. It is not just the more hilly Great Western terrain that accounted for the unusually high number of viaducts and bridges and sparsity of level crossings. Many lines were of course built by small, independent companies and later absorbed, but the local boards of directors usually tapped the same sources for engineering, architectural and other services. Styles varied, but almost everything was solid, built to last. Perhaps nowhere else in the world was so excellent a right of way maintained for so little average traffic.

Stations were mainly substantial buildings, carefully maintained structurally and kept spotlessly clean, as were the public rooms and the platforms. But it was not just for the public. Few homes were as clean and tidy as the average signalbox, where to handle a polished signal or point lever without the protective duster was an unforgiveable offence. The vegetable patch down the embankment was as lovingly cared for and just as orderly as flower beds on the garden, for which soil might well have been brought by specially-ordered truck from 50 or more miles away.

Some station buildings were the first to have prefabricated parts in Britain, and though there was great overall individuality, many standard components were used. The signalling, more elaborate than on some railways, and of course always lower quadrant, also helped make it

Working of Streamlined Rail Cars.

In connection with the running of Streamlined Rail Cars the instructions for Auto Car Service shewn on pages 128 to 131 must be observed except as varied below:—

Clause 1 (fifth paragraph).

Guards must in all cases give the signal to the Driver to start by means of the electric bell communication provided for the purpose, and not by hand signal. In case of failure of the bell communication, the Guard must give a verbal message and must report to his Station Master that the bell communication has failed, the Station Master to notify the Telegraph Lineman immediately.

From the *Great Western Railway Appendix to the Service Time Tables*.

Bugle station between Par and Newquay around 1906 before rebuilding. Not many passengers may have used the train hauled by the 2-4-0T, but clay and coal traffic, not to mention the barrels in the foreground, keep the staff busy, and even at such a wayside station there is an abundance of advertising metal signs.

obvious when you were on Great Western territory. The whole layout was as tidy as that of a well-kept model railway, and especially when viewed from a hill was unusually pleasing to the eye. Not surprisingly, picture postcards of stations were sold by the hundreds along with those of famous beauty spots and castles.

While the physical branch lines were a cut above the average, the trains were not so remarkable. The green locomotives with their sparkling brasswork and the chocolate-and-cream coaches were, of course, also handsome and would have done credit to any model railway. It was their pace that left much to be desired. Rarely was it possible to average much more than 20mph.

Many trains were seriously underpowered, witness the enormous difference in speed when going up or down hill. Locomotives needed frequent and lengthy pauses for drinks. Station work was seldom rushed, and the timetable set for peak rather than average patterns. It was all done with proper dignity rather than haste. Crossing trains at a station with two

Shepton Mallet station on the branch connecting Witham to Yatton on the Bristol main line. Everything is very Great Western from the copper capped chimney on the Dean saddle tank to the station awnings and covered footbridge. Originally this branch to Cheddar was part of the Bristol & Exeter Railway built to the 7ft 0in gauge.

platforms on a single-line route could take an amazing time. Ever conscious of safety on the Great Western, the signalman might bring both trains almost to a complete halt following the carefully framed rules before allowing them (never together) cautiously to enter the platforms. The token would be expeditiously caught, but then the signalman would notice a friend to whom he had to pass a message and two train loads of passengers would wait. Once in his box he would change the road and withdraw the new token with great dexterity, but most GW men being of well above average size, it would be a dignified walk rather than a trot down the platform to the driver.

For many passengers the delay was pure agony, especially on longer branches carrying occasional through services such as that between the Midlands and Ilfracombe on the Taunton to Barnstaple branch. 'Are we nearly there, mummy?' a child would ask. Woe betide the knowledgable local who told the truth! At least through trains had corridors. Ten passengers in a small compartment of a non-corridor train on a scorching day with uphill progress at perhaps 30mph between leisurely station stops was a recipe to drive custom away. 'I'll not answer for him if you don't let him have some', said a mother to a passenger eating prunes her irritable son was eyeing.

Leisurely station times of course ensured it all ran like clockwork and that main-line trains were not delayed by the late arrival of branch connections. That was positively rare on the Great Western, as was mechanical failure, though occasionally passengers would have to be bussed around an obstructed line – usually caused by the derailment of a goods train on catchpoints over-zealously provided in the quest for safety. Not merely did it nearly always run like clockwork, but the mechanism

Presumably waiting for a main-line arrival (though few fast trains stopped), a local for Marlborough waits in the bay at Savernake. The date is 2 August 1918. Except for war-time specials, the double junction with the main line will have been little used for many years since the Midland & South Western Junction became so annoyed by GW delays here that it built a bypass with its own high level station. Passengers for Marlborough had to make sure they presented themselves at the right platform.

Instructions to Stations at Which Homing Pigeons are Liberated.

Birds going in opposite directions must not be liberated within several minutes of each other or until the released birds have got clear away, otherwise large numbers of birds are diverted from their course and in the case of young untrained birds, many are lost by being carried off by birds flying a different course.

From the *Great Western Railway Appendix to the Service Time Tables.*

---

was seldom tampered with, timetables remaining unchanged for decades. In the Wye Valley or Worcestershire or Dorset, you could see goods trains performing identical shunting rites at the same spot at the same time for half a century or more without a break. *Everyone* knew the times of the trains, and many country people got up and went to bed, started and ended work, and had their meals by the Great Western without thinking of consulting clock or watch.

Yet there was still a sophistication of *pattern*, a daily, weekly and seasonal rhythm. Most branches had school traffic and especially in later years carried at least a few people to and from work, a morning and early evening train being busier than the rest. The majority of mainline connection business might be concentrated on one or two trains. The first down train brought the mail, sometimes newspapers, and the heaviest influx of parcels, including empties for those stations despatching perishable traffic, which left by a late afternoon or early evening train bound for London, Birmingham or South Wales. Several of these traffic peaks might be brought together when trains crossed. Every reader must be familiar with the contrast: a country station deserted for an hour, perhaps two, when suddenly everything came to life in readiness for the two approaching trains that were to pass each other. At stations where a branch led off a branch, the peak would be even more intensive, three (in a few places four) trains arriving within minutes. Market day at the next town usually resulted in extra passengers, and Saturdays saw the cinema and fish-and-chip crowds come back on the last train, on many lines a Saturdays-only train added in the 1920s.

In high summer almost everywhere saw people going or coming on holiday, usually staying with friends, or 'doing' the village in the old-fashioned way of arriving by train and walking to the church and pub. Bank Holidays would bring city and town people into the country, the

South Wales branch. Pannier tank No 9634 takes a pick up freight through Cymmer Afan station on the ex Rhonda & Swansea Bay Railway on 7 August 1951. This was the line running from Swansea (High Street) to Treherbert.

188

A scene at Churston on the Kingswear line in a summer of the late 1930s. The 48XX class 0-4-2 tank and two trailers form the Brixham branch train; the whole unit is engaged in van shunting in between services. Each of the very dirty auto trailers carries the Great Western coat of arms. Note the ring-arm signal to the left of the locomotive.

days before Christmas would see country people go shopping further afield than at any other time. Fairs and other agricultural events, carnivals and regattas sent booking office receipts soaring, the normal two-coach auto train perhaps being replaced by a prairie tank and a set of five coaches. Beginnings and ends of school and university terms involved Passengers' Luggage in Advance and frequently questions as to why the tin trunk or bicycle had not yet arrived. In the days when everyone going any distance did so by train, the booking office knew how well the professional broadcaster or local solicitor was doing. And the aftermath of a severe winter spell would be a rush of old people making unusual journeys to attend funerals.

Nearly all these passengers were conscious of their good fortune in being served by the Great Western. Children quickly learned that not all railways were equal, and that the Great Western was stable, prosperous and, above all, safe. A GWR stationmaster, usually a substantially-built man, held his head high. He carried the message of the GWR like a preacher, his tracts being the timetable and numerous other publications sold through his booking office or his rates book from which he could

One of the longer branches, the coast line of the one time Cambrian Railways, with a Dovey Junction train at Barmouth's southbound platform in 1933. The engine is almost certainly No 3213 which was then shedded at Machynlleth and not withdrawn until 1936. It was probably a train originating here (the engine having been turned on the triangle at Barmouth Junction) as the headlamp has not yet been placed in position.

A strengthened branch train at Fowey (terminus of the lines from both Lostwithiel and Par) in July 1949. The engine is No 6417, a 1932 Collett design; the 54XX and 64XX classes were both auto fitted, but the 74XX was not so fitted.

discuss terms for carrying the goods of local traders. A GWR station-master was a person of standing in the village or country town served by the company.

But the people who most counted their luck to be associated with the GWR were the staff. Loyalty was strong throughout the system, but always greatest in country districts, if for no other reason than that the rates of pay were comparatively more attractive here, with fewer other employment possibilities. Getting a job as a lad porter or an engine cleaner was to be set up for life.

If the railway was labour intensive, that was part of its charm. Everyone knew everyone in a club whose main, but by no means, exclusive purpose was to keep the traffic moving. Mutual welfare and self-help figured prominently, and barter helped the lifestyle. Newspapers could be read in three or four signalboxes, eggs would be sent down by one train and beans and lettuce returned on the next, children's clothing was never wasted and seldom allowed even into storage, drivers tipped off gangers about game and mushrooms, and a visit by a headquarters official would quickly be noised throughout the branch.

Much of the romance of the Great Western, and especially of its branch lines, lies in its unique stability, life going on as it was ordained by Paddington, any surprise being a variation of no surprise. Yet all the time the Great Western was proclaiming itself the most go-ahead of businesses, ever in the public eye for its latest innovation. There was of course an enormous difference between the GWR of the crack expresses and the GWR of the single line branches winding through the valleys and over the moors. But some change was felt everywhere, and actually more took

place than the continuity of the overall impression suggested. Some trains, for instance, were modernised. Brand new two-coach non-corridor branch sets, labelled with the name of the lines to which they were allocated, brought relative comfort to West Country villages while country people in most of Britain made do with yesterday's main line left-overs. The diesel railcars were a great innovation. Many were skilfully rostered to work on lines with only light traffic at peak hours and on busier routes at slack times. New halts blossomed in the 1920s. Some stations were served by the GW's own bus services until the railways had partially to sell their bus interests in the 1930s, resulting in the ridiculous stalemate that they could neither compete outright against, nor co-operate with, the rival form of country transport. But services were generally adapted more to meet the challenge than in the rest of Britain, many branch lines carrying their heaviest traffic as well as having their best service well into the bus era.

Practice varied sharply. The holiday areas were not merely the showpiece but generally avoided the worst of the slump. So Castles worked specials up the single line from Plymouth to Yelverton, where up to 6,000 people would go on a busy Sunday or Bank Holiday, in summer the Moretonhampstead line enjoyed a through train from Torbay not calling at Newton Abbot, a restaurant car worked down the Barnstaple branch, and considerable sums were spent improving routes to resorts like Newquay and Aberystwyth.

The Thames Valley branches were smartly kept and mainly had a morning through train to Paddington, while Windsor remained a fully-fledged terminus with numerous specials, mainly school parties. But on most of the cross-country routes in southern England, including the

An unusual scene on the Great Western – a mixed train. Collett 0-6-0 pannier tank No 7431 heads a Bala bound train near Festiniog on a dull 20 September 1949. The service will have been marked in the timetable as '3rd class only'. Note the central position of the locomotive headlamp; any other railway would have placed a branch or stopping train lamp at the base of the chimney.

191

Examination and Collection of Tickets

1. Examination of Lavatories in Trains.—Sufficient importance is not attached to the examination of Lavatories in trains when tickets are being examined, or collected for open stations.

The Staff are particularly requested to bear in mind that, for Ticket Collecting and Examining purposes, A LAVATORY IS A COMPARTMENT, and the following points must receive special attention:—

(a) Lavatories in Corridor Coaches must be examined FROM THE CORRIDOR, whether on the "off" or on the "platform" side of the train.

(b) Lavatories in Non-Corridor Coaches must be systematically examined.

(c) UNDER NO CIRCUMSTANCES IS A LAVATORY TO BE EXAMINED BY LOWERING THE WINDOW FROM THE OUTSIDE.

(d) In the event of difficulty owing to a Lavatory being "engaged," the Station Master, or person in charge, is to be called, in order that his instructions may be obtained for dealing with the case at his discretion.

From the *Great Western Railway Appendix to the Service Time Tables.*

former Midland & South Western Junction and the Didcot, Newbury & Southampton, all attempt at providing speedy links for long-distance passengers had been abandoned and the creeping paralysis that was ultimately to grip the whole countryside network of branches was already obvious by 1930. In North Wales, tourism again helped, though there was an enormous difference between those lines carrying visitors and those – like the mountain line from Blaenau Ffestiniog to Bala Junction – which depended on local support. The depression was felt most strongly in parts of the West Midlands and especially in South Wales, where off the beaten track the glamorous veneer of the Great Western was perhaps thinnest, though virtually the whole of the vast system of duplicate routes that became the GWR's after 1923 continued to run. Each line was its own little world, and at Dowlais Central or Gilfach, Cardiff, let alone Paddington, seemed distant indeed. But it was still from Paddington that the pronouncements affecting local traffic were issued. Throughout the 1920s and 1930s notices about improved services poured forth, the GWR seeking whatever extra traffic it could spot, such as Saturday half-day trips to the cities when multiple stores, such as Burton the tailors, started offering startling value.

Their own little worlds many of the branches, and especially the branches off branches, might have been, yet the system worked as a whole. Seaside excursions were available from virtually every station, and specials for carnival night had connections with special fares from the most unlikely of places. On the freight side, too, the GWR was more concerned to maximise its revenue than reduce its cost. Horseboxes were strategically stabled, cattle trucks quickly supplied for cattle and sheep fairs and markets, farms moved by special train, and household moves by container were ever canvassed. The railway was a business run for profit, and every station, halt and public siding treated with the seriousness it deserved as a trading post.

But it is the individuality of the flavour of the different lines, junctions

The Calne to Chippenham auto train working trailer first with Harris sausage loads in the two trailing four-wheeled Siphon vans. The engine in the middle of an auto train was common practice on the Western when peak loadings were in force.

Opposite:
Inland branch. A4575 class 2-6-2 tank, No 5541 crosses Riverford Viaduct on the long climb through the vale of Bickleigh with the 3.05pm Plymouth to Launceston train on 10 May 1961. In later years the GW trains shared the Southern (ex LSWR) platforms at Launceston where the signalbox had separate lever frames for the two railways.

and stations that commands the greatest nostalgic appeal. Who would not have been excited changing trains at Yelverton for Princetown, the highest station on the system, or working his way up from Newport to Aberystwyth by changing at Three Cocks and Moat Lane Junctions, or catching the non-stop from Aberystwyth to Devil's Bridge, or asking the guard to stop to set you down at Cleobury North Crossing, ten miles from Cleobury Mortimer?

Even today, reading the timetable for the 1930s and 1940s reminds one of boyhood dreams of exploration. The timetable was ever intriguing, with its footnotes (J-Calls on Fridays to pick up passengers for Brecon; W-Runs on Tetbury Monthly Market Day only, second Wednesday in Month) and details of connections to distant parts, and of trains that died for 45 minutes half way along a branch (a common practice where main line connections were made at both ends and the branch effectively operated as two separate feeder units). Reality was seldom disappointing, the stations always welcoming, staff pleased to answer questions about operating curiosities. The rostering of trains and connection facilities often went back into antiquity, yet generally made good sense; they were the days when traffic men believed that if you scrapped the timetable and began again, sooner or later you would evolve exactly the same service. Invitations to footplate or signalbox were a bonus, but it was the general experience that really counted.

How to sum up that experience? The Great Western branch line was, again, well-ordered, neat, in business to make money if only by feeding traffic to the main line. It was run by enthusiastic staff in a tradition of service and self-help. It carried virtually everything country people needed and took away most of their produce to market. Its waiting rooms and carriages enticed you to see more of Great Western land, with their posters and photographs of beauty spots. Above all, the branch was a handsome part of the countryside it served, and from its trains you could see much of the best river, coast and mountain scenery in the West Country, Wales, Cotswolds and Shakespeare's Country. It was unusual not to have a window seat; though well built by international standards, the branches kept closer to rivers and the coast than most main line equivalents, and in hilly areas hugged the contours. They went mainly through areas of sparse population, without either the high hedges or ribbon development along many of the parallel roads. The trains were clean, thanks to the GWR's use of Welsh steam coal. Steam and smoke sometimes obliterated the view, but much less frequently than, say, on an LNER branch, and there was much less chance of nasties on the compartment floor or fleas in the upholstery. The higher standards were reflected in the neatness of signalboxes, information about train changes at public holiday times exhibited at stations and halts, the general bearing of the staff, punctuality and indeed traffic levels.

194

19

NARROW GAUGE

Altogether the Great Western used five separate gauges during its lifetime though at first of course anything less than Brunel's 7ft was regarded as narrow. Of the true narrow gauge lines two were acquired with the 1923 Grouping (Welshpool & Llanfair and Vale of Rheidol) and the third, the Corris, was actually purchased on 4 August 1930. Each of these additions to Paddington's empire had a different gauge; the Welshpool line was 2ft 6in, the Corris 2ft 3in and the Rheidol 1ft 11½in. They were not, however, very prosperous limbs of that empire, and suffered in almost the first wave of economy cuts. At the beginning of 1931 both the Corris and the Welshpool & Llanfair lost their passenger services, though freight traffic continued. The Vale of Rheidol was closed except for the period of the summer timetable each year when a reduced passenger service was maintained. Of all three GWR narrow gauge lines the Rheidol was the only one with any tourist potential, which was realised if not developed.

The Great Western publicity department being what it was there had been little delay in promoting the new Welsh assets. In May 1924 a 30 page

Ex Welshpool & Llanfair Light Railway Beyer Peacock 0-6-0 tank No 823 Countess *with the morning train to Llanfair Caereinion in 1950. Most of the traffic was coal. Both* Countess *and its colleague No 822* The Earl *were 'Swindonised' by the substitution of copper capped chimneys for stovepipes, brass safety valve covers and very Great Western whistles. Both lasted until the end of public service and were acquired by the line's Preservation Society.*

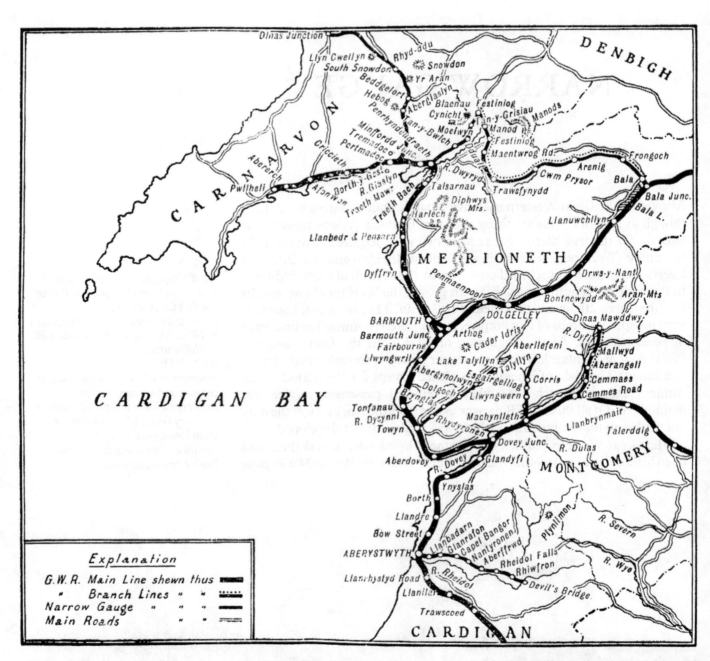

This map showing most of the passenger-carrying narrow gauge lines in Wales was contained in a publicity booklet entitled Welsh Mountain Railways *and issued at Paddington in May 1924. It is the only known GWR map highlighting these lines and it has a nasty crack at the LMS by showing Dinas Junction, the terminus of the then Welsh Highland Railway minus the ex LNWR branch from Afon Wen to Caernarvon.*

booklet illustrated in gravure emerged from Paddington called *Welsh Mountain Railways* and contained the only known GWR map to show the narrow gauge lines from Aberystwyth in the south to Dinas Junction in the north. It did not, of course, show the LMS connection from Dinas and the Welsh Highland Railway to Caernarvon and Bangor. In fact the foreword is very devious, describing the WHR route as 'going right up near Snowdon's summit where it meets the old Welsh Narrow gauge' (meaning the North Wales Narrow Gauge Railway) 'which runs down to Dinas Junction out Caernarvon way'! One wonders if a Welsh mole at Paddington had advocated the publication by extolling the new and what was to be the greatest white elephant of them all, the Welsh Highland Railway. Market traffic on the Welshpool line was ignored – in fact who had ever heard of it, so the W&L was left out. Similarly the Corris line, then owned by the Bristol Tramways & Carriage Co, got pretty short shrift being condensed into 3½ pages along with the Talyllyn.

Welsh Mountain Railways gives better treatment to the Festiniog and Welsh Highland railways but as expected waxes eloquent on the Rheidol which, it says 'in some ways is superior to any, the sublime groups of scenes at Devil's Bridge not being equalled anywhere'. Neither are two other lines forgotten, albeit standard gauge – those from Bala to Blaenau Festiniog and from Cemmes Road to Dinas Mawddwy. Due mention is made of the fact the visitors from Bala can go back down the Festiniog line 'though it provides really too much to see in one day'. Possibly struck by conscience, Paddington saw to it that an article on the Welshpool & Llanfair appeared in the *Great Western Magazine* for May 1937. The passenger service being six years gone this could be regarded as a quaint piece of rural sentiment.

Schoolboy discovery of the Welsh narrow gauge lines in the later 1930s led to a visit to the pillbox-hatted stationmaster at Machynlleth who was lord and master of the Corris. Courtesy (to a pair of 15 year olds) was absolute. Certainly it would be possible to ride up on the train and if next Tuesday would be convenient the stationmaster would be free and would come too. Meanwhile how about looking round the narrow gauge yard and the standard gauge shed? Tuesday came, a glorious and memorable day. After the stationmaster had donned his official hat the small party set off to find 0-4-2 saddle tank No 3, several empty slate wagons and a four-wheeled brake van. The engine crew comprised one cheery Welshman who had brought No 3 down two thirds of the line's length from its shed at Maespoeth. After a little thought the stationmaster suggested that one might see more of the line and scenery riding on three

For many years horses were very much a part of railway life not only for delivery carts and vans but also to act as shunters. Most big stations had their shunting horse, including Birmingham Snow Hill. But this also applied to country branches and the 2ft 3in gauge Corris section acquired by the Great Western was no exception. Just before closure in 1948 a Great Western horse shunts at Aberllefeni, the upper terminus of the Corris Railway. By the end of the year the line had closed, because of a washout on the banks of the River Dovey.

197

separate slate wagons which were duly marshalled at the rear of the train. It was a bumpy but exhilarating ride.

The Great Western never actually abandoned any of its narrow gauge lines. The first to go was the Corris, in 1948, when British Railways had already taken over. Rapidly dwindling traffic had brought the end near but a washout at the Dovey river bridge provided the coup de grace. Corris engines and stock however were not to die. Both the remaining locomotives Nos 3 and 4 together with the brake van, a number of wagons and a reconstituted coach (found in use as a greenhouse) were rescued and are now at work on the Talyllyn Railway, also 2ft 3in gauge. For two and a half years both engines had lain at Machynlleth and it seemed only a matter of time before they were sold for scrap locally or sent to Oswestry or Swindon for breaking up; enterprise proved otherwise. The Talyllyn negotiators who went to Swindon to plead their cause (the works was still in WR hands) were received with open arms – the price was £25 each, as lying. 'If' they said 'we were still Great Western you could have had them for nothing'. Transport to Towyn cost another £50.

The Welshpool & Llanfair was closed on 5 November 1956; the final straw had been the difficulty in recruiting labour for the transhipment of coal in Welshpool yard. Those were the days when everyone was having it good. Closure was marked by the last of many enthusiast specials when participants were conveyed in cleaned out coal wagons, this time to tunes played by the Newtown Silver Prize Band whose music included both 'Pomp and Circumstance' and 'Dead March in Saul' to drown the volcanic lift of *The Earl*'s safety valves and frequent tugging of whistle cords. Autumn in Welshpool had not yet taken on a deathlike wintry look and in the valley there were lovely scenes of red and brown with shades of green amongst the thick woodlands. Farm people turned out carrying their youngest with them 'Have a good look, love, you'll never see this again'. But they were all wrong. As so often happened on the Western the right man turned up at the right moment; Oliver Veltom was at Shrewsbury as District Traffic Superintendent, and the Cambrian had not yet been turned over to the London Midland Region. Sympathetic to the cause of rail preservation he arranged for preservationists to lease the line from

Raven Square to Llanfair, at a very fair price, for a period of 21 years. This lease has now been bought out. Oliver Veltom was one of the last of the real Great Western men, it was *his* railway and he knew virtually everyone on the District. He was well liked and is remembered with pride. It was Veltom who also brought life back to the Rheidol.

Even though the Great Western killed off all other traffic on the Rheidol in the same year (1931) as it reduced its other narrow gauge lines to freight only, it at least made an effort during the summer season, though strangely exempting it from the Holiday (Runabout) Season tickets. Some new coaches were built (on old frames) as late as 1938, and from the mid 1930s to the second world war a good train service was provided – four each way on weekdays and even one on Sundays. There were no services at all during the war, but as early as July 1945 trains were restored. It was a refreshing change for the war weary people who flocked to the Welsh coast, standing in the crowded trains on the Cambrian main line. So, together with the resuscitated Talyllyn, the Rheidol still carried the narrow gauge torch into the hills of Wales, even when the Festiniog lay still after 1946.

But there matters lay; there was no attempt to popularise or even advertise the service beyond the ordinary bills and timetables. It seemed no one really wanted to know and visitors to the district were often totally unaware of the line's existence. In the summer of 1955, with the support of Reggie Hanks, Chairman of the Board at Paddington, Oliver Veltom stepped in, and the line suddenly became advertised widely as the only narrow gauge passenger line owned by BR. Visitors to Aberystwyth were told that their holiday was not complete without a ride on the Rheidol. The train service was improved (even Sunday trains ran) and in 1956 everything reverted to Great Western green, and chocolate and cream. Even the engines were named: Nos 7 and 8, the two pure bred Swindon engines became *Owain Glyndŵr* and *Llywelyn* respectively while the original (but Swindon rebuilt) Davies & Metcalfe engine No 9 had its former Vale of Rheidol name, *Prince of Wales*, restored. And so it remained until the Cambrian was transferred to the London Midland Region; in came 'modernisation' and the age of steam was OUT.

By 1968 all steam had gone on British Railways, except the Rheidol which was a non-profit-making nuisance to Euston. One day this author was asked to lunch with Bobby (later Sir Robert) Lawrence, who was on his way up in the world as General Manager of the LMR. It was a good lunch, not in the Mess but quietly in another room, and the theme was very much in the terms of Henry II considering the removal of Becket – 'who will rid me of this base turbulent priest?' No one at Euston wanted to be seen putting the knife into the Rheidol; politically (and that counted) it was unsound. But then to be seen to be supporting it – and with steam – was to accept a kiss of death to one's career prospects. Lawrence was not, by disposition, a loser. His idea was to hive off the line to a private company of enthusiasts who would love it and care for it. Basically it was sound thinking, but even though it received strong support from a few dedicated people who were prepared to put their money where their

mouths were, it foundered on politics. Welsh suspicion of intruders was only one of the reasons why it shouldn't be done. Two locomotives were purchased from East Germany to augment the stud, and after the failure of the project they were offered to BR for use as extra power. The offer was refused. Having been rapped over the knuckles for proposing something sensible, BR then settled down again to try with the Rheidol. The line was diverted from its original terminus into the old Carmarthen platforms at Aberystwyth station, thus releasing land to the local council, and is still proudly advertised as BR's only steam operated railway. For any railwayman to have done that in 1967, the result would have been instant death.

So, the development of the narrow gauge under Western hands (and their successors) has been a story of ups and downs. The two Corris engines were the first ex-BR engines to be preserved and run, the Welshpool is still almost intact, and the Rheidol runs largely because private enterprise elsewhere showed how it could be done; Wales and the tourist are all better off. If the Great Western had followed the Southern Railway which axed its beautiful Lynton & Barnstaple completely in 1935, who knows, it could have been the beginning of the end for the Welsh narrow gauge.

The Rheidol in London Midland Region hands. Having survived Euston's original plans to close it the Rheidol was 'rationalised'; the Aberystwyth terminus was re-located amid the empty Carmarthen branch platforms of the standard gauge station, the loop was removed at Aberffrwd, the engines painted BR blue and, as a gesture, the coaches in Cambrian olive green.
Swindon-built No 8 Llywelyn takes the morning train out of Aberystwyth and over the river on an autumn day in the early 1970s.

201

20

PRESERVATION

PRESERVATION

Preservation is a thing of the spirit. Keith Grand and his people fought for the spirit of the Great Western for ten increasingly hard years after nationalisation. They fought with the conviction that their traditions were the highest in the country and were supremely worth preserving – which they were – and with the conviction that the equipment of the Great Western was still the best – which it was no longer. Nevertheless, we keep tradition alive not only by the spirit. We need objects from the past to remind us. The Victorians had their locks of hair, the Navy has HMS *Victory*, the RAF has ceremonial Hurricanes and Spitfires, the nation at large has its ancient buildings, its pictures and sculptures.

One of the more controversial things which Sir Brian Robertson did was to delegate more power to the Regions and to appoint Regional Boards of Directors. R. F. Hanks became Chairman of the Western Railway Board. 'Reggie' was an old Swindon hand, tracing back to Churchward and Collett. After many vicissitudes he popped up as Lord Nuffield's Vice Chairman of Morris Motors but now plunged back gratefully into railways. He found *City of Truro*, the first ton-up engine, static in a corner of the old Railway Museum at York. Keith Grand and he arranged her transfer to Swindon, and a huge crowd turned out for the occasion. Swindon restored her to her former glory. Fortunately Swindon *happened* to have a spare boiler. *City of Truro* ran for several years on specials, which were always popular. Eventually she went in to the museum in Swindon Town next to the replica of *North Star* and the real *Lode Star*.

The next steps were virtually simultaneous and at that time modest in scope. The forerunner of the Great Western Society emerged as the 48XX Preservation Society and successfully negotiated the purchase of its first engine, 0-4-2T No 1466 and an auto-trailer. At about the same time Patrick Whitehouse and Patrick Garland, then Secretary and Treasurer of the Talyllyn RPS, began to move with the idea of buying a 45XX 2-6-2 tank engine, restoring it to Great Western livery, and using it on the Middleton Railway in the West Riding. On 4 March 1964, 4555 was waiting orders at Swindon, and she began her new life.

That was a start. But what a start. A year earlier General Manager Raymond agreed in principle to the sale of a Castle. Then a ukase from on high virtually put an end to the idea. One trouble with ukases from on high is that words have so often to be eaten as Moses found with those on the tablets. It took two more years for *Clun Castle* to be offered for sale. Meanwhile 9 May 1964 had come and gone with the 60th anniversary of

Facing page, top:
The preserved small prairie tank No 4555 with the 9.25am Class 7 freight from Bordesley Junction to Leamington leaving Hatton in August 1964. The engine was then temporarily shedded at Tyseley waiting for eventual transfer to the Dart Valley Railway.

Facing page, bottom:
Great Western through and through. Bewdley station on what is now the Severn Valley Railway (once a through link from Kidderminster to Shrewsbury) with Collett 0-6-0 No 3205 at the head of a train to Foley Park. Certainly one of Britain's finest private railways, the Severn Valley now runs from Kidderminster to Bridgnorth (Shropshire).

Farewell to steam on the Western. The then sole survivor of its class, No 7029 Clun Castle, as Gerry Fiennes put it 'blowing a bit' leaves Gloucester for Swindon with the final WR steam train on 27 November 1965. The Western kept it as long as it dared but it was withdrawn on 31 December 1965 and passed into private ownership. No 7029 is now at the Birmingham Railway Museum, Tyseley.

GWR v The Rest

Great Western preservationists out-did those of any other company in initiative, in determination and in the only thing which matters in the end, namely results. The Historical Transport Guide published by the Transport Trust recorded in 1975 that of the preserved railways or railway museums in England, sixteen were wholly or predominantly equipped with Great Western rolling stock. The other three companies only mustered twenty-seven between them. Looking back and having trouble with loyalty to my own origins in the LNER I conclude that a score of 16–9 in favour of the Great Western's enthusiasts is about right. Preservation is a thing of the spirit. This spirit is demonstrably Swindon-built.

G. F. Fiennes

Opposite:
A highly evocative atmospheric and almost timeless Great Western shed scene, magnificently re-created in living form at the Didcot Railway Centre of the Great Western Society, and still to be savoured more than 35 years after the GWR ceased to exist as a company.

City of Truro's ton-up trip marked by the last major Castle fling to Plymouth and back, out via Westbury and home via Bristol sponsored by publisher Ian Allan. *Pendennis, Earl of Ducie*, and *Clun* were the stars plus three Castle standbys. Alas, *Pendennis* going for the ton near Lavington dropped its fire all over the track; the coal was just too hot and it had melted the firebars. So No 6999 *Capel Dewi Hall* standing pilot at Westbury, took the train on and did well. *Clun* on the return ran from Exeter to Bristol four minutes quicker than *City of Truro*. It was a day to remember and a steam record had been broken. In May 1965 *Clun* worked the last steam train out of Paddington; it had earned its place in private preservation. In a few short years the preservation boom had started.

There were locomotives galore, the Great Western Society started its splendid Didcot steam centre where the whole atmosphere of a working Great Western shed is being created; the same has happened at Tyseley. The Severn Valley Railway from Bridgnorth to Kidderminster is now the home of much that was Great Western and provides a real life ride on Great Western trains for much of the year. The Dart Valley has two lines in Devon at Buckfastleigh and between Paignton and Kingswear; the line to Minehead is still alive and so is a little in the Forest of Dean. Great Western coaches abound and there are even bits of broad gauge lovingly retrieved in archeological digs from under almost a century of oblivion. It has been calculated that there are over 60 major sites where GWR material is on display, over 100 locomotives and similarly over 100 coaches have been kept and around 120 miles of GWR route preserved. Just occasionally we can still ride behind a King, the two Castles, Manors and two Halls on a BR main line, savouring Great Western express power unleashed in part if not in full. The spirits of Churchward, Collett and Hawksworth – not forgetting those that came before – must feel proud. As Frank Booker said in his book, *The Great Western Railway, A New History*:

'Today one can travel faster, more cleanly and in immeasurably greater comfort over former Great Western trunk routes than was ever possible in the days of steam. But never again will one travel with the same sense of fulfilment and excitement as when Paddington ordered the coming and going of its servants and the Swindon-designed engine had Welsh coal in its grate and bore on its tender the letters GWR.'

ACKNOWLEDGEMENTS

This book is a tribute to the greatness of the Western, but no corporate body can be great without the people with whom it is associated. Pride of place in this very important section of the book must go to those who served and still serve the railway from Gooch to Barlow, from North Star's driver to HST guard and from Great Western shareholders to those who pay their taxes to Her Majesty's Government. Without these individuals and groups of people there would be no railway, no pride, no nostalgia and no book.

The problem which beset the editors was not that of what to put in but, with the mountains of material available, what to leave out; so much that was absolute in temptation has, sadly, been left read but placed on one side because of sheer volume. Much has been recorded and little can be new but with the help of many who have loved the Great Western, we have been able to make this book live, not only as a place of history marking 150 years of development but also as a window allowing peeps into highlights of the story. To all who have contributed directly or indirectly we are deeply grateful. Particular thanks are due to the amateur enthusiast whose love of things Western has led him to spend countless hours recording and sometimes restoring the things which he has loved. One example is the devotion of members of the Railway Correspondence & Travel Society to produce that thirteen part work entitled *The Locomotives Of The Great Western Railway* – a chronological and statistical survey that has to be any GWR author's or editor's *vade mecum*.

Though most of this book has, of course, been specially written, no work of this nature could be produced without reference to and using extracts from previous publications most of which are listed in the accompanying short bibliography in the form of 'suggested reading'. The editors would however, like to thank the Oxford Publishing Company for permission to use extracts from their unique book *An Historical Survey of Great Western Engine Sheds 1947* by E. Lyons, and the Editors of *The Railway Magazine* for permission to use extracts from that journal, and *The Railway Gazette* for the use of maps and diagrams from the GW 1930s special issues. Reference has also been made to copies of the magazines *Railway and Travel Monthly, The Locomotive, The Engineer* as well as *Trains and Railways*. Others whom the editors would particularly like to thank are M. V. E. Dunn, L. Davis, D. Green, (the last to be in charge of Worcester's locomotive works) and John Edgington of the National Railway Museum, York. Without these and many past and present recorders so numerous that a list would fill a book on its own, this tribute to all things Great Western could never have been completed.

The authors would also like to make acknowledgement to the following photographers or collections for the use of their illustrations: John Adams, 129; P. M. Alexander, 11, 41 (lower), 67 (upper), 78, 79 (upper), 80, 110 (upper), 113, 114 (upper), 115 (lower), 158 (lower), 162; H. J. Ashman, 67 (lower), 112; B. J. Ashworth, 53; Donald R. Barber, 64, 91 (upper); *The Birmingham Post*, 173; P. F. Bowles, 192; British Rail, 58 (lower), 74, 75, 163, 184 (lower); British Rail/OPC, 15, 39, 83, 84, 90; H. W. Burman (P. B. Whitehouse Collection), 16 (top), 87 (upper); W. A. Camwell, 69; D. E. Canning, 141 (lower); C. R. L. Coles, 180; Colour Rail, 42, 43, 44, 77, 79 (lower); K. Connolly, 179; Crown Copyright (National Railway Museum), 12 (upper), 54, 132 (lower), 145, 186 (lower); David & Charles/L&GRP, 6, 8 (upper), 12 (lower), 13, 16 (centre and bottom), 17 (upper), 24 (lower), 33, 35, 36, 48, 56, 57, 62, 125, 131, 134, 186 (upper), 187, 188, 197; M. V. E. Dunn Collection, 30, 146, 147, 151 (lower); M. W. Earley, 87 (lower); D. S. Fish, 22 (upper); J. C. Flemons (P. B. Whitehouse Collection), 107; A. W. Flowers, 52, 58 (upper); P. J. Fowler, 181; Fox Photos, 21; GWR Publicity, 20; W. Leslie Good (P. B. Whitehouse Collection), 91 (lower); Peter W. Gray, 115 (upper), 119; G. F. Heiron, Frontispiece, 8 (lower), 22 (lower), 97 (centre and bottom), 98, 100, 111, 150 (lower), 169, 177, 178 (lower), 182, 183, 203 (lower); Great Western Railway, 66, 81, 132 (upper), 156 (upper); Great Western Society Ltd, 205; P. Hopkins, 118 (upper), 189 (upper); P. Howard, 151 (upper); *Illustrated London News*, 137, 138; G. D. King, 118 (lower); Locomotive Publishing Co Ian Allan Ltd, 32; Courtesy National Railway Museum, 28; Eric Oldham, 120; C. F. H. Oldham, 76, 190, 191; H. F. Prytherch, Courtesy Great Western Society, 167; *Railway Gazette*, 29, 38, 47, 50, 133, 135, 143, 160, 165; G. A. Richardson, 139; Peter J. Robinson, 184 (upper); G. W. Soole/ National Railway Museum, 158 (upper); Eric Treacy, 110 (lower); W. A. Tuplin, 19 (lower), 97 (top); H. F. Wheeller, 189 (lower); C. M. Whitehouse, 150 (upper), 198; P. B. Whitehouse, 41 (upper), 73, 114 (lower), 116, 121, 149, 152, 154, 174, 178 (upper), 195, 199, 201; T. E. Williams (P. B. Whitehouse Collection), 94, 175, 203 (upper), 204; Spencer Yeates, 103.

Many of the chapters are the work of more than one contributor; the first of us is mainly responsible for chapters 19 and 20 but also had a hand in chapters 3, 5, 15, 16, 17, and 20 while the other wrote the introduction and chapters 9, 13, and 18. B. K. Cooper was responsible partly or entirely for chapters 3, 4, 5 (from the original material by E. Lyons in *An Historical Survey of Great Western Engine Sheds*), 7, and 14, G. F. Fiennes for original material in chapters 15, 17, and 20, P. M. Kalla-Bishop for chapter 16, Geoffrey Kichenside for chapter 10, and O. S. Nock for chapters 1, 2, 6, 8, 11, and 12.

P. B. WHITEHOUSE
D. ST. JOHN THOMAS

FURTHER READING

Great Western literature is extensive and growing all the time, especially with more pictorial records, studies on individual branch lines and services, and personal memoirs. But a handful of books covering the railway as a whole deserve special attention. The standard history was commissioned by the railway itself. Originally published in two volumes in 1927, E. T. MacDermot's *History of the Great Western Railway* was revised by C. R. Clinker in 1964 with a third volume by O. S. Nock. It is, however, a ponderous work only for the serious-minded historian. More readers of our book might enjoy going into more detail with Frank Booker in the only one-volume popular yet accurate history, *The Great Western: A New History*, being re-issued with extra plates for the 150th birthday.

L. T. C. Rolt's *Isambard Kingdom Brunel* remains the outstanding biography of the genius behind the railway, and Derrick Beckett's *Brunel's Britain* usefully relates the engineer and his work to the present-day scene, showing how much of

Brunel's work remains in everyday use. Many are the books on Great Western locomotives. Bestselling of all is perhaps O. S. Nock's *Stars, Castles and Kings*, originally published in two volumes but now combined in a single book. O. S. Nock is also author of *Great Western Steam* and *Tales of the Great Western* while *GWR Engines, Names and Numbers* is an omnibus containing several of the famous GWR 'engine books' – part of the company's publicity which is the subject of R. B. Wilson's *Go Great Western*. Finite detail is recorded in the splendid multi-volume series *Locomotives of the Great Western Railway*,

meticulously prepared and published by The Railway Correspondence & Travel Society and its team of editors.

Several volumes in the present publisher's Regional Railway History series cover GWR territory and tell the history of the railway against the social and economic background. *The Great Way West* tells in words and pictures the romantic way in which the railway connected Paddington with Penzance. GWR preservation itself now has a substantial literature including *Great Western Adventure* by J. B. Hollingsworth and Sir Gerald Nabarro's *Severn Valley Steam*.

INDEX

Italic numerals denote illustrations

Aberystwyth, 66, 102
Accidents, 123, 137–9, 142–3
Acworth, Sir William, 34–5
Administration and management, 160 *et seq*, 168 *et seq*
Advanced Passenger Train, 183
Ahrons, E. L., 35–6
Air services, 159
Allen, Cecil J., 86, 101
America, United States of, 55, 60
Armstrong, George, 85
Armstrong, Joseph, 54, 84–5
Ashburton, *116, 141*
Atmospheric system, 156
Automatic Train Control, *140*, 141–3
Avonmouth, 49

Baltimore & Ohio Railroad, 60
Banbury, *15*, 65, 105
Barmouth, *19, 121, 189*
Barnstaple, 27, 191
Barry, 85
Bath, *150*
Bentley Heath, *16*
Birkenhead, 53, 105
Birmingham, *44*, 50–3, *50, 51, 52, 53*, 102, 122, *132*, 173, *173*, 197
Bourne, J. C., *10, 24*, 145
Box Tunnel, *138, 139*
Bridge Rails, 23
Bridgwater, 31, 45
Bristol, *12*, 45–50, *46, 47, 48*, 65, 85, 100, 109, *111, 114*, 144, *158, 177, 182*
Bristol & Exeter Railway, *24*, 31, 34, 45–6, 160–2, *186*
Bristolian, 90, *98*, 100, 112
Britannia Pacifics, 97, 176
British Transport Commission, 168, 170, 171, 172, 176, 177
Broad gauge, *6, 10, 11, 12*, 23 *et seq*, *25, 26, 27, 28, 29, 30*, 31 *et seq*, *32, 33, 35, 36*, 46, 63–4
Brunel, Isambard Kingdom, 25–6, 27, 28, 39, 41, 45, 75, 156, 160
Bugle, *186*

Caerphilly Works, 85
Cambrian Coast, 102, 122
Cambrian Coast Express, 102
Camping coaches, 121
Capitals United Express, *97*
Cardiff, 64, 144, 159
Carriages, 95, 123 *et seq*, *123*
Castle class, *21, 43*, 59, 89–91, *91, 97, 98, 100*, 101, *103*, 106, 107, *111, 113, 114, 115, 169, 175*, 176, 203, 204, *204*
Cathedrals Express, *103*
Cheddar, *24*
Cheltenham, 65, 101
Cheltenham Flyer, 88, 89, 90, *90*, 101–2
Chepstow, 28
Chester, *14*
Chippenham, 78
Churchward, George Jackson, 54, 55, *55*, 56–7, 58–9, 64, 76, 81, 85, 106, 127, 179
Churston, *189*
City class, *8, 41*, 54–5, 86, 92–3, 202, 204
Clark, Daniel Kinnear, 32, 33, 36
Closures, 172, 182
Coal traffic, 13, 15, 133–4, *133*
Collett, C. B., 59
Cornish Riviera Express/Limited, 34, 86, 91, 94–5, *94*, 99, 106, 119, 120, 129, 130, *130, 145*, 146
Cornishman, 49, 94–5, 96, 103
Cornwall Railway, 24, 27, 126
Corris Railway, 195, 197–8, *197*, 201
County class 4-4-0, 57
County class 4-6-0, 62, *79*, 120, 176
Cox, E. S., 108, 176
Cymmer Afan, 188

Dainton, *22, 112, 120, 178*
Dart Valley Railway, 116, 172, 204
Dartmouth, 99
Dawlish, *115, 118, 120*
de Glehn compounds, 55–6, *56*
Dean, William, 54, 64, 81, 126
Dean Goods, *19*, 76, *134*, 155, *166, 167*
Didcot, 32, 33, 34, 50
Diesels, 53, 68, 96, *150*, 177, 177–9, *179, 180, 181*, 183, *184*

Dining/kitchen cars, 95, 96, 98, 102, 105, 111, 112, 127, 129, 130
Directors, Board of, 13
Dividend record, 13
Dovey Junction, 115

Electrification, 176
Exeter, *16*, 31, 34, 63, *64, 91*, 95, 117

Festiniog Railway, 125, 197
Films, feature, 155, 181
Fire Fly Project, 49
Fish traffic, 40
Fishguard, 65, 102
Fowey, *190*
Fox's Wood Tunnel, *10*
France, 55–6
Fraser, William Henry, 147–8
Freight trains, named, 131
Frome, *62*, 95
Fuel consumption tests, 32–3, 35, 36, 108–10, 175

Gas-turbine locomotives, 62, *175*, 176
Gloucester, 23, *27*, 29, 101
Gooch, Daniel, 23, 29, 31, 32, 33, 39, 54, *54*, 75–6, 84–5, 160, 162
Great Central Railway, 50, 105
Great Western Society, 172, 202, 204, *205*
Greenwich Mean Time, 25
Grierson, James, 160, 162

Hall class, *52, 107*, 108–10, *112, 118, 119*, 131
Hammersmith & City Railway, 40
Haverfordwest, 27
Hawksworth, F. W., 62, 108
Hereford, 67, 100–1
High-speed runs, 31, 32–6, 55, 86 *et seq*, 101–2
High Speed Train, *8*, 98, 99, 100, 130, *151*, 174, 183
Holiday traffic, 111 *et seq*, 191, 200
Horses, use of, *197*

Inglis, J., 162–3
Inter-City services, 182

Irish Mail, 28

King class, *22*, 59–62, *61*, *62*, 91, *91*, *94*, 95, 108–9, *110*, *114*, *118*, 144, 175, 176
Knowle & Dorridge, 87

Landore, *63*
Lawn, The, 40, 45
Livestock traffic, 134–5, *136*, 192
Locomotive exchanges, 106 *et seq*, *107*, *110*, 175
Locomotive shed allocations, 68–74
Locomotive testing plant, 76, 81, 175
Locomotives, broad gauge, 6, *25*, 29, 30, *30*, 32–6, *33*, *35*
Locomotives, individual: *The Great Bear*, 56, *57*, 59; *King George V*, 60; *City of Truro*, 36, *41*, 54–5, 202, 204
Locomotives, under BR, 174–9
London Midland & Scottish Railway, 107–10, 155, 171, 198
London & North Eastern Railway, 106–7, *110*, 142, 155
London & North Western Railway, 106, 126, 155
London & South Western Railway, 27, 34, 88, 112
Lynton & Barnstaple Railway, 156, 201

Manor class, *115*
Maps, 29, 143, 164–5, 196
Merchant Venturer, *100*
Metropolitan Railway, 40, 50
Midland Railway, 46, 48, 125, 155, 160–2
Milk traffic, 40, 131, 135–6
Milne, Sir James, 99, 107, 169
Moretonhampstead, *174*, 191

Nationalisation, 168–78
New Milford, 28, *28*, 29, 36
Newbury, *79*
Newport, 65, 144
Newquay, 119, 121, 146
Newton Abbot, 11, *19*, 64, 85, 97, 112, 118, *140*
Nord Atlantics, 55–6, *56*
North British Loco Co, 177
North British Railway, 108–9
North Eastern Railway, 141
North Wales Narrow Gauge Railway, 196
Northern Railway of France, 55–6

Ocean Express, 99
Ocean Mail Specials, 88, 92–3
Oil-firing, 62, 74
Old Oak Common, *57*, 64–5, 85

Oxford, 30, 101
Oxford & Birmingham Railway, 50

Paddington, *16*, 37–45, *37*, *38*, *39*, 63, 67, *103*, 111, 131, 136, 142, 144, 204
Paignton, 118, 119
Pannier tanks, *18*, 67, *119*, *188*, *190*, *191*
Parcels traffic, 40
Pembroke Coast Express, *113*
Penzance, *22*, 65, 96, 103, 105, 119, 135
Perishable traffic, 135–6
Plymouth, 27, *27*, 64, 86, 96
Pole, Sir Felix, 107, 133–4, 147, 153–4, 155, 163, 182
Pontypool Road, 64, 105
Public relations and publicity, 20, 45, 59, 85, 95, 101, 103, 145 *et seq*, 195–6, *196*

Railcars, 74, 129, *129*, 157 *et seq*, *158*, 185, 190
Railway Executive, 168, 169, 171, 172, 176
Railway hotels, 52
Reading, *42*, *43*, 63, 77, 142
Refreshment rooms, 105, 117
Rhymney Railway, 85
Road vehicles, 156 *et seq*, *157*, 191
Robert Stephenson & Co, 29
Royal Albert Bridge, 27
Royal Commission on Railway Gauges, 26–7, 31, 33
Royalty, 20, 27, 39

Saint class, *44*, 55, 76, *90*
Salisbury, 63, 64
Saunders, Charles, 160
Severnake, *187*
Sekon, G. A., 76, 81
Severn Tunnel, *15*, *79*, *80*, 133
Severn Tunnel Junction, 65, 133, *135*
Severn Valley Railway, *203*, 204
Shakespeare Express, 103
Shepton Mallet, *186*
Shrewsbury, *41*, 68, 102, 103–4
Shrewsbury & Birmingham Railway, *10*, 84
Signalling, 49, 78, 137 *et seq*, *138*, *139*, *140*, *143*, *144*
Signals, upper quadrant, *16*
Sleeping cars, 126
Slip coaches, *42*, 87, 88, 95, 96, 98, 102, 103, 117, 128–9, *128*
South Devon Railway, *11*, 126
South Wales Pullman, 97
Southall, 63, 64, 67, 157, 159
Southern Railway, 107, 117, 155, 159, 172, 201

Special wagons, 134, 135
Stafford Road Works, Wolverhampton, 54, *58*, 84–5
Standard time, 25
Stanier, W. A., 142
Star class 4-6-0, *16*, *17*, *41*, *43*, 55–6, 59, 86–8, *87*, 101, 106, 155
Station design, 25, 185
Stationmasters, 20, 189–90
Stratford-on-Avon, 102–3
Streamlining, 61–2, *62*, 158
Swansea, 27, 28
Swindon, 63, 64, *114*
Swindon Works, *44*, 54, *58*, 60, 63, 70–2, 75–84, 125, 126, 176, *178*

Talyllyn Railway, 197, 198
Taunton, 64, 95, 117
Temperance Union (GWR), 153–4
Tenby & Carmarthen Bay Express, 99
Timetables, 94 *et seq*, *104*, 182, 194
Torbay, 99, 118, 119, 121
Torbay Express, *62*, 98, 99, 120
Torbay Limited, 86–7
Torquay, *12*, *119*
Torquay Pullman, 97, 99, 129
Totnes, *11*
Trades unions, 169, 184
Travelling Post Office, 96
Trestle viaducts, 24–5
Truro, 27, 63, 64, 95, 112
Twyford, *32*, *94*
Tyseley, 52, 65, *73*, *83*, *84*, 85, 120, *149*

Uphill, *12*

Vale of Rheidol, 195, 197, *199*, 200–1, *201*

Water-softening, 82
Wellington bank, 36, 55, 92, 117
Welsh Highland Railway, 196, 197
Welshpool & Llanfair Light Railway, 195, *195*, 196–7, 198–200
West Cornwall Railway, 27
West Midland Railway, 84
Westbury, 65, 94, 95, *158*
Weymouth, 25, 64, 68, 69, 95, 96
Williams, Alfred, 82–3
Wilton, *17*
Wolverhampton, 27, 36, 53, 84, 103
Worcester, 85, 100–1
Wyatt, Matthew Digby, 39

Zeiss, 60